URBAN SHADOWS

political urban fantasy
powered by the apocalypse

ANDREW MEDEIROS

MARK DIAZ TRUMAN

Design, Development, and Writing by
Andrew Medeiros and Mark Diaz Truman

Rules editing by Brendan Conway
Copy editing by Amanda Valentine
Proofreading by Shelley Harlan
Art direction by Marissa Kelly
Illustrations by Juan Ochoa
Layout by Thomas Deeny
Indexing by Elizabeth Bauman

The X-Card was originally developed by John Stavropolous to manage difficult and adult content in tabletop roleplaying games. You can read more about the X-Card at tinyurl.com/x-card-rpg.

Intimacy moves were originally developed by Dana Fried in her post titled "Three Small Apocalypse World Hacks" (bit.ly/1ScZQiW). More great design work by Dana can be found at leftoblique.net/wp/games.

The section titled "Asking Great Questions" is drawn from Pete Kautz's work titled "Five Conversational Hypnosis Tools For AW MCs" (bit.ly/1FeF894). Pete—The Black Belt Hypnotist—can be found at alliancemartialarts.com.

The Apocalypse Engine is used courtesy of Vincent Baker and Lumpley Games (lumpley.com). Much of the text of this book was inspired by **Apocalypse World** *directly (as well as* **Monsterhearts** *by Avery McDaldno). Thank you, Vincent. You've given us a new way to see things, and roleplaying will never be the same.*

SPECIAL THANKS

Special thanks to Rob Wakefield and Tommy Rayburn for their early graphic design work on the playbooks and the *Urban Shadows* Kickstarter. We couldn't have made this happen without you two. Thank you!

Thanks to Marissa Kelly, Tristan Price, Justin Rogers, Derrick Kapchinsky, Daniel Fernandez, Robenson Chavez-Arnold, Jim Crocker, Kristin Firth, Jenn Lewis, Mick Bradley, Stephen Bloom, Katherine Fackrell, Ryan Leandres, Aaron Friesen, Sean Horwich, Amelia Broverman, Anthony Van Giessen, Ellen Van Giessen, Mikael Andersson, Sean Dalziel, and more for your live playtesting feedback. Your patience and comments were both greatly appreciated.

Huge thanks to Brand Robins and Mo Turkington for their tireless playtesting efforts throughout multiple drafts of the game; Travis Scott, Eric Mersmann, and Stras Acimovic for their insightful live playtesting feedback at and around Origins 2014; Whitney "Strix" Beltran, Ajit George, and MadJay Brown for their constant cheerleading and critical eyes through Gaming as Other; and Jenn Martin and Richard Rogers for their interest and support through Indie+. You all are amazing.

Thank you to our Kickstarter playtesters! Your feedback was amazing, and the game is so much stronger thanks to your contributions. Please see 294 for a list of our City Champions who went above and beyond in their playtesting support for the game.

If we missed you in these thanks, please let us know. We'll get you in a future printing.

From Andrew:

I'd like to thank my spouse Sonya for the encouragement, patience, and love throughout every step of the *Urban Shadows* project (and for its name!). I'd also like to thank my friend Aaron for some of the original ideas for the rules, which ended up being cornerstones of the final product.

From Mark:

I'd like to thank Marissa for her feedback after dozens of *Urban Shadows* playtests and one-shots; my mom, Rose, for teaching me about urban politics since before I could walk; and Avery McDaldno for pushing me to think about how to engage minority experiences in roleplaying games. Thank you.

TABLE OF CONTENTS

ZERO
THE PREFACE

WHAT THIS IS

Urban Shadows is an urban fantasy story game. When you play it, you and your friends (or acquaintances) tell a story together, a tale of supernatural drama and political intrigue set in a modern-day city. Some of the characters in this story are mortal, but they might also be touched by otherworldly forces, transformed into ghosts, vampires, werewolves, and wizards and locked into a world of supernatural debts and obligations.

Each of you takes on the role of one of these characters in your tale, speaking as they speak and deciding what actions they take, a conversation that will push you to interesting emotional places. Your characters might be lovers, friends, enemies, or allies, but they are inextricably involved with each other, like the cast of a TV show. You sometimes get to feel what your characters feel—if you're lucky—but other times you point the characters toward disaster and delight in the fallout from a safe emotional distance.

The rules of this story involve some negotiation and chance. The conversation will often require that you roll dice to find out what happens, a way of keeping things unpredictable so that the story doesn't stagnate or deflate. The tale you're telling doesn't belong to any one person, anymore than a dinner conversation or a talk over a cup of coffee belongs to the host. Everyone gets to contribute a bit, even the dice. Especially the dice.

The story you're telling isn't random, though. Above all else, *Urban Shadows* is a game about cities, the people who live in them, and the machines that make them run. It's a political game, one that challenges our preconceptions about conflicts between communities, and asks us to navigate complex identities in a demanding social structure. It is personal and political for mortals and monsters alike. It drives hard toward these ideas.

But *Urban Shadows* isn't just a game about race relations at City Hall or tax code regulations on the docket with the city council—although maybe those things will come up in your story. It's a game about monsters—creatures of legends, folklore, and modern-day myths—and the cities they inhabit. Your characters all come from *extremely* different communities, and you have to manage the politics within and between those communities no matter where the rules of the game take you.

A CITY OF MONSTERS

The city isn't safe.

The streets are filled with horrors that will hollow you out for their own pleasure, killers and sadists waiting for a taste of your flesh and your fear, and dark things that linger in the shadows, reflecting back your own hideous wants and desires. The streets are veins of corruption, bubbling up into skyscrapers that watch over the urban landscape like the towers of ancient kings, home to the tyrants of the city who want nothing more than to consume all that you have to offer, leaving nothing behind.

And that's just the mortals.

The city is also filled with "real" monsters: vampires and werewolves, fae and wizards, ghosts and immortals. They are living among us and apart from us, infiltrating our corporate boards and gala fundraisers while holding their own secret gatherings and dark rituals to decide our fate. They're everywhere, but you might not notice them if you're not looking closely. Like the city itself, they are more than they appear to be, dangerous and unkind to those who overstep their bounds.

But the city is not without pleasures. Where else can you hear a century-old vampire play steel string guitar in a riverwalk blues cafe? Where else can you feel the pulse of demonic bodies grinding against each other in the heat of a downtown club? Where else can you learn to call upon the power of blood—yours? someone else's?—under the watchful eyes of a trained coven? Nowhere. That's where. Nowhere.

The city has you now. Whether you were born here or made here or moved here or trapped here as the result of some terrible deal with the wrong people... this is where you belong. We know it. You know it. The city knows it. And as you reach for the power to make this city yours, to own a piece of it the way it owns a piece of you, we hope you remember that all those monsters—mortal and supernatural alike—were once just... like... *you.*

RACE, GENDER, AND QUEERNESS

These types of stories—tales of cities and the monsters who inhabit them—have been told before, in blockbuster movies and serial television and trashy paperback novels available at your local supermarket. They shock and delight audiences by promising something dark and edgy, a glimpse into the deviant fangs of monstrous desire.

Yet for all their purported subversion, they are shockingly normative. A girl who hunts vampires convinces herself that a boy vampire isn't so bad. A wizard who lives on the edge of society realizes that his friends are a kind of family. A werewolf finally masters his beast by falling in love with the right woman. Demons are slain by the just; the innocent escape a terrible fate. The usual.

Almost all of these stories—plastered on billboards and sold in bulk—are about white people.

Isn't that strange? Especially since urban fantasy, as a genre, is about a part of human society—dense, urban environments—that are saturated with diversity. The culture of our cities isn't owned by the norms; it's the product of the gay activists, breakers and graf writers, feminists of every race and creed, and immigrants from every corner of the globe. The story of cities is *by default* the story of exactly these kinds of people. The weirdos. The dreamers. The different.

The divisions that separate communities in *Urban Shadows* are a metaphor for this kind of content. Your characters live at the intersection of different identities, and they have to wrestle with what those identities mean to them, both mortal and supernatural. Some of these identities coalesce into Factions—Mortality, Night, Power, Wild—divisions within the city that draw invisible lines between communities; others are as "normal" as your race, gender, or sexual orientation.

Here are some ideas for making this kind of content a priority in your story:

- Play a character of a different race, gender, or sexual orientation from your own. You're not a wizard or a vampire in real life either. We trust you.
- Establish elements of your character that are culturally inherited. How does your vampire prepare to drink blood? Who taught your wizard magic? What church did you go to as a child?
- Remember that you have origins that extend before this story. Ask each other questions about family history, about immigration status, about the time before now.
- Drive your character toward the boundaries between communities. Explore what it means to love someone your community hates or to violate some norm of your tribe, mortal or supernatural. Try to live with the tensions of flawed community norms.
- Strive for a diverse cast. When you describe residents of the city beyond your characters, include characters from a variety of communities. Let some characters celebrate diversity, but use other characters to remind each other that racism, sexism, homophobia, and bigotry are active forces in the city.

Don't worry about your characters being too different from each other; the mechanics of *Urban Shadows* will consistently push your characters together. You'll owe Debts to people in Factions other than your own, reasons you must cross boundaries to deal with each other's problems, and you'll have relationships that defy the customs of your tribe, mortal or supernatural. As play goes on, you'll also develop loyalties that make you question the boundaries of your identity. You might even join a different community entirely.

But the mechanics of the game will also remind you that you aren't alike. There are differences between vampires and wizards, ghosts and oracles, hunters and fae. Differences that can't so quickly be overcome. Old feuds. Old hatreds. Old fears. History.

And that's what cities are about: difference and boundaries, diversity and exclusion. Each community completely self-sufficient but in desperate need of what other communities have to offer. Chaos at the borders. Cities are the push and pull of progress, messy and violent when you least expect trouble, beautiful and touching in the darkest places. This is the world your characters explore together when you play *Urban Shadows*.

PLAYING TO FIND OUT

As you play *Urban Shadows*, you might be tempted to plot out where you want things to go, to drive the story and the narrative toward some place you think is interesting or fun or satisfying. But the truth is that it's not *your* story. It's not even your group's story.

It's the city's story.

Your group tells your story, of course, but it's not yours to control. You can't plan out the next dramatic scene or plot an arc for your character. The mechanics of the game push you from one conflict to the next, from one messy situation to the next difficult choice, and you only see the story in the rearview mirror. The road ahead is always dark, mysterious, and full of potential.

Playing *Urban Shadows* requires discipline, a commitment to the moment at hand instead of the next ten moments you want. The minute that you know where things are going is the moment that the story feels dead. Trust that you're going somewhere interesting. **Play to find out what happens.** The surprises are most of the fun.

WHERE THIS CAME FROM

Urban Shadows borrows its rules framework—and many ideas about games and stories—from another roleplaying game: *Apocalypse World* by D. Vincent Baker. *Apocalypse World* is about people struggling to survive in a post-apocalyptic wasteland, like *Mad Max* or *Waterworld*. We've found that *Urban Shadows* isn't all that different; the city is as harsh a mistress as any blasted, radioactive flatland, and each character is caught in a tangled web of tricky alliances and explosive grudges that makes gangs of cannibals look downright reasonable.

You don't need *Apocalypse World* to play *Urban Shadows*; we've provided everything you need to play here in this book. But if you're interested in these kinds of stories, you ought to pick up a copy. We refer to it here if we think there's something specific you should check out.

WHAT YOU'LL NEED

In order to play *Urban Shadows*, you need a few friends (or enemies) who want to explore the city with you in two- to four-hour chunks of time. Some groups play the game just once—a one-shot—but some of the best games happen with groups that get together often, following the stories of each character through multiple sessions and a variety of story arcs. It's up to you what kind of commitment you want to make to your characters.

Urban Shadows works best with 4-5 players and a **Master of Ceremonies** (MC), a player devoted to portraying the rest of the world outside of the **player characters** (PCs). More than five players means you'll have trouble spreading the spotlight around; fewer than four players means that you'll struggle a bit to build the chemistry that comes from a rich network of PC relationships and obligations.

Before you start your first session, you also need to gather some supplies that help the game run smoothly. Usually the MC brings these tools to the first session, but the other players are equally welcome to contribute. You'll probably want to have this rulebook on hand as well, in case something comes up that you have a question about during play.

DICE

You need at least two six-sided dice, the kind you find in a board game like *Monopoly* or *Risk*. You can get by with just two dice for the whole group, but it's a lot easier to play if everyone has their own set. After all, you wouldn't want to use up all the luck in someone else's dice...

ARCHETYPES

Urban Shadows comes with ten core **Archetypes** that players can choose from at the start of the game, each one a different staple of urban fantasy fiction. You need to print one copy of each to play, although your group may decide to leave out some core Archetypes or add in a few limited edition Archetypes available other places. We think the Archetypes look great printed on legal-sized paper, but traditional letter-sized paper works fine as well.

PENCILS AND PAPER

The Archetypes provide plenty of space to create characters and keep notes, but you'll want to have other paper on hand for makeshift maps, lists of Debts, sketches, etc. And, of course, you'll want plenty of pencils; you'll be erasing and rewriting things frequently throughout the course of play.

ADDITIONAL MATERIALS

You'll also want to gather up a few additional materials: maps of your city, photographs and portraits of city residents, and the Master of Ceremonies worksheet. Each of these is a useful tool that you'll want to have on hand rather than scrounging for them mid-session.

You can find all the handouts described in this section at www.magpiegames.com/urbanshadows.

ONE

THE BASICS

THE CONVERSATION

When we say in **The Preface** that a roleplaying game is a conversation, we're saying that it's easy. You sit down at a table with sheets and dice and pencils and start talking. For the most part, the conversation revolves around your characters. You say what they do, how they react, what they care about. And since the other players don't live in your head, you broadcast that information to the other players and the MC.

There are times in the conversation when you slip directly into your character's shoes, no longer narrating but actually taking on your character's persona. You make the gestures your character makes; you say things as your character without preface. Most people do this without thinking too much about it. It's pretty natural to damn near *become* your character while you're playing, to want what they want, to fear the outcome of the dice at crucial moments.

The conversation in a roleplaying game evolves naturally over the course of the session. But it's your job—as a group—to keep the conversation interesting. The rules, the techniques, and everything you bring to the table is about driving that conversation toward interesting places. Dark alleys. Dangerous places. Murderous moments. Wherever the fiction takes you.

FRAMING SCENES

The best way to keep the conversation moving toward interesting places is to **frame scenes**. Instead of sitting around the table talking about interesting characters, put those characters into concrete locations with concrete objectives. The MC has the final call on scene structure and flow, but it's really the responsibility of everyone in the group to make sure that scenes start out interesting and go somewhere meaningful.

We bet you're already familiar with this technique; it's been used pretty much since the dawn of time to turn the tales of regular people into interesting stories. *Skip the boring stuff and get right to the meat of what's happening or what's about to happen.* It sounds complicated, but it's no harder than starting any conversation; once you get up and running, the rules of the game will take you the rest of the way.

Mark is MCing **Urban Shadows** *for Tristan, Robey, Marissa, and Justin. He's got a full table of PCs, so he decides to try to* **frame a scene** *that gets lots of them involved with each other right away.*

"How about we get started with a few characters getting together at a club?" Mark says. "I know that Tristan and Justin's characters are still looking for the missing faerie, Onyx, so maybe you all can meet up with Marissa's character, Father Davis, to learn what he's found out about the case."

Tristan and Justin both nod. That sounds good to them.

Marissa says, "I don't know. I think Davis probably would have contacted them immediately when he learned that Onyx was kidnapped. Can we do the scene at their apartment instead?"

Everyone nods at that too. Makes sense to do it there as well.

"Great. Why don't you both tell us what your apartment looks like, since we've never seen it before," says Mark.

And so on. There's no need for us to show the characters getting ready for a meeting unless something interesting might happen. And like any conversation, everyone should contribute, even if it means pushing back a bit against where things are headed. Multiple points of view keep things much more interesting than one person hogging the damn spotlight.

On that same note, scenes end when they aren't interesting any more. The MC might call for a scene to be over, or the players in the scene might realize that the scene's played out as far as it needs to. It's better to cut scenes too short than let them run too long. Leave everyone—including yourself—always wanting more.

»Hard Framing

On occasion, the MC might want to move things along faster or jump right to a tense or difficult situation. Maybe the consequences of an earlier decision come to bear, hard and fast, or perhaps the tone of the story calls for a more aggressive scene. We call this technique **hard scene framing** because there's less room for negotiation; the scene starts and the PCs need to react as best they can.

Robey's character, Wesley Chen, is a third-generation wizard living in the Hyde Park area of Chicago. After Justin, Tristan, and Marissa's characters talk about the missing faerie, Mark decides that he needs to move things along for Wesley a bit more quickly.

"Okay, Wesley. You're probably headed home after a long day of classes, right?"

"Yeah, I usually check on my uncle after school before I do anything else."

"Awesome," Mark says. "When you step off the elevator onto the 8th floor of your apartment building, you immediately know something's wrong. There's trash littered all over the floor—fast food wrappers, paper, all stuff that looks like it's from a dumpster—and you can hear some growling coming from down the hall. It looks like someone has knocked in the door to your apartment."

"Oh shit."

"Yeah. Looks like your uncle's in danger. Probably. Might be dead already. You don't know what the hell kind of trouble he's gotten himself into this time. What do you do?"

There's more in **The Master of Ceremonies** on 179 about hard scene framing and other MC techniques to keep the conversation interesting. It's everyone's job to push for dynamic scenes and conflicts, but the MC has a special responsibility for keeping things moving.

» "What Do You Do?"

The question "What do you do?" comes up again and again and again in *Urban Shadows*. The city demands that you take action, that you respond to creeping darkness and bloody plots; there's little time for you to plan or plot and often you have to decide what matters in a moment. Scene framing is all about getting the PCs to a "What do you do?" moment as quickly as possible; hard scene framing means that the "What do you do?" moment is already upon you.

You might find it interesting to have long conversations about where your characters want to go eat or to reminisce about old relationships with undead lovers. For the most part, though, *Urban Shadows* isn't about that kind of conversation: the rules push you to make decisions, act on your impulses, and deal with the fucking consequences. The city moves forward, and you just have to try to keep up. You can have those conversations—emotional moments that fill in the spaces between dramatic action—but know that they're fleeting and precious.

FICTIONAL POSITIONING

The setup of scenes is important because it plays into the broader **fictional position** of the characters, by which we mean *the things we've agreed upon in the story already*. Each statement, each reveal, each bit of information you say about your character pours into this fictional world you're building together, painting a picture of your characters and the city in which they live. We call this world we're creating **the fiction**, the collection of everything that's happening—and has already happened—in our story.

Remember how we said playing *Urban Shadows* takes discipline? Sticking to what you've contributed to the fiction, even if it's hard or difficult for your character, takes some practice. You've got to let the past define the future, even if you didn't know what you were committing to when you defined the past.

Robey says, "My uncle's in danger, right? I drop my backpack and run into the apartment."

"Are you just charging right in? Ready for action?" Mark asks.

"Yeah. I'm a wizard. I figure whoever broke in here probably isn't that dangerous."

"As you round the corner, you see a mound of trash lift up a desk from your uncle's study and dump the contents onto the floor. It looks up and roars at you, casting the desk to the side."

"Shit. Maybe I don't want to run in there after all..." Robey says.

"Too late. It's already spotted you. What do you do?"

When you play *Urban Shadows*, your characters are constantly walking through doors that close behind them—sometimes literally!—as each decision builds upon the last. You can't take back what you've said before, even if it would be convenient, and it's your job as a group to hold people to the truth of the story, to the position they've taken in the fictional narrative you've constructed together.

Sometimes players will want to **clarify** an action before it's set in stone. If Robey had said, "Huh. Yeah, I guess I should be careful about charging in," and established that Wesley was going to do a little magic to prepare for whatever was around the corner, things would have gone differently. But clarifying isn't rewriting. Once something's agreed upon, there's no taking it back, even when the outcome hurts like hell.

MOVES AND DICE

Framing scenes is the first step in building an interesting conversation, but it's the **moves** that connect your characters to the fiction in exciting ways. Each move is a small set of rules that helps resolve conflicts, answer questions in the fiction, and push the story forward. Moves are like the programming language of the game—"When you do x, then do y"—shaping and defining the fiction when your characters take action.

Everyone can trigger the **basic moves** at the start of the game, but you also get **special moves** attached to your Archetype and might add new moves to your characters as the game goes on. In general, the basic moves cover situations that come up all the time while special moves cover situations that are character specific or much more rare.

Moves don't just go off whenever you think it might be interesting; they have to be **triggered** by something you say in the conversation, usually an action your character takes. If you want to trigger a move, you have to do the thing that triggers it. You can always avoid a move, but then you have to avoid taking that action. Since every move is tied directly to the fiction, we often say that moves are all governed by the same idea: *if you do it, you do it.*

Justin's character, Rashid, is an Iraqi insurgent who fled the Middle East after the Sunni Awakening and ended up as a sociology graduate student at the University of Chicago. His research exposed him to the supernatural, and now he's struggling to keep his mortal life together as he gets more and more involved. When he leaves campus in the middle of the day to investigate some strange fae sightings in Hyde Park, he runs into his advisor, Dr. Pruett.

Mark says, "Dr. Pruett looks concerned when he sees you. 'Rashid, I thought we talked about you wrapping up the grading for my class this week. Where are you off to?'"

Justin rolls his eyes. Pruett is a pain. "Right, Dr. Pruett. I'm actually just going out to pick up some of the surveys from the field team."

Mark grins. "I think you're trying to **mislead** *Dr. Pruett, right? You're headed to a totally different part of town."*

Justin thinks for a moment. He's still got time to change his action so that he doesn't trigger the move, but decides to go ahead with it. "Yeah, I'm going to **mislead** *him. I don't want him to know what I'm up to right now."*

Mark and Justin look at **mislead, distract, or trick**—*a basic move—to find out what they should do next.*

When you commit to a course of action that triggers a move, you usually end up rolling dice. *You don't roll dice any other time.* If a move calls for dice, roll them and consult the move for what happens next. If you want to roll the dice some other time, you have to trigger a move. Sometimes players snap up the dice, ready to roll and do a thing... but the fiction always comes first. Say what you do, then figure out the move that goes with it.

Not all moves use dice. Some moves, like ***workspace*** (96) or **drama moves** (34) tell you and the MC what should happen when they're triggered. No dice needed. No dice rolled.

»Hits and Misses

When a move asks you to roll the dice, pick up two six-sided dice (2d6) and roll them. The moves will tell you to roll *with* something—like Heart or Blood—which means that you should total up your dice and whatever stat the move calls out. A character with Blood +3, for example, adds a +3 to the total from the dice when "rolling with Blood." There are other ways to get bonuses as well, but you can never add more than +4 to a roll.

The outcomes are straightforward: anything 7 or more is a **hit**, anything 6 or less is a **miss**. Some moves give additional options on a 10+ or give you more description for what happens on a 7-9 or 6-. Just follow what the move says, and you'll find your way forward in the game.

In general, a hit means you get what you want. It's not always perfect or pretty, but when you roll a 7+ result, you get at least the minimum you were looking to get out of the situation. When you get just a 7-9—a **weak hit**—there might be some serious costs or complications that go along with your success, but it's not a failure.

A 10+ is sometimes described as a **strong hit**. If a move tells you to do something on a 10+, it usually means that you get some kind of bonus or strong result, well beyond what a 7-9 result would provide. Most of the time, you're hoping for a 10+ when you pick up the dice, especially if the costs associated with a 7-9 aren't costs you want to pay.

A miss isn't a failure either: it means that the MC is about to tell you what happens. It's likely that you won't like what happens, since the MC's job is to push the story in interesting directions, but there's no rule that says it has to be awful or the worst result you can possibly imagine. More often than not, the MC uses misses to tighten the noose...

Justin decides that Rashid will lay it on thick for Pruett. "I'd love to stay and talk, Dr. Pruett, but those field teams are waiting for me." He picks up the dice, notes that he's rolling with Mind—his highest stat at +3—and rolls.

Snake eyes. Justin's total is 5. Way short of the 7 he needs to hit.

Mark says, "Dr. Pruett looks excited when you mention field teams. It dawns on you too late that it was Dr. Pruett who was demanding that you take a more active role in fieldwork. Before you can say anything more, he claps you on the shoulder and says, 'Wonderful! I'll head out with you. I haven't seen anyone on the field team recently. It will be good to get off campus.'"

Justin groans. Now he's got to figure out a way to get rid of Pruett before he can do any snooping at all in Hyde Park. Not to mention that no one from the field team is actually expecting him...

The MC never rolls dice. Instead, the MC gets to make moves when players roll and miss, when a move calls for the MC to contribute in some meaningful way, or when the conversation gets boring. This might seem limiting, but it encourages the MC to create situations and conflicts that require the PCs to take action...and therefore make moves. If you'd like to read more about MC moves, see 189.

»Triggers and Uncertainty

If you're new to using moves in roleplaying, this whole system might strike you as constraining. After all, isn't the best part of roleplaying that you get to do *whatever you want your character to do?* Why would we limit our vampires, werewolves, wizards, and faeries to a prescribed set of actions? Why are there only seven basic moves?

Moves are limits that encourage creativity; they're a structure for uncertainty, a way of signaling what kind of conflicts are going to drive the story. You'll notice that there aren't any moves for hailing a cab or using an elevator in *Urban Shadows*. We figure your group doesn't need moves to figure out what will happen when you do those things. You say what you want your character to do, and the MC tells you what happens because of it. No moves needed.

But when things get uncertain? When you try to perform a magical ritual to banish a crazed spirit to the abyss? When you try to persuade your husband that you aren't sneaking out at night to hunt vampires? When you let out the beast inside you to summon the strength you need to survive the night? Moves help us resolve those moments.

The interesting thing here is that the kind of uncertainty we're talking about isn't one-dimensional. For a move to be triggered, both the player *and the MC* need to be uncertain about the outcome of the action. Player uncertainty is common; players need to go to the MC all the time for how things look, how things taste or smell, and—above all else—what's going to happen. But the MC calls for a move when it's not clear *to the MC* how things are going to move forward.

This doesn't mean that things should be scripted and rote. Just the opposite, in fact. The MC (like the players) is playing to find out what happens while staying true to the fictional positioning of the situation. If a PC knocks an evil demon unconscious and moves to kill him, we're all pretty certain what's going to happen: the demon is toast. On the other hand, knocking that damn demon out in the first place is a mystery for both the player and the MC. What will it take? Will there be any consequences? Will the group's clever plan work? Time for a move.

The moves we've chosen are natural places of uncertainty within our story, beats in which we think that you should stop and reflect on what the characters—and the MC—think is likely to happen. For more on the basic moves, including examples of when they do and do not trigger, see **The Moves** on 37.

STARTING A GAME

Before we get to making characters and rolling dice, there are a few things you need to do when starting a game of *Urban Shadows*:

PREPARING TO PLAY

You can play *Urban Shadows* anywhere, but the game works best when you do a bit of work to prepare the space for play. Get a table large enough that everyone can spread out their dice, paper, and pencils without crowding each other...but not so large that you have to shout to be heard. Draw some boundaries around your game so you're not disturbed; spectators or interruptions can be a pain when you're in a tense and difficult moment. Make sure everyone's had something to eat before you play and take breaks when you need to take breaks. No need to rush.

You might want to find some music that's a good fit for your city. We think local indie rock and hip-hop are good reminders of the undercurrent of a city, especially someplace with iconic musicians like Seattle or New York. Play it as background noise, as a soundtrack for the drama that unfolds. We've made some recommendations for music with each Archetype, starting on 84.

And play at night. Daytime is *their* time: the norms, the normals, the mundane. At night, the murky blackness holds your secrets and your lies. You feel it pressing in on you and it focuses your attention—right here and now—on the city's heartbeat.

CHOOSING A CITY

Before you pass out any Archetypes or start framing scenes, choose a city for your setting. You can play *Urban Shadows* in a fictional city, but we've found that the stories told in real cities are much more interesting. There's history in actual cities—tragic suffering and unfulfilled hopes wrapped up in the shitty reality of the dark streets of any large urban area. It's a shame to waste the pain and promise of Chicago, Los Angeles, Moscow, Paris, or Seattle when there are so many great resources for bringing those cities into your game.

- **Wikipedia**: It's hard to beat the ubiquitous, easy-to-access online encyclopedia. You can find tons of information about any major city in the world, including maps, old history, and current conflicts.
- **Local Newspapers**: Local newspapers are a great way to bring a city to life, and the internet makes it easy to access them. Grab a few of the local headlines and you're well on your way to capturing the feel of a big city.
- **City Guides**: In addition to these resources, our Kickstarter campaign for this book funded the creation of *Dark Streets*, a collection of setting primers for a bunch of urban areas. You can find it at www.magpiegames.com/darkstreets.

»Your City, Your Setting

At the same time, don't get trapped by the reality of your city. *Urban Shadows* is a world filled with undead monsters and supernatural negotiations, a dark reflection of the real world with politics that transcend human dealings. The real Chicago might be going through a contentious runoff election in the real world, but your version of Chicago might have a vampire mayor who's been running the city for forty extremely suspicious years. And if you don't know something about the city you're using, *make it up*.

It's your city. Don't let anyone else tell you how it should run.

You know the *truth*, after all. The truth behind all the lies. The supernatural creatures who lurk in the darkness pulling strings. The sacrifices made by those who wish to keep the peace. The bodies that just won't fucking stay buried, not even when you hex them, bind them, and banish them to another dimension.

SETTING EXPECTATIONS

Before you play, your group should talk a bit about what kind of stories *Urban Shadows* is built to tell. Sometimes folks come to the table expecting it to be *Interview with a Vampire* and get a bit disappointed when they end up with *Underworld* or *Constantine*. It's a matter of taste, you know, of getting what you want from the story you're helping to tell.

In our experience, the tone of the story can vary. Typically, supernatural creatures exist just outside the world of mortals, but it's a thin veneer. The politics of the game are brutal and direct: your enemies are as likely to kill you or magically bind you as they are to try to strike a deal. The city has its own damn rules, even if most mortals don't know what's lurking in the darkness.

But there are very few secrets that stay secrets. Everyone knows who is a werewolf and who is a vampire, who struck an alliance with the fae and who betrayed the wizards. There are lots of mortals with their hands in the supernatural pot, including a few who make their living providing goods and services—blood, drugs, medical attention—to supernaturals who would rather trust a neutral third-party than their own people. Gossip moves fast and revenge moves faster.

»The X-Card

Since the themes and issues that *Urban Shadows* raises are sometimes disturbing and uncomfortable, we encourage you to play with an **X-Card** at your table. The X-Card, designed by John Stavropolous, is a tool that helps groups manage difficult content without setting artificial boundaries or flagging uncomfortable topics in advance.

To quote John:

> *The X-Card is an optional tool that allows anyone in your game (including you) to edit out any content anyone is uncomfortable with as you play. Since most RPGs are improvisational and we won't know what will happen till it happens, it's possible the game will go in a direction people don't want. An X-Card is a simple tool to fix problems as they arise.*
>
> *To use, at the start of your game, simply say:*
>
> *"I'd like your help. Your help to make this game fun for everyone. If anything makes anyone uncomfortable in any way… [draw X on an index card] … just lift this card up, or simply tap it [place card at the center of the table]. You don't have to explain why. It doesn't matter why. When we lift or tap this card, we simply edit out anything X-Carded. And if there is ever an issue, anyone can call for a break and we can talk privately. I know it sounds funny but it will help us play amazing games together and usually I'm the one who uses the X-Card to protect myself from all of you! Thank you!"*

We've found that anything that gets X-Carded during play can be replaced by something equally dark, mysterious, and troubling that doesn't push our group to bad places. We trust your collective imagination to do the same! You'll always think of some other terrible thing the vampire prince was going to do or some other dark ritual the Oracle needs to perform. Don't let yourself be bound by something so mundane as the first thing you thought of in a scene.

More on the X-Card can be found at http://tinyurl.com/x-card-rpg.

WHY PLAY?

But why do this? Why go to all this trouble just to tell a story when you can flip on the television and find thousands of stories—some of them urban fantasy stories!—without having to do any work?

Because the characters are fucking awesome.

Because no matter how awesome the characters might be individually—digging into their part of the city and trying to make it forever theirs—they are even more awesome when they mix it up with each other, when they get in each other's beds and boardrooms, when they cross the borders of race, class, gender, and geography to get what they want.

Because the city wants to eat these characters whole, spit them back out, and make them nothing more than drones doing the awful bidding of the powers-that-be...and we all know you aren't going to let that happen without a goddamn street fight, without striking from below when power makes someone stupid.

Because the city's there for the taking, all wrapped up in the old ways that are just about to give up the ghost any minute now, and maybe, just maybe, your little group of scrappy up-and-comers will be in the right place at the right time to change the face of this fucking city for once and for all.

Because on these dark streets you either die a hero...or live long enough to become a villain.

Your choice.

TWO THE CHARACTERS

CHOOSING AN ARCHETYPE

Creating player characters for a roleplaying game is a bit like casting a new television show or movie: you want each character to be special and unique, but you also want the cast to be more than the sum of its parts. In *Urban Shadows*, we strike that balance through the use of **Archetypes**, templates that capture specific character types found in urban fantasy fiction. This book includes ten core Archetypes—The Aware, The Fae, The Hunter, The Oracle, The Spectre, The Tainted, The Vamp, The Veteran, The Wizard, and The Wolf—but there are other limited edition and fan-created Archetypes available elsewhere as well.

Each player (except for the MC) chooses an Archetype at the start of play and uses it to create their character. No two players can pick the same Archetype; there might be vampires all over your city, but there can only be one vampire protagonist. *Urban Shadows* is about the tensions between communities, which means that our starting cast needs to be as diverse and conflicted as possible. If two or more players want to play the same Archetype, the MC might recommend some other Archetypes that touch on similar themes or adjudicate the decision through a coin flip or dice roll.

It might sound restrictive to pick from a list of character types, but the Archetypes are flexible structures for your imagination rather than limits. A Wizard, for example, might be a classic member of an ancient hermetic order or a modern-day Tesla who crafts etheric machines in his sanctum. It's always up to you to bring your character to life. The Archetypes create a space for player creativity, quickly launching you into play while balancing the need for unique characters and a compelling cast.

When it's time for you to select an Archetype, pick one that resonates with the kinds of stories you want to tell. It's perfectly fine to pick a character type that's typical for your style of play or to try to branch out by picking something that you think goes against your "type." Each Archetype is a collection of strengths and weaknesses designed to thrust you immediately into dramatic situations filled with problems and opportunities; we hope you find that there are no wrong choices. See **The Archetypes** on 80 for a full list of the Archetypes, including a short description of each Archetype and tips on how to play them during the game.

> *Andrew is MCing a game of* **Urban Shadows** *for Jana, Karl, Ryan, and Sophia. Ryan and Karl both seem drawn to The Wolf Archetype at the start of play. Since this is the first time Karl has played the game, Ryan gracefully allows Karl first pick.*
>
> *Andrew asks Ryan, "Why don't you take a look at The Fae? It's got a lot of similar themes to The Wolf because they're both outsiders and outcasts."*

Ryan takes a look through The Fae's Archetype and agrees. It looks like a good fit to him.

YOUR SUPERNATURAL WORLD

As you design your characters for *Urban Shadows*, you'll find yourself needing to answer all kinds of questions about the urban fantasy landscape your characters inhabit: How do vampires react to sunlight? What kind of magic can wizards do? What vulnerabilities do demons have? How many hunters live in the city? Questions, questions, questions.

We've done our best to include in the moves and Archetypes everything we think is necessary to make *Urban Shadows* work at your table. Part of our design philosophy, however, is to leave holes all over the map for your group to fill in. We want you to make the city come to life, to be the kind of vampire or werewolf or wizard or faerie that you want to be, and to tell us what you know about the world. We trust that your answers to those questions will be far more interesting than anything we could set down as hard and fast truth.

After all, you're **playing to find out what happens**. And that means you might find that your answers surprise even you. The city has a will of its own, a heartbeat that pulses through every session of *Urban Shadows*; your answers will feed it and keep it growing, far beyond anything any one of us could dream up. Seize that opportunity.

NAME, LOOK, AND DEMEANOR

After you select an Archetype, start constructing your character by selecting your name, look, and demeanor. Your decisions on these three elements help ground your character, giving you some direction for completing the rest of the Archetype.

Start with your name. We've provided a bunch that we think are a good fit for each Archetype, but feel free to invent your own name. Characters in urban fantasy stories often have mundane or everyday names, but nicknames and callsigns aren't uncommon. You might want to consider your character's look when choosing a name, especially if your character hails from an ethnic group with distinctive naming traditions.

Move to your look next. Your choices here determine how others see you when they encounter you on the streets of the city. Do you have an obvious gender presentation? Are you clearly from one ethnic group or another? What's your style of dress on a typical day? Pick as many from each list as apply, and start thinking about how that particular look has influenced your character's life in the city.

Finally, decide what demeanor your character presents to others. Each Archetype has a unique set of demeanors keyed to the Archetype's specific conflicts and issues; pick from the list instead of creating your own. It's okay to interpret the demeanor broadly—a werewolf who picks *Aggressive* might be eager for a fight or might be a fast-talking, quick-moving salesman, but you've got to pick your demeanor from the list presented. Picking from the provided demeanors is a crucial step toward building a diverse and interesting cast that drives the story toward interesting places.

Ryan doesn't love any of the names on the list of Fae names, so he decides to create his own: Volund. He loves the way it sounds exotic and precise, like European royalty. He decides to match the name with a **Male** *look, and declares that his Fae is a man in his mid-30s who wears fancy suits (***Expensive Clothing***) wherever he goes (***Eccentric Demeanor***). He circles* **Black** *and* **South Asian***, but doesn't make any decisions about Volund's actual ethnicity yet. Ryan didn't think of his faerie as weird or odd at first, but he likes the idea that Volund seems foreign to everyone who meets him.*

THE STATS

Each character has two sets of stats: main stats and Faction stats. The **main stats** describe your character, especially their abilities and weaknesses, while the **Faction stats** describe your character's relationship to the various Factions in the game.

MAIN STATS

There are four main stats: **Blood**, **Heart**, **Mind**, and **Spirit**.

- **Blood** is the measure of your fight or flight instinct. It tells us how tough, dangerous, coiled, and quick to act your character is in a dangerous situation.
- **Heart** is the sum of your passion, charm, and charisma. It tells us how proficient your character is at getting what they want through negotiation and discussion.
- **Mind** is a reflection of your critical thinking, trickery, and observational skills. It tells us how perceptive your character can be and how good they are at manipulating others with deceit.
- **Spirit** gauges your connection to the "other" and your force of will. It tells us how focused and determined your character is under pressure, and what kind of connection they have to the supernatural.

Your character's main stats can never fall below -3, and only in rare cases will one ever exceed +3. It's possible to get small bonuses (+1) to your rolls, but your main stats are the biggest influence on your die rolls while playing the game. Any time you make a basic move (39), you use your main stats.

Each Archetype comes with a set of predetermined stats, usually one rated at -1, one rated at +0, and two rated at +1. Add +1 to any one of the stats and write the final numbers in the boxes in the middle of your playbook. You may want to look at some of the moves on your Archetype to see which stats you'll be rolling more often, but all of the main stats are useful to every character.

As a Fae, Volund's starting main stats are Blood -1, Heart +1, Mind +0, and Spirit +1. Ryan wants Volund to be skilled at escaping dangerous situations; he places his +1 into Blood, raising that stat to a +0. Volund isn't great at dealing with physical situations, but moving Blood from a -1 to a +0 greatly reduces the risks Volund takes when he turns tail in the face of danger or attacks someone to get what he wants.

FACTION STATS

In addition to the main stats, each character also has Faction stats: **Mortality**, **Night**, **Power**, and **Wild**. Factions are loose political groupings that illustrate the differing affiliations and loyalties in the world, each one a community with its own internal politics and dramas. The Factions are:

- **Mortality**: Normal humans without any supernatural ability. Most people fall into this Faction, since mortals are often unaware of the supernatural world around them.
- **Night**: Creatures of the night who were once human but have been irrevocably changed into something dark and unnatural. Vampires, werewolves, and ghosts all belong to the Night Faction.
- **Power**: Human beings who have obtained supernatural power or gifts through training, blessing, or curse. Wizards, oracles, and immortals all belong to the Power Faction.
- **Wild**: Otherworldly beings, strange peoples, and demonic creatures that originate from outside our world. The Wild Faction is most heavily populated by faeries and demons, but creatures bizarre and strange sometimes find a home in this Faction as well.

Each Faction stat represents how well your character understands a specific community. A character with a high stat in one of the Factions has contacts and connections, and can easily interpret political information within a Faction; a character with a low stat in a particular Faction doesn't understand how that Faction works or who the power players are within that community. These stats—like the main stats—range from -3 to +3, and whenever you make a Faction move you use them instead of your main stats.

Your Archetype defines your starting Faction stats; add +1 to any one of them and write the final numbers in the middle of your playbook. Your character's relationships with these communities change a bit more often than the main stats, so write these stats in pencil. They'll likely change by the end of the first session!

Volund's starting Faction stats are Mortality +0, Night -1, Power +1, and Wild +1. As a Fae, Volund has typically had more dealings with his own kind and others like him from Wild, and with mortals that carry the mantle of Power. Ryan decides that Volund has lived among regular humans for several years and has had a lot of interaction with Mortality, so adds +1 to Mortality. His Faction range at the start of the story is Mortality +1, Night -1, Power +1, and Wild +1.

INTRO QUESTIONS

Once you've finished choosing your character's stats, take a few moments to look over the **intro questions** for your Archetype. Each set of questions is a collection of prompts to get you thinking about your character, especially about how your character relates to the city itself. You don't have to type up fancy answers to these questions, but try to jot down a few quick answers so that you can mention them during character introductions.

Ryan jots down the following answers to The Fae's intro questions:

Who are you?

I am Volund, a famed smith of the Storm Court of faerie.

How long have you been in the city?

I was exiled here by my king nearly fifty years ago for a crime I did not commit.

What do you love most about humanity?

Their ability to surprise me. I find it most amusing.

Who is your closest confidante in the city?

Laurella, she is a powerful practitioner and healer. She understands my people well, for a human.

What do you desperately need?

I need to regain access to my homelands and be reunited with my beloved.

GEAR

All the characters in *Urban Shadows* start with some gear. It's pretty tough to survive in the city if you don't have the shit you need to get by. For some folks, we're talking about weapons—the shotguns, knives, and handguns that keep the darkness at bay. Others are less violent; they have gear that helps them connect with the mystic and magical forces that lie just outside of mortal sight.

Sometimes your gear will come from a list, like The Oracle's "set of unique items" or The Wolf's "2 practical weapons." In these cases, pick as many off the list as indicated. You can get more of those kinds of items later in the story, but your character only starts with whatever the Archetype instructs you to select. No fair to start with more than your share.

On the other hand, some gear prompts you to say much more about your stuff. The Spectre, for example, has "Whatever was on your person when you died, albeit spiritual versions of each." In these cases, you can describe whatever makes sense for your character to have at the start of the story.

Finally, there are a few characters who have gear that tells them to **detail** the gear more explicitly, like The Hunter's custom weapons or The Veteran's workspace. When a playbook asks you to detail a piece of gear, look for a section of the Archetype dedicated to that piece of gear and make choices appropriately.

> *Volund gets a nice apartment, a car, and a smart phone by default, but Ryan still has to pick a relic from his homelands and a symbol of his court. He decides that his relic will be a* **hammer and anvil used to forge faerie objects**, *an important tool for his work as a fae smith. For his symbol, he chooses* **a bronze bracer etched with a lightning bolt**. *Volund doesn't wear it every day, but it's an important gift from the king of his faerie court.*

PICKING MOVES

At the start of play, any character can trigger any of the basic moves, including ***unleash***; ***escape a situation***; ***persuade an NPC***; ***figure someone out***; ***mislead, distract, or trick***; ***keep your cool***; and ***let it out***. Each of these moves triggers when the characters take actions in the fiction that match the move.

In addition to these basic moves, each Archetype also gets **Archetype moves** that grant them new powers or expand on what the basic moves can do. Some of these require a roll with one of the stats, but many of them are simple additions to your existing abilities or powers that work without a roll. For example, The Hunter can choose ***Deadly*** to inflict one more harm whenever they inflict harm.

Each Archetype has special instructions for how many Archetype moves you have to start and how many moves you select at the start of play. Follow the instructions provided, but remember to look at how the Archetype moves match up with the main and Faction stats you selected earlier. It's okay to go back and change those stats before you introduce your characters, if you find a move you love or realize that you want to emphasize something different about your character.

Most of the Archetypes also have **extras**, features that are unique to that particular Archetype. The Wizard has a sanctum and a focus, for example, while The Hunter has a set of custom weapons and The Vamp has a web that slowly draws in their prey. Make whatever decisions need to be made about these extras when you decide which moves to take from your playbook.

Over the course of play, you may take moves from other Archetypes through advancements. We left some room for you to write new moves on each Archetype under the section *Other Moves*.

> *Ryan takes a look at his moves and finds out that he gets* **Faerie Magic**. *The Fae Archetype says he gets two more moves, so he also takes* **Scales of Justice**, *a move that allows him to use faerie magic he doesn't know by spending Debts, and* **Words Are Wind**, *a move that gives him Debts on people that lie to him or break promises. He finishes off his choices by selecting* **Nature's Caress**, **Bedlam**, *and* **Glamours** *from the list of faerie magic.*

DRAMA MOVES

In addition to their Archetype moves, each character also gets a set of **drama moves**: a **corruption move**, an **intimacy move**, and an **end move**. There aren't any choices to be made about these moves when making characters, but it's good for players to be familiar with what these will mean for their character. Check out 73 for more on drama moves, including all the mechanics for corruption, intimacy, and death.

> *Ryan briefly notes Volund's drama moves. His corruption and intimacy moves both involve promises and lies; Ryan can see that truth telling and deception are going to be major elements of his character. Ryan's not too worried about the end move for now, though. Volund's death—if it ever comes—is a long time away.*

INTRODUCTIONS AND DEBTS

Once everyone has finished filling out their Archetypes, it's time to introduce the characters and assign starting **Debts**, a network of favors and obligations that bind the characters to each other amidst the chaos of the city.

First, each player takes a minute or two to introduce their character, sharing their name, look, demeanor, and answers to intro questions, as well as any additional information that the other characters might know about them. If your character has a reputation in the city for a particular kind of work or behavior, now's a good time to note that. Other players, especially the MC, might ask you a few questions about your character to help the group get a better grasp of your life in the city.

Once each character has been introduced, assign Debts. Begin with the person to the left of the MC and go around the circle, each player reading aloud one of the Debt moves listed on their Archetype. Each **Debt move** establishes a connection between the PC and another character in the form of backstory and ongoing relationships. Most of these relationships will be with other PCs, but it's fine for some of them to be directed at characters controlled by the MC (**non-player characters** or NPCs), especially if there are a small number of PCs.

When it's your turn to assign a Debt, choose one of the Debt moves listed on your Archetype, decide which character the move is describing, and read it out loud to the group. Then work with that player and the MC to make the Debt make sense given what you already know about the characters. Remember that we want you to build on what's said before, drawing connections whenever you see an opportunity to enrich the story.

Think carefully about what kind of relationships you want to establish in the fiction when you assign Debts. Giving away Debts to other characters means that you're giving them the opportunity to demand favors, gifts, and information down the road; getting Debts from other characters means that you will have those same kind of opportunities. Debts tie characters together, usually beyond the simple transaction of the Debt, so look for opportunities to get mixed up with characters you find compelling and intriguing at the start of play. It might seem interesting to focus on NPCs when you assign Debts, but remember that your fellow PCs are the protagonists; their contributions to your story will always be more vital, more dynamic, and more interesting than what NPCs have to offer.

Ryan decides to start with the first Debt move on the Fae Archetype; he says "I think Veronica, The Vamp, broke an important promise to me, and swore she would make it up to me. She owes me two Debts." He looks to Veronica's player, Sophia, to see what she thinks of that Debt. Ryan liked her introduction, and he thinks that Volund probably has big plans for such a… useful beast.

Sophia grins. Veronica is a street kid vampire determined to move up in the world, and breaking a promise sounds like exactly something she would do. "Maybe I told you I would protect you from something and bailed at the last minute?" Sophia's put her extra stat point in Blood, and she likes the idea that the other characters would come to her for protection.

Ryan nods. "Yeah, I've been trying to deal with a gang of demons, and you promised that you'd be there when I scheduled a meeting with them. But on the day of the meeting, you were nowhere to be found. Sound good?"

"Yup! I felt really bad about it later, though. I probably brought you some shitty beers or something to say I was sorry."

Ryan notes the Debt on his Archetype: "Veronica owes me for breaking her promise to keep me safe from the demon gang." Ryan and Sophia will continue to assign Debts and fill in other relationships, but they both know that Veronica owes Volund a favor or two for this broken promise. Ryan looks forward to cashing in that Debt later when he needs some muscle!

When someone owes you a Debt, write down both *who owes you* and *what you did for them* on your Archetype. In order to ***cash in a Debt*** later, you'll need to remind them why they owe you a favor. The person that owes the Debt doesn't have to mark down anything, but they might want to keep a record anyway. See 64 for more on using Debts during the game.

Once you're done assigning Debts, you're ready to start. The city awaits!

THREE
THE MOVES

USING MOVES IN PLAY

The golden rule of moves is simple: *to do it, you do it.*

No move triggers without an action. Want to ***unleash an attack*** on someone? You've got to get your fists, knives, and guns out first. Want to ***figure someone out***? You've got to watch their every move for long enough to get your bearings. Want to ***hit the streets***? You've got to get out of your apartment, my friend. To do it, you do it.

Sometimes the moves prompt you to think about pushing your character to action. You might be sitting there thinking that you've had enough talk, that it's time to get the hell out of this bad situation...when you spot ***escape a situation*** on the basic moves sheet. Next thing you know, you're telling the MC that you want to try to make a break for it at the next opportunity, that you want to push past the opposition and get the hell gone.

Urban Shadows encourages this kind of thinking, provided that you turn your desire to make a move into some action in the fiction that triggers the move. You can't simply say "I escape!" or "I mislead them!" and expect to roll dice. You've got to do something in the fiction that triggers the move or the move doesn't trigger. If the move doesn't trigger, no dice.

At the same time, one of the MC's primary jobs is to watch for those moments when you trigger a move without thinking about it, when you start watching another character closely enough to ***figure them out***, or when you try to ***keep your cool*** in a tense situation. You don't have to worry too much about what moves your character might be triggering; say what you want to do, and the mechanics of the game will kick in when they're needed.

HOLD, +1 FORWARD, AND +1 ONGOING

Some moves describe your character getting **hold** as a result of the move, such as "hold 1" or "hold 3." These are resources that you can spend according to the move—such as "spend the hold one-for-one to ask the MC questions"—but once the holds are spent they're gone. Usually hold has to be spent during a given conversation or scene, but moves tell you how long you have before the hold expires. If there's some ambiguity to how long hold should last, ask your MC for clarification.

Other moves describe your character "taking +1 forward" or "taking +1 ongoing." **+1 forward** means your character gets +1 to the next applicable roll; **+1 ongoing** means your character gets +1 to all rolls that fit the situation the move describes. Like hold, these bonuses only last as long as the move indicates.

BASIC MOVES

Throughout the story, every player character makes use of the basic moves. Your Archetype has other moves that might also come into play (or alter the basic moves), but the majority of the moves characters make during a session are basic moves. Remember that the basic moves are essentially narrative triggers that bring the rules into play.

The seven basic moves are ***unleash an attack***; ***escape a situation***; ***persuade an NPC***; ***figure someone out***; ***mislead, distract, or trick***; ***keep your cool***; and ***let it out***. In this section, we explain each of the moves in greater detail, discuss some of the options the moves present, and provide some helpful examples to show them at work.

UNLEASH AN ATTACK

When you ***unleash an attack*** on someone, roll with Blood. On a hit, you inflict harm as established and choose 1:

- Inflict terrible harm
- Take something from them

On a 7-9, choose 1 from below as well:

- They inflict harm on you
- You find yourself in a bad spot

Unleash an attack is for those times when violence is the answer. Or at least it's your character's answer. And we're not talking about threats or some pushing and shoving. ***Unleash an attack*** triggers when you get down to the business of hurting people—breaking bones, pulling triggers, and generally trying to fuck up your opposition before they do the same to you.

You usually ***unleash*** with a weapon, but you can also trigger this move with your own body—provided you have the right training—or magical attacks, so long as the goal is to harm another character. The latter part is key: this move is about hurting people, full stop. Note that you can't ***unleash*** on inanimate objects like barriers; the move doesn't trigger if your goal is to knock down or move through stuff that can't fight back.

Inflicting harm as established means that you do as much **harm** to your target as makes sense given the fiction. If you're fighting with nothing but your empty fists (1-harm or 0-harm), you do a lot less damage than someone holding a shotgun (3-harm) or a grenade (4-harm). See 148 for more on harm and damage.

»Options for *Unleash an Attack*

Inflicting terrible harm means that you escalate your attack to something really serious—adding +1 harm to whatever you would normally inflict—even if you're already using a lethal weapon. If you're punching someone out, you keep punching even when your target is curled up in a ball; if you're shooting someone, you're pulling the trigger until the clip is exhausted. Inflicting terrible harm is the cold crunch of broken bones in a street fight, the rattling gasp of someone sliced open with a knife at close range. Use it carefully.

Taking something from your opponent is a bit broader; it can represent literally taking an object they're holding or it can be more conceptual, such as seizing the high ground, unseating their footing on a precarious surface, or capturing their complete attention when your ally is trying to escape. In many cases, you can use this option to open an opportunity for someone else to ***unleash an attack*** or ***escape a situation***. When you pick this option, the MC works with you to describe how the situation changes because of your dominance.

When you select *They inflict harm on you* after rolling a 7-9, your opponent is able to perform a counterattack against you while you're unleashing your attack on them. They get their punches, shots, and stabbings in, same as you. It can also represent their allies, if present, inflicting harm on you. The MC tells you how much harm you suffer.

When you select *You find yourself in a bad spot* after rolling a 7-9, you find yourself in a worse position than you held before you made the roll. The MC ups the ante somehow and further complicates the scenario. Sometimes that means that you're physically threatened by the existing opposition or new forces, but it can also mean that you're socially or emotionally vulnerable after striking out.

»Examples for *Unleash an Attack*

While investigating the disappearance of a close friend, Solomon comes face to face with a deadly vampire. He draws his wooden stake and charges the bloodsucker. The MC, Andrew, asks Solomon's player, Victoria, to roll **unleash an attack**, *since Solomon is turning to violence to try to deal with the undead threat.*

Victoria rolls **unleash** *and gets a 7. She chooses to* **inflict terrible harm** *and to* **put Solomon in a bad spot**. *Solomon's stake inflicts 2-harm normally, but since Victoria chose to inflict terrible harm, the stake inflicts 3-harm on the vampire. Andrew, as the MC, describes Solomon quickly stabbing his target in its chest, expertly avoiding the vampire's terrible fangs. The vampire falls back onto the floor shuddering in pain and slowly turning to ash. However, Andrew tells Victoria that Solomon suddenly notices two more vampires in the room, blocking both exits. Looks like The Hunter's night just got messy.*

Gareth is battling his rival Merijke and her goons in a construction site. Andrew tells Miguel, Gareth's player, that there's a deep foundation pit filled with liquid cement at the center of the site; Merijke was planning on dumping Gareth and leaving him trapped for centuries!

Gareth will have none of that. Miguel tells Andrew that Gareth pulls out his 9mm and unleashes on Merijke, who is standing near the gaping hole. Miguel rolls **unleash** *and gets an 11!*

In addition to **inflicting his harm as established**, *Miguel chooses to* **take something from Merijke**. *He wants to take her footing on the edge, causing her to fall into the foundation. Andrew describes Merijke buckling from pain as Gareth shoots her legs several times. She falls into the hole, and unable to stand, sinks slowly into the cement…*

Marissa's Spectre, Father Davis, is looking for a young boy taken by Watanabe, an elder vampire lord. A tip from one of Watanabe's rivals has led Davis to a set of storage units near the docks, but he arrives to find that he's not the only one looking for the boy. Mark tells Marissa that Davis discovers one of Watanabe's guards injured and unconscious outside the facility.

"I kill him. I don't want him waking up and causing trouble. I guess I roll **unleash***?"*

Mark thinks about the situation and says, "Nah, I don't think you're really **unleashing an attack** *here. He's just a human, so he can't fight back or stop you while he's unconscious. If he were a vampire goon, you might be unleashing an attack, but just killing a defenseless mortal isn't really an attack. You snap his neck before he can react. What do you do next?"*

ESCAPE A SITUATION

When you take advantage of an opening to ***escape a situation***, roll with Blood. On a hit, you get away. On a 10+, choose 1. On a 7-9, choose 2:

- You suffer harm during your escape
- You end up in another dangerous situation
- You leave something important behind
- You owe someone a Debt for your escape
- You give in to your base nature and mark corruption

Escape is how you get out of a situation that you would prefer to avoid. It doesn't matter how dangerous the circumstance is, so long as your leaving could be considered risky. It's obvious that you're escaping if you're running from bullets, but attempting to flee from a tense family gathering or a difficult emotional situation also triggers this move.

In order to trigger ***escape a situation*** you need to either create or take advantage of an opening—a difficult task when you're cornered and have no clear avenue of escape. ***Unleash an attack***; ***mislead, distract, or trick***; and ***let it out*** are all excellent ways to create the opening you need to trigger ***escape***.

»Options for *Escape a Situation*

Suffering harm during an escape might be the result of your pursuers attacking you on your way out or because you run into something that blocks your path; the MC tells you how much harm you take. As always, you suffer harm as established, which makes choosing this option much more dangerous when the people chasing you are using automatic weapons or the path in front of you is riddled with deadly magical traps.

Ending up in another dangerous situation puts your fate into the hands of the MC. The new danger may be an old foe catching up to you or some novel threat presenting itself for the first time. The type of danger may change as well; you might get out of an awful professional situation and run right into a group of thugs sent by a rival.

Leaving something important behind means that you drop, forget, or leave something on your way out of the situation. Note that this doesn't give the MC carte blanche to ruin your day; you're much more likely to leave something incriminating or personally significant than you are to leave a priceless magical item or the very object you were trying to get out of the scene in the first place.

Owing someone a Debt for your escape signals that someone—perhaps a character who wasn't even in the scene previously—provides a crucial resource or opportunity that enables your escape. Often this will be an obvious choice, especially when another PC helps you get out the door by covering your escape, but it's the MC's final call who you owe. Perhaps one of your enemies within the city is suddenly eager to help at just the right moment...

Giving in to your base nature and marking corruption means that you call upon whatever darkness lurks inside your character to get to safety. This seems cheap compared to suffering harm or owing Debts, but corruption is more costly than it might initially appear to be. See 176 for more on marking corruption.

»Examples for *Escape a Situation*

> *Convinced that his uncle isn't even in his apartment, Wesley decides to* **escape a situation** *by fleeing through the door away from the trash monster.*

Mark says, "Yeah, that sounds fair. He just noticed you, so you've still got a clear path out."

Robey rolls with Blood and gets a 7, just enough for a hit. He chooses two options off the list: **owe someone a Debt** *and* **leave something important behind***. He's not sure he wants to find out how much harm this thing can do, and he's not interested in more danger or corruption.*

"Cool. The trash monster hurls a jumble of books, but you turn your body so they bounce off your shoulder and you stumble out into the hall. At the end of the hall, you see a man holding the elevator open for you. He gestures to you and shouts, 'Wesley! Come this way!'"

"I run toward him!"

Mark nods. "You reach the elevator without any trouble, but you totally owe this guy." Mark writes down the Debt on his MC sheet. "You also realize that you dropped your cell phone when you got hit with the books. You'll have to find some other way to get in contact with your uncle."

Colby and Liam are freeing their friend Sayed in a dark warehouse where he's been held captive by a wendigo. As they finish untying Sayed's chains, they hear the roar of the beast approaching. Liam tells Colby to run while he holds the creature off.

Andrew, the MC, says "Great. That definitely gives Colby an explicit opening for the **escape***."*

Colby helps Sayed to his feet, and they both flee the warehouse together. Erica, Colby's player, rolls with Blood and gets a result of 11. Colby escapes with her friend in tow but Erica must choose one option for Colby's escape. Erica chooses to **give in to her base nature and mark corruption**.

Andrew asks her, "What does that look like?"

Erica describes Colby and Sayed moving through the warehouse, Colby's pulse racing, every shadow she sees filling her heart with dread. Colby, The Aware, is caught up in the supernatural; it has a hold on her now, and it isn't letting go.

Maeve realizes too late that the meeting with a local oracle is a trap. By the time she figures out that the soothsayer sold her out to a rival faerie court, trolls are already blocking the door.

"I think it's time for me to **escape***," says Tristan, Maeve's player. "This is... not my scene."*

Mark says, "Okay, what do you do?"

"Uh… I try to run past the trolls?"

"Doesn't sound like you have an opening yet. You've probably got to create one before you can roll to **escape***."*

Tristan sighs. "This day is getting baaaad…"

PERSUADE AN NPC

When you ***persuade an NPC*** through seduction, promises, or threats, roll with Heart. On a hit, they do what you ask. On a 7-9, they modify the terms or demand a Debt.

If you ***cash in a Debt*** you have with them before rolling, you may add +3 to your roll.

Persuade an NPC triggers when you try to get an NPC to do something for you by seducing them, promising them something, or threatening their interests. Simply talking isn't enough here; you have to have some leverage for the move to trigger. In other words, they have to want something you're offering or be afraid of the consequences you can bring to bear.

At the same time, your request has to be proportional to your leverage. It's absurd to think that an NPC will betray a close friend because you *asked* them to flip. Promising them something they want, seducing them with your charms, or threatening their safety might work, but *the leverage has to match the request*. The MC is the final judge on what counts as proper leverage.

When you spend a Debt to add +3 your roll, explain how you're bringing that Debt into play. Just saying "I spend the Debt" isn't enough; you have to include it in your persuasion, perhaps by referencing the Debt that has yet to be paid or threatening to reveal secrets kept or go back on promises made. Spending a Debt always counts as providing moderate leverage for this move, such that most NPCs will consider moderate favors and demands.

When you hit this move with a 10+, NPCs generally accede to your wishes, albeit with their own idea of how to give you what you want. If you ask a violent werewolf to find someone for you, there's no guarantee they're going to play nice with that person unless you make that part of your request. Wolves be wolves, after all. Nothing changing that.

On a 7-9, though, the NPC has some more input on the deal itself. It's their choice: they can either modify the terms of the deal—essentially making you a reasonable counter offer on the spot—or take a Debt up front to follow your plan. If they modify the terms, you can still back down from the arrangement, but you won't be able to propose anything new until the situation has changed.

»Examples for *Persuade an NPC*

Lianne has cornered the vampire doctor she believes has information as to the whereabouts of her missing fiancé, sneaking into his office during the middle of the day and catching him by surprise when he opens the office at night. The spirits she consulted told her that she could catch him alone, provided she took a few risks. She draws her revolver and orders the vampire to tell her all that he knows about her fiancé's location.

As MC, Andrew thinks about it for a moment. The vampire could probably take a few bullets, but pain is pain, right? "Okay, he hesitates for a second when he sees the gun. Roll with Heart, and we'll see if you can **persuade** *him."*

Jana, Lianne's player, rolls the dice and gets an 11. The vampire shrugs his shoulders and tells Lianne all he knows. It's not really worth getting shot over.

Roxy is trying to get her wolf pack to lie low because she knows trouble is coming and she wants them to stay safe. But wolves be wolves: they would rather face their enemies on the street.

Vivian, Roxy's player, says, "Okay, I round up the wolves and call out my beta, Zach. I tell him 'Nobody does shit until I say so. I promise I'll look into things, and I'll give you all a howl when I find out more.'"

Mark nods. Her promise is legitimate leverage—she is their alpha, after all—and it doesn't really matter if she's telling the truth or not. Wolves be wolves. He has her roll with Heart to **persuade** *Zack; she hits an 8.*

Mark says, "Zach says, 'I don't know, Rox. This is some serious shit. How about we lay low, but me and Aliah come with you. Keep you safe.' You get the feeling he also wants to say 'And honest,' but he knows better. What do you do?"

"Shit. I don't really want to deal with Zach. But this keeps everyone else off the streets, right?" Mark nods. "I say 'Fine, Zach. We leave in 10 minutes.' Maybe I can ditch him when we get on the road..."

Volund's been doing his best to get back to Arcadia, but all the doors are locked, all the entrances sealed. And damn his luck, his last attempt put the Wild Hunt to his scent. The fucking Hunt.

As Volund steps out of a movie theater on a Tuesday night, Andrew hard frames a scene: "You try to light up a cigarette, but the wind sweeps down the street and puts out the match, as if someone was reaching out to shut you down. You see the darkness light up with the glowing eyes of the Wild Hunt."

Ryan says, "I shout into the darkness, 'It's not me you want! I'm an exile. I'm off-limits!' Can I roll **persuade***?"*

"Sorry, brother. Doesn't look like there's any leverage there. The Wild Hunt's on orders from your king. Logic doesn't move them. Got anything else?"

Ryan frowns. "Nope. I'm not even carrying a weapon. Maybe I should run? Yeah. I think I'm going to run."

FIGURE SOMEONE OUT

When you try to ***figure someone out***, roll with Mind. On a hit, hold 2. On a 7-9, they hold 1 on you as well. While you're interacting with them, spend your hold 1-for-1 to ask their player a question:

- Who's pulling your character's strings?
- What's your character's beef with _______?
- What's your character hoping to get from _____?
- How could I get your character to _____?
- What does your character worry might happen?
- How could I put your character in my Debt?

If you're in their Faction, ask an additional question, even on a miss.

Figure someone out involves learning another character's motivations and worries by scrutinizing their body language, tone of voice, smell, or other telltale clues. In order to trigger the move, you have to narrate how you're studying the other character, including what kinds of things you're looking for in their behavior and appearance.

Note that you get to ask the *player* of the character your questions, so the focus here is on the data your character takes in from the environment—info that might be unspoken or subtle. You might also ask the question in character, but the player has to respond truthfully to the question, even when you're figuring out an NPC and that player is the MC.

Figure someone out usually requires interacting with your target, but there may be cases where you can trigger the move by watching them at a distance or rifling through their belongings. As with other moves, the way you trigger the move shapes the outcomes, so the answers you get from the character may be a little more vague when you're working at a distance.

When you hit this move on a 10+, you're in complete control of your observations. On a 7-9, you let something slip, giving your target a chance to ask questions about you as well. If you're reading them at a distance, you might leave something behind at the scene or disturb the location in such a way that your target gets some information about your machinations.

Remember that you get an additional question, even on a miss, if the character you're figuring out is in your Faction. You know a bit more about how people from your own community act and think, so it's easier for you to piece together what they're up to, even when you don't get a full read on them.

»Examples for *Figure Someone Out*

Liam is questioning the owner of Club Café regarding a shooting outside the club that Liam suspects was the result of some clashes between Night and Wild. The NPC owner, Yolanda, seems a little nervous but answers his questions directly and quickly, giving very little information.

Liam's player, Troi, describes Liam as being skeptical of Yolanda's answers. "I'm going to watch her breathing and eye movement closely, searching for any signs of deceit. I'm The Veteran, so I'm going to rely on my police training from when I worked homicide." He rolls to **figure someone out** *and gets a 14! Liam holds 2.*

Troi starts by asking, "What does your character worry might happen?" Andrew, the MC, tells Troi that Yolanda's clearly worried that if she tells the truth she'll be in danger.

Liam wants to know who she's afraid of and Troi follows up with his second question: "Who's pulling your character's strings?"

Andrew says, "She saw something powerful. It's clear that it scared her and gave her the impression that she should keep her mouth shut or else."

Because Liam and the owner are both members of Mortality, Troi gets to ask Yolanda an additional question. He asks, "How could I get your character to tell me exactly what she saw?"

Andrew tells him, "You'd need to give her a sense of safety, that the thing she saw tonight can't hurt her anymore."

Troi nods, satisfied with the answers.

Father Davis is lost in the spirit world, trapped by a dark ritual with few ways back to the other side. As he tries to find his way home, he runs into a spirit haunting a spirit door, a guardian to keep ghosts and spirits from crossing over.

"I want to watch it from a distance, so I can learn something about it before it sees me. Does that trigger **figure someone out**?*" Mark nods, and Marissa, playing Father Davis, rolls an 8.*

"Okay," Mark says, "you get to hold 2 and it gets to hold 1; it's Wild so you don't get any additional hold. Remember that your questions are pretty limited here while you're only watching it. Do you want to get closer?"

"Yeah, I step out and wave my hands. I'll also spend a hold to ask 'How could I put your character in my Debt?'"

Mark says, "As the spirit gets closer, you see that its mouth is caked with corpus. It eats other spirits, and it would certainly value a meal. If you gave up a bit of yourself to it, it would owe you."

"Eww. No thanks. Who's pulling this character's strings?"

"It's Drik. This spirit wears her brand. Good chance she left it here to guard the door. Here's my question for you: 'What are you worried might happen?'"

Marissa thinks for a moment, then answers. "I'm worried that the spirit is going to tip off Drik before I can get out of here. It's clear from the way I look at the door that I want out of this place. **Now.***"*

Rashid is doing his best to figure out why Elan is running drugs for the faeries, but Elan isn't being cooperative. Despite the fact that Rashid caught him with a trunk full of cocaine and meth, Elan doesn't have anything to say. Mark tells Justin, Rashid's player, that Elan isn't going to talk.

"Fine," says Justin. "I pull out my gun and get real close to Elan. I look him dead in the eye and say, 'Tell me something useful.'"

"Are you trying to intimidate him?"

"No, I want to figure him out," says Justin. "I want to ask, 'Who is pulling your strings?'"

"Sounds to me like you're trying to threaten him. He'd probably give up the information you want, but you'll have to roll **persuade an NPC** *instead. If you want to* **figure him out***, you'll need to deescalate the situation a bit."*

"Yeah, that makes sense," says Justin. "I'm pretty pissed at him, so I think I'll start by threatening him. **Persuade** *it is." He picks up the dice to roll* **persuade**.

MISLEAD, DISTRACT, OR TRICK

When you try to ***mislead, distract, or trick*** someone, roll with Mind. On a hit, they are fooled, at least for a moment. On a 10+, pick 3. On a 7-9, pick 2:

- You create an opportunity
- You expose a weakness or flaw
- You confuse them for some time
- You avoid further entanglement

Mislead, distract, or trick is used whenever your character tries to gain the upper hand over another character through deception. The goal could be to deflect someone's attention away from or toward something, convince someone that the lie you're offering them is the whole truth, or fool them into taking an action—or not taking an action—by your prompting.

Triggering this move, however, involves offering a plausible lie, distraction, or trick. You can't walk into a bar full of vampires and pretend to be one of them if you've previously established that all vampires in the city know each other... unless you've got a magic spell that makes you look like a particular vampire. You've got to offer some plausible falsehood that makes it possible for your target to believe your lie, especially when you're facing some long odds of successfully deceiving another character. You haven't reached the point of uncertainty—the point at which a move triggers—if it's obvious you're not telling the truth.

That said, the move has a broad trigger based on intent: throwing a rock at the cops to distract them is definitely ***mislead, distract, or trick***, but throwing rocks with the intention of hurting the cops would probably be ***unleash***. ***Mislead, distract, or trick*** triggers any time you're trying to put one over on another character and it seems possible that they'd fall for it. If you're being sneaky while trying to accomplish another goal—like harming someone—you need to roll ***mislead*** first, knowing that it might tip your hand, or just go straight for the jugular with whatever you're trying to do.

»Options for *Mislead, Distract, or Trick*

Creating an opportunity gives you a chance to act when you otherwise wouldn't be able to act—an escape route in tight quarters—or makes an action you were going to take considerably more successful—fooling your pursuers for long enough to hail a cab. When you choose this option, your MC tells you what opportunity you get as a result of your trickery.

Exposing a weakness or flaw lets you discover a vulnerability within your opposition. Sometimes this is because you mislead them into revealing a particular weakness or distract them long enough for you to observe something meaningful that they would rather keep secret. It's up to you to act on the weakness, which may lead you to trigger another move.

Confusing them for some time means your gambit lasts longer than it would normally. The deception may last until you're ready to act on it, or may extend for several scenes or sessions. Note that *not* picking this option means that your opposition is only fooled for a short time. If you want your tricks to stick, you need to give up one of the other options.

Avoiding further entanglement allows you to get away more or less clean. After this, the attention is no longer on you and is unlikely to return or your enemy can't quite pin you down. Your opposition may blame someone else or simply overlook you, but their focus falls elsewhere. Further engagement might reopen their interest.

»Examples for *Mislead, Distract, or Trick*

Nathaniel is negotiating with his vampire allies about feeding rights in his territory. One of the older vampires, Riker, demands that Nathaniel make the territory available to his entire clan. When Nathaniel hesitates, Riker gets aggressive: "You wouldn't hold out on us, would you?"

"No. Of course not! It's just that my territory is so small. And unpopulated. You all would drain it dry."

Mark, the MC, says, "That's a lie, though. You just learned that they're opening up the housing complex in the middle of your territory. **Mislead***?"*

Derrick, Nathaniel's player, smirks. "Yeah. Totally a lie." He rolls **mislead, distract, or trick** *and gets a 10. He's very convincing. "I'll take* **expose a weakness or flaw**, **confuse them for some time**, *and* **avoid further entanglement**. *I don't think I need to* **create an opportunity** *here."*

Mark nods and says, "Cool. Riker doesn't look happy, but you can see that he's already willing to give up here. He says, 'I heard rumors that things were getting thin around here. Just didn't want to believe it. Fine, though. We'll go somewhere else.' You're pretty sure he's not going to bring it up again."

"What about the weakness or flaw?" Derrick asks.

"Right. As Riker backs down, you can see that one of the other vampires, Celina, is eyeing him like prey. It looks like Riker doesn't have as tight a grip on his gang as he thinks."

Matt's been changing into a wolf on the regular to keep an eye on Volund's sister, paying off a Debt he owes to the faerie. One night, he notices a group of men park their van across the street from her apartment. As he moves in closer, they exit the vehicle, armed to the teeth.

Andrew, the MC, asks, "What do you do, Matt? They're probably 20-30 feet away from the door."

Karl, Matt's player, says, "I want to move in real close to them. Can I get the jump on a few before they realize I'm here?"

Andrew says, "Yeah, roll **mislead, distract, or trick***. You might be able to catch them off guard."*

Karl rolls and gets an 8. "High enough to hit, but not quite a 10+. I get two options off the list?" Andrew nods. "Okay, I'm choosing **create an opportunity** *and* **avoid further entanglement***. I don't want to get into a fight in the middle of the street."*

"Sounds good," says Andrew. "You move silently along the road, avoiding their line of sight, until you're close enough to grab one of them. While the others are distracted, you dart out of the darkness and knock him to the ground. He's out cold. You pull his body into a shadow. One of them is down, and they don't know where the hell you are."

Karl grins. "Awesome. Can I do it again?"

"They're on the lookout now. I think any further attacks on the group mean **unleashing***, even if you keep your head down. They keep moving toward the apartment door. What do you do?"*

Yuri, a ghost who haunts the local high school, has been passing herself off as a new teacher to get close to some students she thinks might know something about her death. Andrew, the MC, tells her that one day she sees a priest wandering the halls, looking lost.

Blaine, Yuri's player, says, "I'll try to be helpful. I'll manifest so that I can be seen and heard. 'Can I help you, Father?'"

"His eyes open wide when he sees you. He withdraws his crucifix and says, 'I didn't believe it. But it's true. You haunt this place!' You realize too late that you know this priest. He was the one who presided over your funeral!"

"Shit. I try to laugh and dismiss it. 'What are you talking about, Father?' Can I **trick** *him?"*

"I don't know," Andrew says. "He came here looking for you after someone tipped him off that there was a ghost haunting the high school. Pretty tough to trick him when he's on the lookout for you. Do you have a story maybe?"

"Yeah, yeah. How about 'Oh my god. You were...the priest at my twin's funeral. I remember you!' Does that do it?"

"Yeah, go ahead and roll. That's plausible enough that it might buy you a few moments. Might even fool him totally if you're lucky."

KEEP YOUR COOL

When things get real and you ***keep your cool***, tell the MC what situation you want to avoid and roll with Spirit. On a 10+, all's well. On a 7–9, the MC will tell you what it's gonna cost you.

Keep your cool triggers when your character's focus and willpower are needed to accomplish an important goal or avoid serious danger. Note that the move only triggers when the pressure is on, so you won't have to roll this move unless something else in the scene has already brought some pressure to bear on your character.

When you do trigger ***keep your cool***, you set the stakes by declaring what situation you're trying to avoid. If you're worried about the guns already drawn in a gunfight, you might say, "I don't want to get shot"; if you're nervous about your spouse's reaction to some terrible news, you might say, "I'm trying avoid a misunderstanding about what happened last night."

When you roll a 10+ with ***keep your cool***, you see the stressful situation through, dodging bullets, avoiding calamity, and generally coping with shit. On a 7-9, you find yourself in a bit deeper than you expected—the MC will always provide a way out for you...but you might not like the costs. Remember, though, a hit is a hit. A 7-9 result here offers a real way forward, provided you're willing to pay the cost. The MC isn't obligated to bring that threat to bear on a miss, but they are obligated to give you a way out if you get a hit.

Keep your cool is one of the most flexible moves in the game. When your MC is looking for a move but not sure which one to use, they'll probably choose this one. If you're looking for another move instead of ***keep your cool***, push back a little and explain why you think another move ought to trigger instead. Anytime there's some uncertainty in the fiction that's not covered by an existing move, ***keep your cool*** is a solid way to find out what happens next.

»Examples for *Keep Your Cool*

Elora has taken cover in the middle of a firefight against some vamps she was hunting by the docks. She'd hoped to take them by surprise, but things went to hell and now she's got to get out alive before they call in the cavalry.

Mark, the MC, says, "You've got decent cover, but you know it can't last. Your truck is parked a few dozen feet away, and the space between here and there is filled with bullets. The vamps are playing it safe by shooting from cover, but you know they're ready for you to make a move. What do you do?"

Elora's player, Tomas, says, "I think I've got to make a run for it. Should I **keep my cool**? *This shit seems pretty real, and I'd like to avoid getting shot. My* **Slayer** *move lets me roll with Blood instead of Spirit if I'm on a hunt."*

"You're totally still on a hunt. Go ahead and roll with Blood."

Tomas rolls a 12. Mark says, "You break from cover, running fast toward your truck. A bullet nicks your neck, but you otherwise arrive unharmed. You fumble for your keys for a moment, then get the truck running. You see a bunch of vamps breaking cover to pursue. What do you do?"

Hadi is playing Olivia, an Oracle who had delved deep into the spirit wilds to find out the truth behind her mother's murder. After a long journey, she finally comes face to face with Fenrir, the Norse wolf of myth and legend, and begins to demand answers.

"I walk as close to him as I can, shouting, 'Tell me what you know, wolf! No more secrets.'"

Andrew, the MC, grimaces. "That's tough to do. He's enormous. His teeth look like they're each a foot long, at least. He growls as you approach. I think you're going to have to **keep your cool** *to pull that off."*

Hadi rolls with Spirit and gets a 7. She looks back to Andrew. "What's the cost?"

Andrew says, "He's a spirit lord, and you're showing him a lot of disrespect. Fenrir will take a Debt against you—he's not likely to forget this insult—or you need to show weakness and submission before his majesty. Your choice."

Hadi doesn't hesitate. "Take the Debt. I want my answers."

Andrew laughs. "Very well. Fenrir snorts, and turns toward you. You've got his attention, and he looks mildly *interested. What do you do?"*

Skylar is an adjunct professor of psychology at the local university...but not that long ago she was a vigilante who worked to free women from sex trafficking. While tracking down a lead for Rashid, she finds herself back on her old stomping grounds, face to face with a trafficker she thought was dead. There's a reason she got out of this business.

Mark says, "As his goons move to surround you, you realize that your old foe...isn't human. He's probably a vampire. Maybe something worse. Before you can react, he grabs you by the neck. What do you do? Do you want to try to **keep your cool** *here?*

"Fuck that. I want to hurt this guy. I draw my gun and shoot him in the stomach."

"Yeah, I don't think he's expecting that. Go ahead and make your **unleash** *roll. Just remember that you're already in a bad spot here, and a miss is going to make it a whole lot worse."*

LET IT OUT

When you ***let out the power within you***, roll with Spirit. On a hit, choose 1 and mark corruption. On a 10+, ignore the corruption or choose another from the list.

- Take +1 forward on your next roll
- Extend your senses, supernatural or otherwise
- Frighten, intimidate, or impress your opposition
- Take definite hold of something vulnerable or exposed

Let it out is the catch-all supernatural and preternatural move. If you're wondering how to mesmerize a mortal with your vampiric powers or tear off a car door with your werewolf strength, look no further: ***let it out*** allows your character to access whatever strange powers and abilities you don't find elsewhere on your Archetype.

On occasion, you might find that there's some overlap between ***letting it out*** and using an Archetype move. A faerie, for example, might decide to get in touch with their connection to Arcadia rather than casting faerie magic. Remember that triggering ***let it out*** isn't just activating magic powers; you're actively letting out the darkness within you, giving it control to get what you want. The risks and rewards of such an opening are greater, and you might decide you want these options rather than the ones tied to an Archetype move.

Unlike the other basic moves (and many Archetype moves), ***let it out*** has an inherent cost—marking a corruption—because your character is opening up a floodgate to the darkness in exchange for power. Unless you can maintain strict control by rolling a 10+, the darkness gains a stronger hold on your heart and soul, pushing you closer to the abyss. Check out *Corruption* on 176 to learn more about corruption and your corruption track.

Mortals might be hesitant to use this move, but the lack of supernatural abilities isn't an impediment to triggering ***let it out***. Mortals have power supernaturals don't have: human instinct, adaptability, untapped potential, etc. Find a way to tap into the power within you, no matter how overt or subtle it may be. You might surprise yourself.

»Options for *Let It Out*

Taking a +1 forward to your next roll means that you're using your abilities to gain an immediate advantage on the next move you make. You might tap your inner wolf before you ***unleash*** on an enemy or open up your third eye to see clearly before you ***figure someone out***. Work with your MC to describe what it looks like when you choose this option.

Extending your senses, supernatural or otherwise gives you direct information about the situation at hand. The MC tells you what you find, depending on the fiction. An Oracle investigating a murder scene might get glimpses of what happened, while a Hunter might notice an overlooked clue that points toward the supernatural. Note that there's no guarantee you'll find anything when you open up your senses; sometimes there's nothing there for you to find.

Frightening, intimidating, or impressing your opposition causes them to rethink their current course of action or sets you up to make them vulnerable or exposed. This effect can be subtle—a vampire's hypnotic gaze—but it generally gets the attention of those around you. Work with your MC to describe what it looks like when you choose this option.

Taking definite hold of something vulnerable or exposed allows you to seize what others have, including their possessions, their position, or their life. It's similar to choosing "take something from them" from ***unleash***, but it allows for more nuance. You can use this to rip off a car door or to push a demon back to a hellplane with an arcane ritual. Note that the target must be vulnerable or exposed; you can't affect secure targets. What's vulnerable or exposed depends on the situation and your character's native talents and abilities.

»Examples for *Let It Out*

Veronica is out at a nightclub, hoping to pick up something to eat. She's found a nice young man, Donald, who is already interested in taking her home for the evening. On their way out of the club, however, she notices a few demons following them. She's in no shape to fight them toe-to-toe—not until she's eaten—so she scrambles for a new plan.

Sophia, Veronica's player, says, "I want to use Donald against them. Can I try to grab hold of his mind with my vampiric powers?"

Andrew, the MC, says, "Yeah, sure. Sounds like you're **letting it out***. What does that look like?"*

"I grab his head with both hands, kiss him deeply, and then look him straight in the eyes. I say 'Those bad men there want to hurt me. Can you please take care of them for me?' Does that work?"

Andrew nods and tells her to roll with Spirit. She hits a 10. "Great. He's totally captivated by you, enthralled by your presence. Which options do you want?"

"I want my hold on his mind to be solid. I think I'll go with **take definite hold of something vulnerable or exposed***. I don't mind marking corruption, so I'll also choose* **take +1 forward on your next roll** *for when I* **escape** *this awful situation."*

"All right," says Andrew. "Donald's eyes cloud, and he turns away from you toward the demons. You see his body tense as he gets ready to throw a punch. How do you **escape***?"*

Gareth is trying his best to deliver a message for his demonic patron, but the woman he's been sent to intimidate is hard to reach. So far, he hasn't had any luck getting past the security at her office. After a few more subtle attempts fail, he decides to take a forward approach.

"I walk right up to the security staff by the front door and summon some fire from a hellplane. I want to scare the shit out of them."

"You **letting it out** *or activating your demon form?" asks Andrew.*

*"***Letting it out** *for now. I don't want to activate my demon form unless I need that kind of power."*

"Sounds good. Go ahead and roll with Spirit."

Miguel, Gareth's player, rolls and hits a 7, barely enough to pull off his plan. "I'll take **frighten, intimidate, or impress your opposition***. I want these guys gone."*

Andrew says, "Sure. Your hands catch fire, brimstone and darkness swirling around them. The two guards take one look at you and bail, running away as fast as they can. They don't even draw their weapons." Miguel smiles.

"But you feel the hellfire seep into your heart. And it burns something up inside of you, something precious. Already you can't remember what it was, the thing you cared about. It's gone now. Just hellfire remains."

Rashid and Skylar have come to Pythia with a request: they want her to use her supernatural foresight to help them figure out who shot their friend, Sun-Hi. They have the murder weapon, but they don't have any way to get answers from the gun. It was wiped clean of prints and the serial numbers are long gone.

Pythia takes the gun and holds it in her hands. "I think I want to **let it out** *here to extend my supernatural senses. I want to get in touch with the gun."*

Mark, the MC, nods and says, "Don't you have **Psychometry***, though? If you use that move, you get multiple, specific questions that are totally in line with the information you want. If you* **let it out***, you'll only get vague impressions and you might end up marking corruption."*

Pythia's player, Lucia, says, "Oh, I totally forgot about **Psychometry***. I think I'll use that instead."*

LEND A HAND OR GET IN THE WAY

When you ***lend a hand*** or ***get in the way*** after a PC has rolled, roll with their Faction. On a hit, give them a +1 or -2 to their roll. On a 7-9, you expose yourself to danger, entanglement, or cost.

Each move in *Urban Shadows* is a moment in the fiction, an event that needs to resolve before you can move on to the next event. Only one character can have that kind of spotlight at a time, so you resolve one move at a time. If you try to ***escape a situation***, we need to see how that resolves before you can ***let it out*** or ***unleash*** on the opposition. One move at a time.

After a player rolls, however, other players can jump in to help or interfere with their plans, provided they are fictionally available to do so. (You can't help someone beat up a demon while you're on the phone—unless you've got some secret knowledge about demons that would be meaningful to the other character!) Some of these actions might normally trigger a basic move—like trying to trick another character or beat them up—but since you're acting while another player has the spotlight, you roll with their Faction instead of rolling the basic move.

The bonuses and penalties for these rolls tell you when they're useful—you can't help when someone has rolled a 4, and you can't interfere when someone has rolled a 12. Your character can obviously undertake whatever fictional action they deem appropriate, like providing cover fire or intimidating an NPC, but these two moves only trigger when they make sense for the situation *and* have mechanical meaning. If you can't help or interfere, it's likely that your assistance can trigger a new move after the current one is resolved, lashing out with violence or attempting to persuade the NPC yourself.

When you roll a 10+ while ***lending a hand*** or ***getting in the way***, things go smoothly and you can apply your bonus or penalty to the other player's roll without cost. On a 7-9, you still get the bonus, but you find yourself in a tough spot as a result of your interference in the situation. On a miss, the MC tells you what happens, just like with any other basic move. You roll with Faction because your character is trying to evaluate the best way to help or interfere with a person from this particular community; misses here may indicate misperceptions about other communities (or your own).

This move is crucial when the players oppose each other. Since ***unleash*** isn't an opposed roll, whoever unleashes first might do a lot of damage before the other player's character can react. ***Getting in the way*** allows players targeted by other players to weaken attacks and resist trickery without everyone rolling dice all at once. It's not uncommon for the MC to turn a move back on someone who misses when they're targeting another player, effectively giving them a 10+ on the same move in reverse. If you'd like to read more about these kinds of conflicts in *Urban Shadows*, check out *Player vs. Player* on 207 in **The Master of Ceremonies**.

Only one character can successfully lend a hand and only one character can successfully interfere on any given roll. All the characters can try, but you can't keep racking up the +1s as every other PC lends a hand (or -2s if everyone jumps in to get in the way). If a player misses while ***lending a hand*** or ***getting in the way***, however, other characters can jump in and try, exposing themselves to the potential costs and complications that result from these kinds of rolls.

Note that ***lending a hand*** or ***getting in the way*** has to make sense within the fiction. You can't interfere by silently thinking evil thoughts (unless you've got mind magic or telepathy!) when someone ***unleashes an attack*** with a machete, and you can't help someone ***escape a situation*** by whispering encouragement across a room. You also can't ***lend a hand*** or ***get in the way*** with Faction moves (198) as those moves center around a character's relationship with an entire faction.

»Examples for *Lend a Hand* or *Get in the Way*

Roxy has agreed to help out Elora the Hunter with clearing out a vampire nest she's discovered behind a punk rock club. As they break down the front door, Elora is confronted by a pair of vampires, both of whom leap up at her with their teeth bared.

Tomas, Elora's player, says, "I blast both of them with my shotgun." Mark, the MC, nods and tells her to roll **unleash**. *Despite Elora's high Blood, Tomas only rolls a 9; he'll have to pick between taking harm or getting put in a spot.*

"Can I **lend a hand**?" *asks Roxy's player, Vivian.*

"Of course! How are you helping?"

"I throw my head back and let out an unnatural howl as we enter to frighten the vampires.

"Sounds great. You're helping a Hunter, so roll with Mortality." Roxy gets a 9. Elora gets to add +1 to her roll—making her result a 10+—but Roxy has exposed herself to danger, entanglement, or cost by **lending a hand**.

Mark says, "Okay, one of them takes a full blast from the shotgun and stumbles backward, already turning to ash. The other moves at lightning speed, dodging the blast from the shotgun and tackling Roxy to the ground, its teeth an inch away from her neck. Roxy, what do you do?"

After Lianne discovers that Yuri was responsible for her fiancé's death, she decides that the only just punishment is an eye for an eye; she decides to kill Yuri's niece to teach the ghost a lesson. Luckily for Yuri, Colby tips her off to the plan, giving her enough time to get to her niece just as Lianne arrives to execute her revenge.

Blaine, Yuri's player, says, "I immediately manifest, grab a knife off the counter in the kitchen, and attack Lianne." Andrew, the MC, nods and Blaine rolls to **unleash** *on the wizard. He rolls an 8, just within the range that Lianne can alter.*

Lianne's player, Jana, says, "I definitely want to interfere. How do I do that?"

Andrew says, "You can try to push her away with magic or just roll out of the way. Anything that's going to keep her away from you."

"I like pushing her away with magic. I'll let loose an uncontrolled burst of energy to push her away from me." Jana rolls with Night, and hits a 10+. Blaine shakes his head. Tough break.

Andrew says, "The blast of energy catches Yuri off guard. You push her back further than you expected, slamming her hard into the wall. Go ahead and pick some options off the **unleash** *list as if you rolled a 10+."*

Jana says, "I don't think I really want to hurt her. I think I want to take something from her. Maybe force her to de-manifest?"

Andrew nods. "Seems pretty reasonable. You slam her up against the wall—Yuri, mark 1-harm—and then slowly pull her apart, scattering her corpus. She's going to have to **keep her cool** *to manifest again this scene. What do you do next?"*

FACTION MOVES

Faction moves complement the basic moves, allowing your character to interact more broadly with the Factions that vie for power within the city. Instead of rolling with a main stat when you trigger one of these moves, you roll with a Faction stat that describes your relationship with the community you're engaging.

The three core Faction moves are ***hit the streets***, ***put a face to a name***, and ***investigate a place of power***. Other moves might also make use of the Faction stats on your Archetype, but only these count as Faction moves.

HIT THE STREETS

When you ***hit the streets*** to get what you need, name who you're going to and roll with their Faction. On a hit, they're available and have the stuff. On a 7-9, choose 1:

- Whoever you're going to is juggling their own problems
- Whatever you need is more costly than anticipated

Hit the streets lets you seek out contacts and connections within the city to help you get what you need: info, magical items, information, your nightly fix, whatever. Any time your character grabs their coat and hat to get out and pound the pavement for resources, roll ***hit the streets***.

You must say who you're making contact with before you roll; it should be reasonable that they can provide you with whatever you need. Whenever possible, try to circle back to existing characters with this move: the city gets a little crowded if there's a knowledgeable demon hunter on every corner. Better to go to the person everyone knows.

Notice that you actually have to get out into the city to trigger this move. It's not enough to make a few phone calls or post on an internet forum and hope that the goods come directly to you. Supernatural creatures—and the mortals who deal with them on a daily basis—are always skeptical of impersonal communication. Phone calls are too easily monitored by their enemies. Emails are vulnerable to hackers and police. Best to see someone in the flesh. Safer.

»Options for *Hit the Streets*

If *whoever you go to is juggling their own problems*, it doesn't mean they can't or won't help you. In fact, they might be more open to bargaining because they've got a ticking time bomb on their hands, some situation that they can't resolve on their own because they lack the resources or skills needed to get out from under the rock. Your request for help is certainly messier when you drag their business into it, but they definitely have whatever you're looking to get from them.

If *whatever you need is more costly than anticipated*, then either your contact is suffering some sort of shortage or scarcity or you don't know the real value of what you're requesting. Maybe whatever you're looking for is more dangerous than you realize or you overlooked something obvious about the costs of the thing in question. Your contact may need you to pay with more than just Debts or money, like immediate favors or valuable items, magical or mundane. They have it, but it's going to cost you.

»Examples for *Hit the Streets*

Veronica, a vampire still associated with the Night Faction, has recently learned that a group of demons are looking for her. She wants to find out who they are before they catch up to her.

"I want to go visit my Power contact, Jean Paul," says Sophia, Veronica's player. "He's a human wizard who sometimes feeds me information."

"Sounds like you're **hitting the streets** *to me," says Andrew, the MC. "Where does he live?"*

"He has an apartment downtown near a subway stop. It's not far from my place." Sophia rolls with Power and gets a 9. Even though she's close to a full success, she can't get help on a Faction roll. Sophia chooses that **the cost will be higher than she anticipated**.

Andrew smiles and describes Veronica reaching Jean Paul's apartment. "His staff lets you in, telling you he's inside his study. As you walk to that part of the apartment, your supernatural hearing picks up Jean Paul whispering: 'She's here! Yes. Be ready. I'll let you know as soon as she leaves.' It sounds to you like Jean Paul is already mixed up in the situation; getting the truth out of him will be more difficult than you thought."

PUT A FACE TO A NAME

When you ***put a face to a name*** or vice versa, roll with their Faction. On a hit, you know their reputation; the GM tells you what most people know about them. On a 10+, you've dealt with them before; learn something interesting and useful about them or they owe you a Debt. On a miss, you don't know them or you owe them; the MC will tell you which.

The city is filled with more people than anyone can possibly know, but your character is bound to have met—or at least heard of—most of the movers and shakers in the city. This move lets you establish history or learn someone's reputation upon seeing them or hearing about them for the first time. The question "What do I know about them?" or "Have I heard of this person?" is going to come up often while playing *Urban Shadows*; this move lets you answer the question and build on the answer quickly.

You only roll this move the first time you meet someone new or hear a new name. It's not something that you can trigger later when you sit down to really think about the person that you met earlier. Either the name (or face) hits you and you remember something, or you proceed in the fiction to build a new relationship with that character. It's always an option to say, "I don't know this person" and skip the roll.

If you get a hit on this move, you're familiar with the person in question, but they might not know who you are at all. They've got a reputation, but information isn't always a two-way street. On a strong hit, you get their reputation and a little bit more: choose a Debt for services previously rendered or dig a bit deeper into their story. On a miss, the MC tells you if they're a stranger or someone you owe.

»Examples for *Put a Face to a Name*

Liam is scoping out a meeting between powerful wizards and werewolves, a peace meeting that he's worried might turn ugly. He's found a safe space in a building across the street, and he's set up surveillance equipment to get solid sounds from the meeting.

Andrew, the MC, says, "You see a car pull up to the building across the street. A tall woman gets out, lanky and thin, her red hair cropped short to her head, wearing a white suit. She says something to the driver and starts to walk up the stairs to the front door."

Troi, Liam's player, says, "I'd like to **put a name to a face**. *I want to know if I know her." Mark nods and tells Liam that the woman is in the Wild Faction. Liam rolls with Wild and gets an 11.*

"Yup. You know her. Do you want a Debt or something interesting and useful?"

"I'll take something interesting and useful!"

"Awesome. Her name is Raquel. She's a werewolf, but she left Night a long time ago to join the Wild faction. She represents the demon Ortalix in business dealings here in the city. You've probably seen her around a number of times, and she always wears the same exact outfit. What most people don't know about her is that she's eager to get out of her service to Ortalix.

She signed a contract she didn't understand, and now she's in a tough spot. Maybe she's here to find some way out of her shitty deal?"

Pythia, paying off a Debt to Rashid, takes Maeve to a local meeting of wizards in the hopes that one of them will know who has cast a curse on the faeries that live near the Heights. As they enter the meeting, Pythia says, "Whatever you do, don't tell Dr. Flint that Rashid asked me to do this."

Tristan, playing Maeve, nods and turns to the MC, Mark. "Do I know Dr. Flint?"

"Not sure. Go ahead and roll **put a face to a name***. He's part of Power, obviously." Tristan rolls and gets a 9, not quite enough for a 10+. "Looks like you only know his reputation. He's a wizard of some repute. He's been in the city a long time, but lately he's been showing up to fewer and fewer events. There's some rumor that he was leaving the Council, but nothing's come of it."*

INVESTIGATE A PLACE OF POWER

When you ***investigate a place of power***, roll with the Faction that owns it. On a hit, you see below the surface to the reality underneath. On a 10+, you can ask the MC one question about the schemes and politics of the Faction in question.

Investigating a place of power comes in many forms: you might literally go through the files in someone's study or subtly observe the dance floor in a mortal nightclub. In order to trigger the move, you've got to be looking for answers beyond what you can see with a quick glance. Walking through a crowded room doesn't trigger the move; you've got to slow down and really *look around* at the place.

Sometimes other moves might offer you unique opportunities to investigate places of power, triggering the move when it would otherwise be difficult to trigger. For example, a vampire might ***let it out*** to supercharge their senses and listen closely to what individuals are whispering to each other. These other moves don't do the investigating all on their own, but they set you up to trigger ***investigate a place of power*** in a difficult situation.

A place of power is one that others in that Faction would consider important: a werewolf bar, the law office owned by a demon lord, the fae's tattoo parlor, the police precinct, you get the idea. The question you can ask on a 10+ should fit within the context of the place and situation, but your MC might allow you to ask broader questions if the location might offer clues to the Faction's larger political machinations.

»Examples for *Investigate a Place of Power*

After weeks of searching, Solomon has located the haven of a nest of demons that have been preying upon the local neighborhood. When he arrives to investigate—and possibly harm them—no one is home. He breaks in anyway, and starts looking around their place.

The MC, Andrew, asks, "Are you actually digging into stuff or looking for something in particular?"

Victoria, Solomon's player, says, "I'm mostly looking for information about their dealings. Why are they here? What are they trying to do? I think that's **investigating a place of power***?" Andrew nods. Victoria rolls and gets a 10.*

"This nest of demons has left this place a mess. It's like all they do is come back here to eat and sleep. The rest of the time they don't want anything to do with this place. As you get a better sense of the space, you realize that they're preparing a ritual here. At the center of the nest is an altar, pieces of flesh and bone scattered around it. Whatever it is, even the demons don't like the power it holds."

"Jesus. I get a question, right? How about 'How can I stop this ritual?'"

Andrew nods. "Good question. You see that the altar bears the mark of one of the demons who lives here, Erakthu. If you kill him, this whole ritual falls apart. Easier said than done, though. What do you do?"

DEBT MOVES

There's no way to *make* another player character dance to your tune in *Urban Shadows* besides Debt. You can't persuade them with logic or intimidate them with violence; you might get them to go along with you, but only because it's easier than fighting with you. There's no way to roll the dice to make folks make tough choices.

Unless you've got a Debt. Once people owe you, you can ask them for all kinds of things. And when you put the weight of a Debt behind something, it carries all new meaning. If they want to be taken seriously in the city, then they need to pay what they owe. Only someone who can't be trusted—who isn't worth saving when the chips are down—goes back on their accounts.

Debt moves deal with interactions fueled by Debt. There are four Debt moves: ***do someone a favor***, ***cash in a Debt***, ***refuse to honor a Debt***, and ***drop someone's name***. None of these moves come up as often as the basic moves, but you'll see them multiple times a session. In this section, we offer some examples and explanations for Debt moves to help you integrate them into your sessions.

DO SOMEONE A FAVOR

When you do someone a favor, they owe you a Debt.

Gaining Debts means going out of your way to ***do a favor*** for other characters. Anytime you help someone out without recompense, you get to claim a Debt from them that can be cashed in at a later time. You can claim Debts from both PCs and NPCs, provided you do something useful for them.

A favor has to be acknowledged by the other party or it isn't a Debt; you can't do something for someone and claim a Debt if they don't really care about your efforts. It's cool to work this out in the fiction in advance—"Yeah, I can totally help you out, but you're going to owe me"—or to step out of character and draw attention to something that happens in the moment—"I just saved your Fae's life. I think she owes me a Debt." If you forget to call out a Debt in the moment, don't fret. You have a chance at the end of each session to collect Debts you think you're owed if you miss them in the moment.

If you do someone a favor because you're already getting something from them, it doesn't count. Consider that a wash. No need to keep the books when everybody's breaking even. That said, one-sided deals—"Rat out your friends, and I'll give you a ride across town"—don't count as even exchanges. You can't avoid a Debt by offering something paltry.

»Examples for *Do Someone a Favor*

During a lengthy negotiation with some local demons, Volund uses faerie magic to distract them long enough to steal a cell phone off one of their goons. Later, he brings the cell phone to Gareth, hoping to push Gareth further into his Debt by sharing crucial information.

"So I'll give you this phone, but you owe me, right?" says Ryan, Volund's player.

"Yeah, that's fine," says Miguel, Gareth's player. "I definitely want the phone, so I'll owe you the Debt."

Ryan writes the Debt down on Volund's sheet. He can call it in later when it's useful to him.

Nathaniel and Elora have teamed up to take down Watanabe, working to kill enough of his vamps to draw him out of hiding and kill him before he hurts anyone else. Nathaniel's got his own reasons for wanting the vampire lord dead, but Elora isn't asking too many questions.

The two of them get in over their heads at the local police station when they're trapped in a cell with a vampire who tries to kill them both. Nathaniel manages to rip the vampire's head off, but they're both wounded in the scuffle.

Derrick, Nathaniel's player, says, "Since I killed him, I think you owe me a Debt. If I wasn't here, you'd be dead."

Tomas, Elora's player, says, "I think I would have been okay. Also, he was trying to kill you too. You didn't do me any favors."

The MC, Mark, nods. "Yeah, I think Elora has dealt with this kind of thing before. No Debts for this. You're not doing her a favor by saving her life when yours is also on the line."

CASH IN A DEBT

When you ***cash in a Debt***, remind your debtor why they owe you in order to...

...make a PC:

- Do you a favor at moderate cost
- ***Lend a hand*** to your efforts
- ***Get in the way*** of someone else
- Answer a question honestly
- Erase a Debt they hold on someone
- Give you a Debt they hold on someone else

...make an NPC:

- Answer a question honestly about their Faction
- Introduce you to a powerful member of their Faction
- Give you a worthy and useful gift without cost
- Erase a Debt they hold on someone
- Give you a Debt they have on someone else
- Give you +3 to ***persuade*** them (choose before rolling)

Cashing in a Debt is easy. Whenever you want something from someone who owes you a Debt, remind them why they owe you and tell them what you want. Anything from the list is legit at all times, including making them answer questions honestly or giving you a Debt they're holding on someone else. Provided they follow through on your request, the Debt is used up and erased.

You don't need to quote the reason for the Debt exactly when you ***cash in a Debt***; alluding to the favor owed is plenty reason enough to trigger the move. What matters is that both parties recall the Debt and acknowledge it, and that they both know that it's been spent if the debtor honors the Debt. Of course, PC debtors can always ***refuse to honor a Debt*** with all the cost and consequences that come with going back on their word.

»Options for *Cash In a Debt* with PCs

Getting a *favor at moderate cost* is a broad option, encompassing all sorts of favors that aren't already on the list. You might ask someone to hide something sensitive for you, steal something valuable, or back you up in a tough situation. It's all dependent on the skills and talents of the character who owes you the Debt. For some characters, killing someone is a favor they can perform at moderate cost. As always, the MC arbitrates any disputes on what's moderate, but look to the fiction to get a sense of what might be moderate for any given character.

Lending a hand or ***getting in the way*** both involve engaging with another PC's roll. If you want another character to help you in the moment, this is the option to choose. Note that this means that you might resolve ***cashing in a Debt*** in the middle of another move to determine if someone will ***lend you a hand*** or ***get in the way*** of someone else.

Demanding that a PC *answer a question honestly* is the only way to get the absolute truth from another PC. None of the options on ***figure someone out*** tell you if a character is lying about any particular statement—***figure someone out*** focuses on the political situation a character is in, not the truth—but you can force another PC to be honest by cashing in Debts. If the PC honors the Debt, their answer to the question must be full and complete: no misleading or tricks!

Erasing Debts means that you're spending a Debt to erase a Debt, effectively clearing the books. You lose a bit of your control over the person who owes you the Debt, but you can get out—or get someone else out—from under their thumb, assuming they don't hold other Debts over you or the person you're trying to save.

Transferring Debts requires that you know about the Debts in question. Most people are pretty open with who owes them, but you've got to get the information before you start asking people to hand over their Debts to you.

»Examples for *Cash In a Debt* with PCs

> *Late at night, Volund decides that he needs to get some real answers out of Gareth. He calls him and says, "Remember how I gave you that phone earlier? I need you to help me out. Tell me what you know about Michael's death."*
>
> *Miguel groans. He doesn't want to tell Volund that Gareth killed Michael, even though he had good reasons for his actions. But he also doesn't*

want to try to refuse the Debt. He decides to honor the Debt and weather the consequences.

"Volund... It was me. I killed Michael. I'm sorry. It had to happen..."

On the run from a powerful wizard, Pythia finds Skylar in her office at the local university, just before Skylar's class starts. Skylar isn't happy to see Pythia: one more "incident" on campus and Skylar's likely to lose her teaching position at the university. Yet, as Pythia tries to explain her situation, there's a loud knock at the door.

"I try to climb out the window. I gotta stay on the move," says Lucia, Pythia's player. She rolls **escape** *and hits a 6. Not quite enough.*

Lucia turns to Reiko, Skylar's player, and says "Maybe you can help?" Reiko shakes her head. No need to get involved in this business.

Lucia isn't deterred. "I'm **cashing in a Debt** *to make her* **lend me a hand** *here."*

Mark, the MC, says, "Okay. What do you say? Remember you've got to make reference to the Debt."

"Pythia says, 'Dammit, Skylar. Do you remember when I used my second sight on that gun you found? It led you right to the murderer. You gotta help me out here.'"

Reiko nods and sighs. "Okay, okay. I'll **lend a hand**.*"*

Mark says, "How? What do you do to help her out?"

"I'll shout 'Hold on a minute!' at the door, and help Pythia climb out the window. We're on the second floor, but there are some vines she can climb down."

Skylar rolls and gets a 7, just enough to help, but not enough to get away clean. Pythia gets to **escape** *out the window with a few complications—she chooses to suffer harm and mark corruption—but Skylar is on the hook for some serious drama. It looks like whoever is looking for Pythia is going to want to ask Skylar a few questions...*

»Options for *Cash In a Debt* with NPCs

Demanding that an NPC *answer a question honestly* is a bit narrower than demanding an answer from the PC. The question must be about their Faction, either broadly about the politics of the Faction or confirmation of gossip or rumors about individual members. If you want NPCs to answer questions about themselves honestly, you'll have to ***persuade*** them.

Getting an NPC to *introduce you to a powerful member of their Faction* allows you to bypass the obstacles such NPCs usually put up to avoid dealing with riffraff. Your debtor may not like you, but they must give you a friendly introduction and guarantee safe passage to the powerful NPC. If you screw things up while you're surrounded by the NPC's goons, though, that's on you. Try to play nice.

Demanding they *give you a worthy or useful gift without cost* means that you're offering the NPC a chance to pay off their Debt by giving you material goods. NPCs don't have to honor specific requests, but they do have to give you something that you actually want. If they make an offer and you reject it, however, you can't go back and demand it after you see a few more things.

Erasing and transferring Debts with NPCs works exactly the same as it does with PCs. Remember that you have to know a Debt exists in the fiction before you can cancel it or get the NPC to give it to you.

Adding a +3 to your ***persuade*** *roll before rolling* is essentially asking for a moderate favor from the NPC. Since NPCs can't roll to ***refuse to honor a Debt***, ***persuading*** them with a +3 is effectively calling in a moderate favor with the Debt. A miss on a ***persuade*** roll can sometimes mean that the NPC weasels out of the Debt, returning the Debt to you as if they had successfully refused it. You always have leverage if you're willing to ***cash in the Debt*** and take the +3 before you roll.

»Examples for *Cash In a Debt* with NPCs

Fahad has been working for his demonic patron long enough to stack up a few Debts. When the Wild faction goes to war with Power, he tries to get some answers from the dark lord who pulls his strings. The next time he meets with Razerk, he **cashes in a Debt** *to* **get some honest answers**.

Bryan, Fahad's player, says, "I've done all your dirty work for months now. You have to tell me the truth for me to do my damn job. Why is Wild striking out at Power? What's going on?"

Mark, the MC, says, "Razerk hesitates, but then shakes his head...and caves. 'I am not the only demon with plans for the mortal world. Onrathen's agents seek to steal a relic from the wizards and open a door to hell. I would advise that you stay out of their way.'"

Matt is a wolf on a mission; he's in debt to Yuri, a ghost who wants him to help her find out who was responsible for her murder. Matt decides that the best path forward is to contact an oracle he knows, Carlos, who might be able to peer back into the past.

Carlos isn't having it: "I told you, cabrón, *I don't do that shit. The future* solamente*."*

Matt is insistent. Karl, Matt's player, says, "You remember that time I backed you up when the cops tried to rough you up and close your store? You owe me, man. Time to pay up."

Andrew, the MC, says, "Sounds like you're **cashing in a Debt** *to* **persuade** *him, right?"*

"Yeah. I need this." Matt rolls, but comes up short—even with his +3, he only gets a 6.

"Carlos just shakes his head. 'Sorry. I can't do it. You'll have to find someone else. Looking backward is dangerous business. I can't pay you back in full if I'm dead, right?'"

"Damn. Do I still lose the Debt?"

Andrew says, "No, I think Carlos still owes you. He just weaseled his way out this time. You can call in the Debt again later. What do you do now?"

REFUSE TO HONOR A DEBT

When you ***refuse to honor a debt***, roll with Heart. On a hit, you weasel out of the current deal, but still owe the Debt. On a 7-9, you choose 1:

- You owe them an additional Debt
- You lose face with their Faction
- You mark corruption

On a miss, you can't avoid the noose. You either honor your Debt or face the consequences: they pick two from the list above or force you to lose all the Debts owed to you.

Just because someone has a Debt over you doesn't mean you have to honor it...right now. Maybe it's not a good time or the thing they're asking for is just out of your reach at the moment. You can't be all things to all people all the time. And sometimes people ask for "reasonable" things that are going to cost you more than you want to pay.

Refuse to honor a Debt lets you try to slip out of your obligations. It won't mean you no longer owe the other character—the best you can hope for is delaying the payback for another time—but it might keep you out of the fire until you can sort the situation out. Live to fight another day and all that shit.

When you try to push off your Debts and miss, you face a tough choice: honor the Debt or face the consequences. Your debtor gets to pick two different options off the list for you or cancel all the Debts you hold over other people. If you won't honor a Debt, then why should anyone honor their Debts to you? Best be careful.

If you successfully refuse a Debt, the character who tried to cash in a Debt can't cash another in with you until the situation changes. After all, they already asked for one favor, right? No point in asking again so soon. You've already said "no" once.

»Options for *Refuse to Honor a Debt*

Owing another Debt means that the owner of the Debt gets to mark down another Debt on their Archetype sheet with your name on it. Basically, you're getting out of what you owe now by owing more in the future. Interest, we call that.

Losing face with their Faction means that other characters from their Faction start to think less of you because you didn't pay up when asked. This is a subtle cost, but it means that the Faction is a little colder to your advances, a little less likely to go out on a limb for you when it really matters. Best of luck surviving in the city when roughly a quarter of the folks who matter think you're a fuckoff.

Marking corruption means that you shut out the Debt with the sheer force of your will...at the cost of a bit of your soul. Relationships are what keep us grounded; when you push them away, you might find yourself drifting toward the worst parts of yourself. At some point, you won't be able to come back toward the light.

»Examples for *Refuse to Honor a Debt*

> *Solomon's got wind that someone from the Trinity Group has put out a contract on his life. He asks his ghost friend, Yuri, to help him out by sneaking into their corporate offices and stealing the information he needs to figure out who's trying to kill him. She says it's too dangerous, so he calls in a Debt: "Remember that time I saved your niece, Yuri? Come on. You've got to do this for me."*
>
> *Andrew, the MC, says, "Sounds like he's* **cashing in a Debt** *for a moderate favor."*
>
> *Blaine, Yuri's player says, "I don't know. It sounds like a huge favor. Trinity Group is serious business."*

Andrew says, "Yeah, but you're a ghost. You can get in and out a lot easier than most people. I think you'll need to **refuse to honor the Debt** *if you want out of this."*

Blaine says, "I'm not going to honor the Debt then." He rolls and gets a 9. "Hmm. I guess I'll choose **You owe them an additional Debt**. *I say 'Look, Solomon, I just can't do it. It's too dangerous, even for me. I'll owe you, though. Let me know when you need something else. Happy to help.'"*

Elora and Nathaniel manage to get close enough to Watanabe to capture one of his thralls, a woman named Alexis. Nathaniel moves to kill her, draining her blood so that he can heal some of his injuries.

"Stop," says Tomas, Elora's player. "We need her alive. I'm **cashing in a Debt** *to keep you from killing her."*

Derrick, Nathaniel's player, says, "I'm hungry! I **refuse to honor the Debt**.*" He rolls...but comes up with snake eyes for a total of 5.*

Mark, the MC, says, "Ouch. Up to you. Do you honor the Debt or risk the consequences?"

"Sigh. I don't really want to be pushed around by hunters. I kill her."

Tomas sighs. "Okay, fine. I choose two options of the list. You **owe me another Debt** *and you* **mark corruption**. *I can't believe you just killed her. Asshole."*

DROP SOMEONE'S NAME

When you ***drop the name*** of someone who owes you a Debt, roll with their Faction. On a hit, their name carries weight and gives you an opening or opportunity. On a 10+, you keep the Debt and mark their Faction. On a 7-9, you have to cash in the Debt. On a miss, erase the Debt and brace yourself.

Dropping someone's name means using it as leverage against your opposition, granting a moment's advantage or hesitation and creating an opening that was previously closed. You might use it to get someone to rethink hurting your character or to gain access to a sensitive location. It's useful any place you think the person's name might help you get by.

Just saying the name of the person who owes you isn't enough; you've got to inform your opposition that who you're naming owes you and you could call in that favor against them specifically. On a hit, that threat carries a serious amount of weight, enough to get you an opening or opportunity. When you miss, you find out too late that you've overstepped your bounds, that the name you dropped isn't going to offer you much assistance. In fact, it might even get you killed.

You have to cash in the Debt on a 7-9, marking it off your sheet and marking Faction, because you've already used up that favor; you have to erase the Debt on a miss because you've been throwing the Debt around recklessly. No one wants their name dragged through the mud every time you want something. Erasing the Debt means that you don't get to mark Faction for spending it. See *Advancement* on 162 for more on marking Faction.

»Examples for *Drop Someone's Name*

Rashid and Roxy arrive at The Silver Moon, a werewolf bar, to try to get some answers out of the other packs. The bouncer stops them at the door: "No mortals. Boss's orders."

Vivian, Roxy's player, says, "I get up in his face and say 'Your boss owes *me for the Icarus thing. Want me to go upstairs and tell him you're giving me and my friends shit? I'm* happy *to go tell him his guard dog is slipping up.'"*

Mark, the MC, says, "Sounds like you're **dropping a name**. *You didn't say his name, but you both know who you're talking about. Roll it."*

Vivian rolls with Night and gets an 8. She erases the Debt from her sheet and marks Night.

Mark says, "The bouncer looks back and forth. 'Fine. But if I get in trouble, I'm sending him to talk to you. Not my problem if this guy'—he points at Rashid—'gets gutted.'"

DRAMA MOVES

Drama moves are central and unique to your Archetype; they describe how your character responds to the big stuff, like slipping toward the darkness, getting intimate with others, and...dying.

Each Archetype includes three drama moves: a corruption move, an intimacy move, and an end move. In this section, we detail how these moves work and provide a few examples to help you make use of them in your sessions.

CORRUPTION MOVES

Every Archetype has a unique **corruption move** written specifically for that Archetype, aimed at exploring the major themes of darkness associated with their story. Corruption is more than just *darkness* or *evil*. It represents your character slipping toward the worst parts of their nature, becoming that which should be feared instead of respected, hated instead of loved. Yet, as your corruption mounts, your powers only grow...

When the conditions of your corruption move are met, mark off a box on your corruption track. If you're unsure if the conditions have been met, ask the MC. There might be other moves that call for you to mark corruption—or other times that the MC tells you to mark corruption based on your terrible actions—but the primary source of corruption for your character is your corruption move. Look carefully for it during your story. The MC can help remind you, but it's tough for them to watch everyone's corruption moves.

When your corruption track fills, mark a corruption advance and clear the track. You get some new moves, but at the cost of your soul. Eventually you won't be able to fight the darkness any longer...

See *Corruption* on 176 for more information on how corruption affects PCs, including more on corruption advances and examples of corruption moves triggering.

INTIMACY MOVES

Intimacy moves are also unique to each Archetype, reflecting how your character connects with others during moments of closeness. What defines a moment of emotional, mental, or physical intimacy is up to the parties involved, but the MC might ask, "Is this a moment of intimacy?" if no one is bringing it up. Intimacy moves require both or all parties to agree intimacy occurred: it means they've shared a poignant and personal moment with one another.

There are obvious moments of intimacy—sex, vampires feeding, transcendental psychic experiences—but urban fantasy is filled with a broader set of emotional connections. Two characters might get drunk together or tell each other a painful secret or open up about their real desires in the face of the city's daily grind. Any and all of these moments are triggers for the characters to go deeper into their connection by activating their intimacy move.

When you trigger an intimacy move, both players should read their intimacy moves out loud and follow the instructions given. If an intimacy move requires you to hold one, note that on your Archetype sheet. Sometimes an intimacy move gives other characters moves or bonuses. Tell them to note those on their Archetype sheet as well.

> *Olivia is snooping around Veronica's apartment when she finds Veronica is huddled in a ball near her car, unconscious after barely escaping a vicious beating at the hands of some local demons. Olivia picks Veronica up off the ground and gets her upstairs to safety.*
>
> *Andrew, the MC, says, "Veronica, you start to wake up. You're a bit defensive, but you see that it's Olivia who saved you."*

Sophia, Veronica's player, nods and says, "Veronica chokes out 'Thank you...' and you can see she's really grateful. You've never seen her this vulnerable."

Andrew jumps on that statement. "Great! Sounds like a moment of intimacy to me! Right?" Both players nod. "Let's have you both read your intimacy moves aloud and then we'll see how they turn out."

Sophia says, "Okay, I have to tell you a secret or I owe you a Debt. I think I'll tell you a secret. Veronica says 'I lied to Liam when I said that I didn't know about Yolanda's plan. I just thought you should know the truth.' It also says here that you enter my web and owe me a Debt." Sophia marks down both on her sheet.

Hadi, Olivia's player, says, "Huh. I thought you were telling the truth! My move says that I get a 'specific and clear vision' about Veronica, and that I can mark corruption to ask more questions. What do I see?"

Andrew thinks for a moment, then says, "You see Veronica feeding on Liam! They're in a dark room, and Liam is opening himself up to her, as if he wants her to feed on him. Do you want to mark corruption to ask a question?"

"Yeah, I want to know 'When is this going to happen?'"

"Tonight. You just know it's going to be tonight. What do you do?"

END MOVES

End moves may only trigger when your character dies or—in many cases—**retires**. Retirement is only available as a result of character advancement (see 162), but death might strike at any time. Note that faking your death doesn't trigger the move. You've got to go for real if you want your end move to happen.

When your character fulfills the criteria of their end move—death or retirement—they're removed from the story and their end move triggers (unless they have a way to come back from the dead). Read the move out loud and follow the instruction as written, like any other move. Some end moves involve a quick resolution in the scene that triggered the move; others have long term effects on the remainder of the story.

Wesley's in a bad way. He's stuck on the 15th floor of an office building that houses a secret wizard club, caught in the middle of a bizarre turf war between Wild and Power. He's suffered five harm, completely filling up his harm track, and it doesn't look like there's any way out of the office building.

Mark tells Robey, Wesley's player, "Okay, Wesley. Looks like medical attention isn't available. You're knocking on death's door. Time for your end move."

Robey smiles. "Let's see… 'When you die, you may place a devastating curse on someone nearby. Specify the effects of the curse and how they may end it.' How close is Belanzaer? I can curse her, right? Even though she's a demon?"

"Yeah, she's fighting with Nathaniel now. He seems to be having some trouble with her. You see her throw him into a wall as things start to go dark. She's still fair game."

"Perfect. I curse her."

"What do you say?"

"I curse you, *Belanzaer, to be mortal until you repent for your sins."*

"Whoa. Nice." Mark is impressed. He didn't see that coming. "Belanzaer screams. You see her horns pulling back into her head, her eyes turning from solid black to a soft blue, her skin softening to a light pink. She's definitely vulnerable. Nathaniel, what do you do?"

Derrick smiles. "She's mortal now? I eat her."

ADVANCEMENT

When you make a Faction move, trigger an intimacy move, cash in a Debt, or honor a Debt, mark the Faction involved. When you've marked all four Factions, erase the marks and advance.

Advancement allows you to improve your character's stats, gain new moves, and unlock additional improvements outside of corruption. When you make a Faction move, it doesn't matter if it's a hit or miss; rolling for a Faction move allows you to mark the Faction. ***Cashing in a Debt*** on someone who successfully ***refuses the Debt*** allows you to mark Faction, although the character that refuses the Debt doesn't get to mark Faction, since they didn't honor the Debt.

Note that you can only mark a Faction one time until you advance and clear all your marks. Marking Mortality twice in a row isn't helpful; you've got to mark the other three Factions and advance before marking Mortality is useful to you.

You can read more about *Advancement* on 162 in **The Long Game**.

SESSION MOVES

Given the long-term nature of *Urban Shadows*, we like to think of each session as an episode of a television show or entry into a series of novels. Each story stands on its own, but they link up together into something broader and grander. Debts accumulate, feuds build, and the city watches over every bloody street.

In order to open and close these episodes, we've provided **session moves**, mechanics that your group will use to start and finish each session of play. These moves aren't tied to any one character; each character triggers the move when sessions open and close.

SESSION INTRO

At the beginning of every session, announce which character your character trusts the least; their player will spotlight a Faction for your character (that isn't already marked). Mark that Faction. Tell the MC about a rumor or conflict that you've heard about that Faction, building on previous established information if you'd like, and roll with the Faction.

On a 10+, you're prepared for the conflict you laid out: you've got a Debt on someone in that Faction or a useful piece of information or equipment, your choice. On a 7-9, you're neck deep in it: you owe someone in that Faction a Debt, and someone in that Faction owes a Debt to you. On a miss, you're caught flat-footed, unprepared, or unaware: the MC will tell you who is coming at you.

If you start a session in the middle of a chaotic situation or with plenty going on already, the MC might decide to skip this move.

The session start move is used to expand upon or create new threats and conflicts in the city. The move puts some pressure on you as the player to create story, but don't let this intimidate you. The rumor or conflict you choose to create or build upon can be simple and direct: maybe a powerful supernatural is angry at an ally or some hunters are getting ready to move on a nest of vampires. Feel free to ask your fellow players or MC for help if you need it.

Session start is also an opportunity for you to create threads in the story that interest you personally. If your Hunter targets demons and faeries, then introduce a conflict or rumor that ties into those two groups. The MC will take those threads and run with them, building a story that fits your interests. Be direct about the kinds of stories you want to tell!

SESSION END

At the end of every session, if you learned something meaningful about a Faction, increase your score in that Faction by 1 and decrease your score in a different Faction by 1. Tell the MC how your relationships to those communities have changed.

If someone did you a favor at a cost, tell the group; you owe them a Debt. If you did someone a favor without redress, tell the group; they owe you a Debt.

What defines something as *meaningful* is entirely up to you: this is always in your hands, no one else gets to make this call. You decrease your score in another Faction because it's impossible to keep up with everyone—the more time you spend with one group, the less you can spend with another.

Debts are exchanged at the end of the session to catch up on any missed Debts that should have been collected during play. Afterward, you may realize you owe or are owed a Debt from actions taken in the story: this is your chance to correct that. That said, some sessions will end without you collecting or owing any new Debts.

If you'd like to see an example of session moves in play, head over to 237 in **The First Session** for a longer example called *The Long Example*.

CUSTOM MOVES

In addition to the moves listed here—and the moves specifically attached to your Archetype—you might also use custom moves in your sessions. Each custom move is designed to handle a unique situation, crafted by your MC just for your game. As with all other moves, you have to trigger the move by doing something in the fiction. See **The Shadows** on 271 to learn more about expanding on these moves with your own custom work.

FOUR

THE ARCHETYPES

THE LIST

In **The Characters**, we talked about **Archetypes**, the character templates that ground the fiction in *Urban Shadows* by providing a flexible structure for character creation. Each Archetype houses a unique story—a character arc with its own dramatic tension and opportunities—ready for you to pick up and make your own.

Below is a list of all the core Archetypes for *Urban Shadows*, accompanied by a short summary that tells you a bit about each Archetype, including the Archetype's high and low stats. There are additional limited edition and fan-created Archetypes available for use with *Urban Shadows*, but we don't cover them in this book.

Like the city itself, the list of Archetypes is divided up into the four Factions: Mortality, Night, Power, and Wild. Each of these Factions has sway over a different facet of city life, and they often come into conflict as they vie for resources and control.

MORTALITY

Archetypes from Mortality live on the edge of mortal society, still connected to the rest of their Faction, the slumbering fools who don't know about the supernatural world that surrounds them. With all their connections, these Archetypes are in too deep to ever go back to a mundane, normal life.

»The Aware

Inquisitive, resourceful, intuitive, lucky. The Aware is a mortal investigator who has come to see the supernatural world for what it really is. They understand humanity isn't alone in the city and they're entranced by the shadows.

- High stats: Heart, Mind. Low stat: Blood.

»The Hunter

Dangerous, focused, deadly, solitary. The Hunter is a mortal who has mastered the art of the kill through intense training. They are direct and violent, never to be taken lightly.

- High stats: Blood, Mind. Low stat: Spirit.

»The Veteran

Experienced, tenacious, knowledgeable, clever. The Veteran is a has-been who uses their hard-won talents to remain relevant in city politics. They have a workspace in which they can create all manner of things that others might need.

- High stats: Heart, Mind. Low stat: Blood.

NIGHT

Archetypes from Night operate at the level of the street, contesting for territory, drugs, money, and blood. They are the things that go bump in the night, the monsters that live in the shadows of the city.

»The Spectre

Vengeful, alienated, incorporeal, alone. The Spectre is the ghost of someone who died, their spirit trapped on this side of eternity. They are an echo of what they once were, knowing only restlessness and loneliness.

- High stat: Blood, Spirit. Low stat: Mind.

»The Vamp

Seductive, merciless, eternal, hungry. The Vamp is a creature that must feed on humanity to survive. Their web draws in prey, linking them to their assets, minions, and debtors in order to keep their undead hunger satiated.

- High stat: Blood, Heart. Low stat: Spirit.

»The Wolf

Primal, unstoppable, brutal, unlucky. The Wolf is capable of transforming into a deadly werebeast when the moon rises into the sky. Little stands in their way, but they often find more trouble than they bargained for when they prowl the city's streets.

- High stat: Blood, Spirit. Low stat: Heart.

POWER

Archetypes from Power see the truth behind the lies the city tells, the push and sway of politics that drive change amidst the concrete and darkness. They have access to power—great power—and many intend to use it to control the future of the city itself.

»The Oracle

Prophetic, blessed, cursed, intense. The Oracle is a seer, mystic, or psychic, gifted with sight beyond sight. They can see beyond the present, beyond this reality, but they cannot turn away, no matter how terrible their visions become.

- High stats: Mind, Spirit. Low stat: Heart.

»The Wizard

Powerful, dedicated, hermetic, strange. The Wizard relies on years of training to channel intense magics. With enough preparation, these mages can move mountains...or turn them to dust. When caught alone and unprepared, they are still painfully mortal.

- High stats: Mind, Spirit. Low stat: Blood.

WILD

Archetypes from Wild are foreign to these lands, touched and altered by forces beyond this reality. They have contracts and arrangements that bind them and give them power, ties to ancient and epic beings from beyond.

»The Fae

Fickle, enigmatic, cold, illogical. The Fae is a being from beyond this world or the offspring of a creature with ties to distant realities. They are able to draw upon the logic of their native world, tying themselves to oaths and promises in exchange for great power.

- High stats: Heart, Spirit. Low stat: Blood.

»The Tainted

Brutal, intense, callous, manipulative. The Tainted was a mortal who sold their soul in exchange for power, wealth, or security. They are of two worlds, torn between their human compassion and demonic obligations.

- High stats: Blood, Heart. Low stat: Mind.

introducing mortality

THE AWARE

Most people walk around all day with no idea of the power the darkness holds or what truly takes place in the shadows. Those who are Aware, awakened to the world as it truly is, have the power to stand up and fight for their people, to spit in the eyes of the dark beasts that roam their world, and—if they're very lucky—live to see tomorrow.

NAME

(pick one)

Alisa, Anthony, Cam, Cleo, Cole, Datu, Devon, Galina, Hairi, Hans, Julius, Kim, Kirsten, Laasya, Lara, Marisa, Miguel, Philip, Rashid, Veronica

LOOK

(pick as many as apply)

- Ambiguous, Female, Male, Transgressing
- Asian or South Asian, Black, Hispanic/Latino, Indigenous, Middle Eastern, White, __________
- Business Casual Clothing, Everyday Clothing, Inconspicuous Clothing, Uniform Clothing

DEMEANOR

(pick one)

Aggressive, Charming, Paranoid, Serene

STARTING CHARACTER STATS

(Add 1 to one of these)

Blood -1 Heart 1 Mind 1 Spirit 0

STARTING FACTIONS

(Add 1 to one of these)

Mortality 1 Night 0 Power 1 Wild -1

INTRO QUESTIONS

- Who are you?
- How long have you been in the city?
- How did you learn about the supernatural?
- Why is this city worth saving?
- What mystery are you currently investigating?

GEAR

- A simple apartment, a decent car, a smart phone
- 1 self-defense weapon
    - ☐ 9mm Beretta (2-harm close loud)
    - ☐ Taser (stun-harm hand)
    - ☐ Snub-nosed revolver (2-harm close loud reload concealable)

DEBTS

- Someone told you their secrets and you haven't told anyone about them yet. They owe you 2 Debts.
- Someone thinks they're protecting you, but it's really more like you're protecting them. You owe each other a Debt.
- You're leveraging dirt you have on someone to get their help with something. You owe them a Debt.

AWARE MOVES

You get this one:

☑ **Snoop:** When you keep an eye out for trouble, roll with Mind. On a 10+, hold 3. On a 7-9, hold 1. While you're there, spend your hold to ask the MC questions, 1 for 1:

- What's my best way in/out?
- Who or what here is not what they seem?
- What happened here recently?
- What here is the greatest danger to me?
- Whose turf is this?

On a miss, you find yourself in over your head. The MC will tell you why this is a bad spot.

And choose two more:

☐ **Did Your Homework:** When you ***put a face to a name*** with someone politically important (your call), roll with Mind instead of Faction. On a hit, you know a dangerous secret about them or their political machinations. On a 10+, you know how to leverage that information; take a Debt on them as well. On a miss, your snooping has already landed you in hot water with your target; they know you've been looking into their business.

☐ **I Know a Guy:** When you ***hit the streets*** or ***put a face to a name*** with Mortality, roll with Mind instead of Faction.

☐ **I Brought Friends:** When you ***cash in a Debt*** with an NPC, add this option to the list:

- Back you up in a dangerous situation

☐ **Sharpshooter:** When you ***unleash an attack*** with a firearm, roll with Mind instead of Blood.

☐ **Hard-Boiled:** When you get into trouble while chasing down a lead, gain armor+1.

DRAMA MOVES

»Aware Corruption Move

When you ignore your mortal responsibilities to deal with the supernatural, mark corruption.

»Intimacy Move

When you share a moment of intimacy—physical or emotional—with someone who isn't mortal, mark corruption.

»End Move

When you die, each character chooses whether your death inspires or corrupts a part of their being. If it inspires, they erase a corruption advance they've taken (if any). If it corrupts, they immediately take a corruption advance.

STANDARD ADVANCES

Advances available at beginning of play:

- ☐ +1 Blood (max +3)
- ☐ +1 Heart (max +3)
- ☐ +1 Mind (max +3)
- ☐ +1 Spirit (max +3)
- ☐ A new Aware move
- ☐ A new Aware move
- ☐ A move from another Archetype
- ☐ A move from another Archetype
- ☐ Change your Faction

After 5 advances you may select:

- ☐ +1 to any stat (max +3)
- ☐ +1 any Faction (max +3)
- ☐ Erase a scar
- ☐ Join or lead a watcher's society
- ☐ Erase a corruption advance
- ☐ Erase a corruption advance
- ☐ Advance 3 basic moves
- ☐ Advance 3 basic moves
- ☐ Change to a new Archetype

CORRUPTION ADVANCES

- ☐ Take a corruption move
- ☐ Take a corruption move
- ☐ Take a corruption move
- ☐ Take a corruption move from another Archetype
- ☐ Retire your character. They may return as a Threat

CORRUPTION MOVES

- ☐ **In Too Deep:** When a non-mortal tries to ***lend you a hand*** or ***get in your way***, mark corruption to add or subtract 3 from their roll.
- ☐ **Eyes on the Door:** When in danger from the supernatural, you can mark corruption to ***escape a situation*** as if you rolled a 12+.
- ☐ **Free Agent:** Mark corruption to ***refuse to honor a Debt*** owed to a non-mortal as if you rolled a 10+.
- ☐ **If You Can't Beat 'Em:** Take two moves from non-mortal Archetypes. Whenever you use these moves, mark corruption.

PLAYING THE AWARE

Inquisitive, resourceful, intuitive, lucky. The Aware is a mortal investigator who has come to see the supernatural world for what it really is. They understand humanity isn't alone in the city and they're entranced by the shadows.

Unlike some of the more established Archetypes (The Vamp, The Wizard), your character is new to the world of the supernatural, driven to push past the veil that keeps most mortals out. You're not just "aware" of the larger world; you're actively working to discover the truth about the monsters that lurk in the dark. As you build and play your character, seek opportunities to be the truth-seeking protagonist of the story, solving mysteries or saving those in danger.

Of course, all of these drives leave you on a crash course with the supernatural world; each time you step away from your mortal responsibilities, you take another step closer to becoming a Threat to your friends and family on both sides of the veil. You can't retire to safety; you might find it easier to change Archetypes than to stop yourself from going over the edge.

»Notes on Your Moves

Snoop is often undervalued by players. It's incredibly powerful—you get information that's hard to get any other way—but you've got to use it before you step into a situation. Once you're in the thick of things, you'll have more trouble acting on the answers the MC gives you.

Did Your Homework still counts as a Faction move for the purposes of advancement. Mark the Faction of your target when you make this move as if you ***put a name to a face*** as normal.

I Know a Guy might not seem that useful at first, but you're not going to stay connected to Mortality for very long. Chances are you're going to get mixed up in everyone else's business; this move lets you keep up with the important members of your Faction despite that distance. Like ***Did Your Homework***, it still counts as a Faction move for purposes of advancement.

When you ***cash in a Debt*** to get an NPC to back you up in a dangerous situation using ***I Brought Friends***, the NPC shows up with whatever resources they typically rely on for support: a werewolf might bring her pack, a wizard will have a spell or two prepared. Don't fucking expect them to die for you, though. If things get really rough, they'll bail to save their own skin.

»Inspiration for The Aware

- Books: Fever series (Karen Marie Moning), H & W Investigations series (Jess Haines), Twilight series (Stephenie Meyer)
- Music: "All of the Lights" (Kanye West), "Help I'm Alive" (Metric), "Littlest Things" (Toh Kay), "Welcome to the Jungle" (Guns N' Roses)
- Movies: *Drag Me to Hell, Kiss the Girls, Manhunter, Se7en*
- Television: *Sherlock, Sleepy Hollow, True Detective*

THE HUNTER

Determined and fearless, the Hunter is a mortal who has taken up a cause against the darkness around them, perhaps because they were trained to stalk the night or because they were born with the power to protect their people. They carry a heavy burden, one that would eventually crush anyone. How long can they keep from becoming what they hunt?

NAME

(pick one)

Abimbola, Amanda, Anwar, Beatrice, Bianca, Christopher, Elora, Eugene, Flaco, Ilyas, Jason, Jessica, Marcus, Moriko, Patty, Paul, Samuel, Sarah, Sean, Solomon, Susan

LOOK

(pick as many as apply)

- Ambiguous, Female, Male, Transgressing
- Asian or South Asian, Black, Hispanic/Latino, Indigenous, Middle Eastern, White, ___________
- Camo Clothing, Casual Clothing, Dark Clothing, Dirty Clothing

DEMEANOR

(pick one)

Calculating, Detached, Friendly, Volatile

CHARACTER STATS

(Add 1 to one of these)

Blood 1 Heart 0 Mind 1 Spirit -1

STARTING FACTIONS

(Add 1 to one of these)

Mortality 1 Night 1 Power 0 Wild -1

INTRO QUESTIONS

- Who are you?
- How long have you been in the city?
- How did you become a hunter?

YOUR PREY

- What do you hunt, primarily?
- What are their strengths and weaknesses?
- What terrible thing have you done to yourself to help even the playing field?
- How are you like them?

GEAR

- A shitty apartment, a pick-up truck or muscle car, a cell phone
- 3 custom weapons (detail)

CUSTOM WEAPONS

»Ranged Weapons

- ☐ Bow (2-harm close/far reload)
- ☐ Shotgun (2-harm close loud reload messy)
- ☐ SMG (2-harm close area loud)
- ☐ Pistol (2-harm close loud)
- ☐ Rifle (2-harm far loud)

Add-ons (choose 2 for each weapon):

- Silenced (-loud)
- Big (+1 harm)
- Semi-automatic (-reload)
- Automatic (+autofire)
- Antique/Ornate (+valuable)
- High-powered (+1 harm)
- Scoped (+far or +1 harm at far)
- Silvered (+silver)
- Cold Iron (+cold iron)
- Blessed (+holy)

»Hand Weapons

- ☐ Staff (1-harm hand/close)
- ☐ Haft (1-harm hand)
- ☐ Handle (1-harm hand)
- ☐ Chain (1-harm hand area)

Add-ons (choose 2 for each weapon):

- Head (+1 harm)
- Bladed (+1 harm)
- Antique/Ornate (+valuable)
- Famed (+reputation)
- Extendable (+close)
- Enchanted (+anchored)
- Silvered (+silver)
- Cold Iron (+cold iron)
- Blessed (+holy)
- Hidden (+concealable)

DEBTS

- Someone has enlisted you to protect them from something very dangerous. They owe you a Debt.
- Someone keeps you equipped and supplied. You owe them 2 Debts.
- You consider someone a friend even though the friendship keeps bringing you trouble. They owe you a Debt.

HUNTER MOVES

Choose three:

- ☐ **Slayer:** When you ***keep your cool*** while on a hunt, roll with Blood instead of Spirit.
- ☐ **Deadly:** When you inflict harm, increase the harm by 1.
- ☐ **Book Learnin':** When you encounter a new type of supernatural creature, roll with Mind. On a hit, the MC will tell you a bit about it and how it can be killed. On a 10+, ask the MC a follow-up question; they will answer it honestly. On a miss, you misread the creature; the MC tells you how.
- ☐ **Safe House:** You have a secure location that you can hole up in. Detail it and choose 3:
  - ☐ High-tech surveillance
  - ☐ A mystical prison
  - ☐ Fortified walls/windows/doors
  - ☐ A week's worth of food and water
  - ☐ Explosives set to blow the place
- ☐ **This Way!:** When you lead people out of danger, roll with Blood. On a 10+, you all get away safely. On a 7-9, you get hurt or one of them gets hurt (you choose). On a miss, everyone's safe but you; you're left behind and the way out is closed to you.
- ☐ **Do You Feel Lucky?:** When you ***persuade an NPC*** while wielding a 2-harm or greater weapon, roll with Blood instead of Heart.
- ☐ **Prepared for Anything:** You have a well-stocked armory, full of modern and ancient weapons. Take another custom weapon or add another add-on to each of your custom weapons.

DRAMA MOVES

»Hunter Corruption Move

When you injure a mortal while pursuing the supernatural, mark corruption.

»Intimacy Move

When you share a moment of intimacy—physical or emotional—with another person, ask them a question; they must answer it honestly. They will ask you a question in return; answer it honestly or mark corruption.

»End Move

When you die or retire your character, choose a character belonging to another player and give them one of your chosen Hunter moves. It's theirs for keeps.

STANDARD ADVANCES

Advances available at beginning of play:

- ☐ +1 Blood (max +3)
- ☐ +1 Heart (max +3)
- ☐ +1 Spirit (max +3)
- ☐ A new Hunter move
- ☐ A new Hunter move
- ☐ A new Hunter move
- ☐ A move from another Archetype
- ☐ A move from another Archetype
- ☐ Change your Faction

After 5 advances you may select:

- ☐ +1 to any stat (max +3)
- ☐ +1 any Faction (max +3)
- ☐ Erase a scar
- ☐ Get a workspace
- ☐ Erase a corruption advance
- ☐ Advance 3 basic moves
- ☐ Advance 3 basic moves
- ☐ Advance 1 basic move

CORRUPTION ADVANCES

- ☐ Take a corruption move
- ☐ Take a corruption move
- ☐ Take a corruption move
- ☐ Take a corruption move from another Archetype
- ☐ Retire your character. They may return as a Threat

CORRUPTION MOVES

- ☐ **Divided I Stand:** When you turn down help and enter a dangerous situation alone, mark corruption to advance ***unleash an attack*** and ***keep your cool*** for the scene.
- ☐ **Hard to Kill:** Choose a Faction. Mark corruption to gain armor+1 against that Faction until the end of the scene.
- ☐ **Perfect Timing:** Mark corruption to arrive in a scene. Mark an additional corruption to show up in a superior position.
- ☐ **Death Wish:** If someone nearby is about to suffer harm, you may mark corruption to suffer the harm instead.

PLAYING THE HUNTER

Dangerous, focused, deadly, solitary. The Hunter is a mortal who has mastered the art of the kill through intense training. They are direct and violent, never to be taken lightly.

Hunters burn bright, tragic figures of righteousness on the dark streets of the city. You can't retire to safety. You can't give up on the hunt. This is the only life you'll ever know and it's almost certainly going to kill you.

What you hunt is up to you. Your prey can be typical fare—vampires or demons—or have a more esoteric focus: ghosts, spirits, etc. If you say you hunt a type of supernatural creature, it's the MC's job to make sure that such creatures appear often.

If you decide that you hunt a type of supernatural creature selected by another player, come up with a few reasons why you haven't decided to hunt them down yet. You don't have to be friends, but it's not a good idea to start with that kind of animosity. Give that kind of conflict some time to develop.

»Notes on Your Moves

For the purposes of ***Slayer***, the MC decides if you're "on a hunt." Generally, you've got to be armed and looking for a particular supernatural target.

Deadly means you do +1 harm each time you harm another character. This isn't optional; you can't shoot someone with the intent to do less harm than normal.

If you haven't met a vampire, wizard, fae, etc. at the start of the game, you might decide that you trigger ***Book Learnin'*** the first time you meet one in person. Tell the MC if you think a supernatural creature should trigger the move.

This Way! replaces ***escape*** when you're leading a group of folks away from danger. If you're by yourself or they refuse to follow, the move doesn't trigger. You'll have to roll ***escape*** instead.

If you want to use ***Do You Feel Lucky?*** to ***persuade an NPC*** with Blood, you have to brandish the weapon in a threatening way. You don't have to point it at them or hurt them, but they need to know that you'd be willing to pull the trigger.

»Inspiration for The Hunter

- Books: Anita Blake series (Laurell K. Hamilton), *Dracula* (Bram Stoker), The Mortal Instruments series (Cassandra Clare)
- Music: "Don't Fear The Reaper" (Blue Oyster Cult), "The Howling" (Within Temptation), "Paranoid" (Black Sabbath), "Rebel Without a Pause" (Public Enemy), "Wayward Son" (Kansas)
- Movies: *Blade, Dredd, Solomon Kane*
- Television: *Buffy the Vampire Slayer, Grimm, Supernatural, Vampire Hunter D*

THE VETERAN

Once upon a time, you were someone important…and dangerous. People knew you and gave you a wide berth. You were a force to be reckoned with in this city. And then you got old, broken, or both.

NAME

(pick one)
Alejandro, Bartholomew, Beth, Constance, Danuta, David, Emma, Frank, Joanne, Jose, Julie, Kimiko, Leo, Mahinder, Michelle, Regis, Skylar, Tabitha, Terry, Yakub

LOOK

(pick as many as apply)

- Ambiguous, Female, Male, Transgressing
- Asian or South Asian, Black, Hispanic/Latino, Indigenous, Middle Eastern, White, __________
- Dirty Clothing, Everyday Clothing, Formal Clothing, Uniform Clothing

DEMEANOR

(pick one)
Charming, Crass, Professional, Reserved

CHARACTER STATS

(Add 1 to one of these)
Blood -1 Heart 1 Mind 1 Spirit 0

STARTING FACTIONS

(Add 1 to one of these)
Mortality 1 Night 0 Power 0 Wild 0

INTRO QUESTIONS

- Who are you?
- How long have you been in the city?
- What was your greatest accomplishment in the city?
- Why did you stop?
- What do you desperately need?

GEAR

- An apartment or warehouse hideout, a nice car or old pick-up truck, a smart phone, a workspace (detail)
- 1 self-defense weapon
    - ☐ 9mm Beretta (2-harm close loud)
    - ☐ Pump-action shotgun (3-harm close loud reload messy)
    - ☐ Magnum revolver (3-harm close loud reload)

WORKSPACE

You have a workspace that includes a large space for your tools and/or supplies. When you go into your workspace to work on something, the MC tells you what it will take to complete.

Choose and underline 3 features that your workspace includes:

automotive hoist and tools, a darkroom, a regulated growing environment, two or three skilled assistants, a junkyard of raw materials, machining tools, transmitters & receivers, a testing ground, deadly booby traps, a library of old books, a scattering of ancient relics, a mystical focus, magical wards, a medical station, an operating room, high-tech electronics and computers, an advanced surveillance system, a forge, a science lab, a portal to another dimension.

Items created in your workspace are safe from the MC. They can't be destroyed or taken without your permission, even if you sell or give them away to another character.

DEBTS

- Someone relies on you for training or knowledge. They owe you 2 Debts.
- You're working on something big for someone, and it's nearly ready. They owe you a Debt.
- Someone keeps pulling your ass out of the fire. You owe them 2 Debts.

VETERAN MOVES

You get this one:

☑ **Old Friends, Old Favors:** When you first encounter an NPC—rather than ***putting a face to a name***—you may declare them an old friend and roll with Mind. On a hit, they offer you comfort and aid, even if it exposes them to danger or retribution. On a 7-9, tell the MC why you owe them a Debt. On a miss, tell the MC why they want you dead.

And choose two more:

☐ **True Artist:** When you create something for someone using your workspace, mark their Faction.

☐ **Invested:** When someone owes you 2 or more Debts and you ***lend them a hand*** or ***get in their way***, roll with Mind instead of Faction.

☐ **Too Old for this Shit!:** When you get caught up in a fight you tried to prevent, you get armor+1 and take +1 ongoing to seeing yourself and others to safety.

☐ **The Best Laid Plans:** When you work out a plan with someone, roll with Mind. On a 10+, hold 3. On a 7-9, hold 2. You can spend your hold 1-for-1, regardless of distance, while the plan is being carried out to:

- Add +1 to someone's roll (choose after rolling)
- Dismiss all harm someone suffers from a single attack
- Ensure your people have the exact gear they need on hand

On a miss, hold 1, but your plan falls apart at the worst possible moment.

☐ **Gun to a Knife Fight:** When you ***unleash an attack*** on someone by seriously escalating the conflict, roll with Mind instead of Blood.

DRAMA MOVES

»Veteran Corruption Move

When you knowingly head straight into danger, mark corruption.

»Intimacy Move

When you share a moment of intimacy—physical or emotional—with another person, tell them a story about the past and the lessons you learned. Choose 1:

- You both take +1 forward
- You take +1 forward and they take -1 forward
- Hold 1. Spend the hold to ***lend a hand*** to that character from any distance

»End Move

When you die or retire your character, choose a character to inherit your workspace and ***True Artist***.

STANDARD ADVANCES

Advances available at beginning of play:

- ☐ +1 Heart (max +3)
- ☐ +1 Mind (max +3)
- ☐ +1 Spirit (max +3)
- ☐ A new Veteran move
- ☐ A new Veteran move
- ☐ Add 2 more features to your workspace
- ☐ A move from another Archetype
- ☐ A move from another Archetype
- ☐ Change your Faction

After 5 advances you may select:

- ☐ +1 to any stat (max +3)
- ☐ +1 any Faction (max +3)
- ☐ Erase a scar
- ☐ Erase a corruption advance
- ☐ Erase a corruption advance
- ☐ Advance 3 basic moves
- ☐ Advance 3 basic moves
- ☐ Retire your character to safety
- ☐ Change to a new Archetype

CORRUPTION ADVANCES

- ☐ Take a corruption move
- ☐ Take a corruption move
- ☐ Take a corruption move
- ☐ Take a corruption move from another Archetype
- ☐ Retire your character. They may return as a Threat

CORRUPTION MOVES

- ☐ **Back at It:** Take a standard move and a corruption move from another Archetype. Whenever you use those moves, mark corruption.
- ☐ **Pack Rat:** You may mark corruption to reach into your kit and find just the thing you need to deal with your current situation.
- ☐ **Catch You Fuckers at a Bad Time?:** Mark corruption to arrive in a scene. Mark an additional corruption to bring someone with you.

☐ **Dark Experiments:** When you "work over" someone (alive or dead) in your workspace, mark corruption and roll with Mind. On a 10+, ask 3. On a 7-9, ask 2:

- What is your weakness?
- What are you hiding?
- What are you afraid of?
- What are you, really?
- What are you planning?

On a miss, ask 1, but someone from their Faction knows what you did.

PLAYING THE VETERAN

Experienced, tenacious, knowledgeable, clever. The Veteran is a has-been who uses their hard-won talents to remain relevant in city politics. They have a workspace in which they can create all manner of things that others might need.

You might feel like a support character, but—like all Mortality Archetypes—The Veteran is on an unsustainable path. You can't be retired and still relevant; you can't be half in and half out of the game. You're going to have to make a choice sooner or later: do you want to matter or do you want to be happy?

Unlike The Aware and The Hunter, The Veteran can retire to safety. Usually this means leaving the city, taking that retirement that you've always talked about, moving in with your kids in the suburbs, or traveling Europe for a few months that turn into years. Anything short of that means you're going to get pulled right back in.

»Notes on Your Moves

When you use your workspace, the MC may give you requirements that are extremely difficult to fulfill; you may need to turn to allies and cash in Debts to get what you need. If you do finish a project, whatever you create is safe; the MC can't destroy it or weaken it without good cause.

Old Friends, Old Favors still counts as a Faction move for the purposes of advancement. Mark the Faction of your target when you make this move as if you ***put a name to a face*** as normal.

The Best Laid Plans allows you to skip the tedious process of trying to plan for anything the MC might throw at you. When you spend your hold, it's assumed that you thought of that particular contingency while laying out your strategy.

Escalating a conflict for ***Gun to a Knife Fight*** means that you seriously escalate a violent conflict—pulling a gun or a knife when verbally threatened or drawing a shotgun when threatened by a pistol.

If your intimacy move is triggered by you telling a story to another character, there's no need to tell a second story. The first one will suffice.

Whatever you pull out of your kit using ***Pack Rat*** has to be compact enough to fit in whatever storage you've got with you—a bag, your truck, etc. It should probably be cheap too, but sometimes it makes sense for you to have something rare on hand.

Dark Experiments requires you to get your hands dirty. Working over someone living usually means torture; working over someone dead usually means dissection.

»Inspiration for The Veteran

- Books: Bourne series (Robert Ludlum), *Disturbed Earth* (E.E. Richardson), *Tea with the Black Dragon* (R.A. MacAvoy),
- Music: "Can't Find My Way Home" (Blind Faith), "I Shall Not Be Moved" (Johnny Cash), "Rusty Cage" (Soundgarden), "Straight Outta Compton" (N.W.A.)
- Movies: *Blade, Crouching Tiger, Hidden Dragon, Taken*
- Television: *The Blacklist, Buffy the Vampire Slayer, The Equalizer*

introducing night

THE SPECTRE

Poltergeist, ghost, spirit—they go by many names in every corner of the world. They are our secret fears and unfulfilled dreams. They are the echo of one who died, but their essence hasn't moved on for some reason. They are the audience of our secret pains and guilty pleasures.

NAME

(pick one)

Bert, Cathy, Clarita, Clark, Davis, Emily, Eric, Grace, Grey Light, Hiro, Isabelle, Joy, Karl, Mohammed, Moises, Monica, Patricia, Rebecca, Thomas, Yuri

LOOK

(pick as many as apply)

- Ambiguous, Female, Male, Transgressing
- Asian or South Asian, Black, Hispanic/Latino, Indigenous, Middle Eastern, White, __________
- Blood-Stained Clothing, Dark Clothing, Everyday Clothing, Vintage Clothing

DEMEANOR

(pick one)

Antiquated, Confused, Meek, Volatile

CHARACTER STATS

(Add 1 to one of these)

Blood 1 Heart 0 Mind -1 Spirit 1

STARTING FACTIONS

(Add 1 to one of these)

Mortality -1 Night 1 Power 0 Wild 1

INTRO QUESTIONS

- Who are you?
- How long have you been in the city?
- Who do you still love?
- What makes your afterlife worth living?
- What do you desperately need?

GEAR

Whatever was on your person when you died, albeit spiritual versions of each

DEBTS

- Someone, or someone's progenitor, was involved in your death. They owe you a Debt.
- Someone is watching out for a family member of yours. You owe them 2 Debts.
- You are haunting someone and they know it. You owe them a Debt.

SPECTRE MOVES

You get this one:

☑ **Manifest:** Regular people can't sense or interact with you unless you manifest. You manifest by spending a few quiet moments concentrating and choosing 2:

- You can be heard
- You can be seen
- You can touch and be touched by the physical world

You may mark corruption to instead choose 1 or all 3.

And choose two more:

☐ **Won't Be Ignored:** When you ***get in the way*** of someone, treat your roll as a 10+ without rolling. If you ***distract*** an NPC, roll with Spirit instead of Mind.

☐ **Ghost Town:** When you ***hit the streets*** with ghosts, take +1 ongoing to dealing with them.

☐ **Phantasm:** Take +1 Spirit (max +3).

☐ **"Wall? What Wall?":** You always have an opening to ***escape a situation***. You can choose an additional option off the list to bring someone with you. On a miss, you attract the attention of dangerous spirits and ghosts in the area.

☐ **Link:** Something keeps you from passing on: a **Link**. When in the presence of your Link, advance ***let it out***. When your Link is in danger, you have access to all your corruption moves until you see it to safety. If your Link is ever destroyed, so are you.

DRAMA MOVES

»Spectre Corruption Move

When you witness a scene of victimization and do nothing, mark corruption.

»Intimacy Move

When you share a moment of intimacy—physical or emotional—with another person, you hold 1. Whenever they get into trouble, you can spend your hold to be there.

»End Move

When you fill up on harm, your corpus is scattered and dispersed. You'll reform in a few days. When your spirit passes on permanently or you retire your character, any characters present gain +1 Spirit (max +3).

STANDARD ADVANCES

Advances available at beginning of play:

- ☐ +1 Blood (max +3)
- ☐ +1 Mind (max +3)
- ☐ +1 Spirit (max +3)
- ☐ A new Spectre move
- ☐ A new Spectre move
- ☐ A move from another Archetype
- ☐ A move from another Archetype
- ☐ Change your Faction
- ☐ Join or lead a body of ghosts

After 5 advances you may select:

- ☐ +1 to any stat (max +3)
- ☐ +1 any Faction (max +3)
- ☐ Erase a scar
- ☐ Erase a corruption advance
- ☐ Erase a corruption advance
- ☐ Advance 3 basic moves
- ☐ Advance 3 basic moves
- ☐ Move on through to the other side
- ☐ Change to a new Archetype

CORRUPTION ADVANCES

- ☐ Take a corruption move
- ☐ Take a corruption move
- ☐ Take a corruption move
- ☐ Take a corruption move from another Archetype
- ☐ Retire your character. They may return as a Threat

CORRUPTION MOVES

- ☐ **Possession:** Mark corruption to enter the mind of a weak-minded person (MC's call) in your presence and control their movements and speech for a short time.
- ☐ **Telekinesis:** You can move and lift small objects at a distance by concentrating. Mark corruption to move an object up to the size of a car.
- ☐ **Nightmare:** Mark corruption to enter the dreams of someone sleeping in your presence. While you're there, you can interact with them and their dreams as if they were spirits.
- ☐ **Siphon:** Mark corruption to reach into someone's body, inflict 2-harm (ap) on them, and heal 1-harm of your corpus.

PLAYING THE SPECTRE

Vengeful, alienated, incorporeal, alone. The Spectre is the ghost of someone who died, their spirit trapped on this side of eternity. They are an echo of what they once were, knowing only restlessness and loneliness.

You are the watcher, the silent witness to the horrors of the modern world. The apathy. The greed. The lust that leaks out from behind the mask when nobody's looking. You see it all. After all, you can go anywhere. No place is truly safe from your eyes.

But you are a solitary witness. And against the horrors of the city, you are often alone and outgunned. It would be foolish to try to stop them all, to try to stand against the whole city without allies or resources.

The less you do about the horrors you witness, however, the more you slide toward oblivion, a kind of hopelessness from which you know you will never recover. You'll remain in this world, of course, but whatever vestigial personhood you have will crumble and wilt. You know this fate to be true.

The central question of your existence is clear: do you care enough to save a world that has already forgotten you?

»Notes on Your Moves

In order to ***Manifest***, you need a few moments to yourself; you need similar amounts of time to manifest a second time in a scene to choose new options. If you mark corruption, the process is nearly instantaneous. The MC decides who is "regular people" for the purposes of this move, but you should assume that most supernatural creatures can at least sense your presence.

The Spectre is a surprisingly physical character. Between your starting Blood +1 and ***Won't Be Ignored***, you can ***unleash an attack*** on opponents when they're at their most vulnerable. If you're not carrying a weapon, their weapon will work just fine, assuming you take it from them.

If your corpus is destroyed, it takes you a number of days to heal and regroup. That's the price you pay for being nigh immortal. Serious magics and some spirits or ghosts may have the ability to damage you or force you to pass on against your will, even when you aren't manifested.

When you use ***Nightmare***, your target is especially vulnerable to you. You don't have to manifest to interact with them, nor can they escape the dream. That said, you may find other things in their dreams that endanger you both.

»Inspiration for The Spectre

- Books: *Her Fearful Symmetry* (Audrey Niffenegger), *The Lovely Bones* (Alice Sebold), *The Shining* (Stephen King)
- Music: "Knockin' on Heaven's Door" (Bob Dylan), "Night Tide" (Scorn), "Tha Crossroads" (Bone Thugs-n-Harmony), "Who Wants to Live Forever" (Queen)
- Movies: *Ghost, The Sixth Sense, Stir of Echoes*
- Television: *American Horror Story: Murder House, Being Human* (UK), *Twin Peaks*

THE VAMP

Strong, fast, eternal in age, and insatiable in hunger, the vampire is a pure, unadulterated predator. They are a monster, a twisted reflection of the person they once were, doomed to walk the earth and feed their hungers. Keep your distance.

NAME

(pick one)

Adel, Ash, Bilal, Clara, Cleopatra, Damon, Danielle, Hadier, Isa, Joseph, Klaus, Leanne, Marta, Maximillian, Monique, Nathaniel, Orion, Salim, Reginald, Zoe

LOOK

(pick as many as apply)

- Ambiguous, Female, Male, Transgressing
- Asian or South Asian, Black, Hispanic/Latino, Indigenous, Middle Eastern, White, __________
- Concealing Clothing, Everyday Clothing, Formal Clothing, Vintage Clothing

DEMEANOR

(pick one)

Antiquated, Feral, Seductive, Volatile

CHARACTER STATS

(Add 1 to one of these)

Blood 1 Heart 1 Mind 0 Spirit -1

STARTING FACTIONS

(Add 1 to one of these)

Mortality 1 Night 1 Power -1 Wild 0

INTRO QUESTIONS

- Who are you?
- How long have you been in the city?
- How do you keep your cravings in check?
- Who turned you?
- What scheme are you invested in now?

GEAR

- A secluded apartment, a comfortable car, a smart phone
- 1 stylish weapon
    - ☐ Sword (3-harm hand messy)
    - ☐ Dual 9mm Glocks (2-harm close loud)
    - ☐ Walther PPK (2-harm close reload concealable)

THE VAMP'S WEB

When someone comes to you to ask for a favor, look for advice/info, or threaten your interests, they enter your **web** and owe you a Debt. When someone is in your web, you gain the following when dealing with them:

- Get +1 ongoing to ***lend a hand*** or ***get in the way*** of their efforts
- Add this question to ***figure someone out***: "What is your character's true hunger?"

At the start of a session, choose someone in your web and learn a secret about them that they'd rather keep buried.

They leave your web only when they no longer owe you a Debt.

DEBTS

- Someone makes sure you get fed regularly. You owe them 2 Debts.
- Someone relies on you for their fix. They owe you a Debt.
- Someone bears responsibility for you becoming a vampire. They owe you a Debt.

VAMP MOVES

You get this one:

☑ **Eternal Hunger:** You hunger for human blood, flesh, or emotions, pick one. When you feed, roll with Blood. On a 10+, choose 3. On a 7-9, choose 2:

- You heal 1-harm
- You learn a secret about them
- You take +1 forward
- They don't die

On a miss, something goes terribly wrong.

And choose two more:

☐ **Irresistible:** When you ***persuade an NPC*** using promises or seduction, treat a 7-9 as a 10+ result. On a miss, your machinations succeed as though you rolled a 7-9, but attract the attention of a rival or enemy.

☐ **Haven:** You have a safe place, secure from outside dangers. It has emergency rations, a few ghouls, and an escape vector. When someone willingly comes to your haven, they enter your web.

☐ **Cold-Blooded:** When you ***keep your cool*** under emotional duress, roll with Blood instead of Spirit.

☐ **Keep Your Friends Close:** When you ***figure someone out*** by indulging their vices, roll with Blood instead of Mind.

☐ **Put Out the Word:** When you ***cash in a Debt*** with someone in your web, add this option to the list:

- Put out the word with their Faction that you want something. You get +3 forward to ***hit the streets*** with that Faction.

DRAMA MOVES

»Vamp Corruption Move

When you feed on an unwilling victim, mark corruption.

»Intimacy Move

When you share a moment of intimacy—physical or emotional—with another person, tell them a secret about yourself or owe them a Debt. Either way, they enter your web and owe you a Debt.

»End Move

When you die or retire your character, name someone in the scene you want dead; your agents and allies relentlessly pursue them.

STANDARD ADVANCES

Advances available at beginning of play:

- ☐ +1 Blood (max +3)
- ☐ +1 Heart (max +3)
- ☐ +1 Mind (max +3)
- ☐ +1 Spirit (max +3)
- ☐ A new Vamp move
- ☐ A new Vamp move
- ☐ A move from another Archetype
- ☐ A move from another Archetype
- ☐ Change your Faction

After 5 advances you may select:

- ☐ +1 to any stat (max +3)
- ☐ +1 any Faction (max +3)
- ☐ Erase a scar
- ☐ Join or lead a vampire clan
- ☐ Erase a corruption advance
- ☐ Advance 3 basic moves
- ☐ Advance 3 basic moves
- ☐ Retire your character to safety
- ☐ Change to a new Archetype

CORRUPTION ADVANCES

- ☐ Take a corruption move
- ☐ Take a corruption move
- ☐ Take a corruption move
- ☐ Take a corruption move from another Archetype
- ☐ Retire your character. They may return as a Threat

CORRUPTION MOVES

- ☐ **True Hunter:** Mark corruption when pursuing a human NPC at night. Your prey cannot escape you, no matter where they attempt to flee, and you can prey on them or kill them at will.
- ☐ **Adaptable Palate:** You can feed on any creature, not just humans. Feeding on something wildly different than a human will have unexpected side effects.
- ☐ **Pull Them Back In:** When you ***cash in your last Debt*** on someone in your web, mark corruption to keep the Debt and keep them in your web.
- ☐ **Blood Magic:** Choose 2 faerie powers. Mark corruption to use one of these powers.

PLAYING THE VAMP

Seductive, merciless, eternal, hungry. The Vamp is a creature that must feed on humanity to survive. Their web draws in prey, linking them to their assets, minions, and debtors in order to keep their undead hunger satiated.

You are not a noble lord of the night or a beautiful predator. You are a parasite, an unholy tick feasting on the blood of the living to sustain your unlife. There is no grace in what you have to do to feed, no matter how you dress it up.

But none of that makes you a monster. There are chances for redemption on the streets, should you lift your head from the trough long enough to look for them. The other characters need your influence and your muscle to get things done, and in return they might help you hold off the darkness for a little longer.

»Notes on Your Moves

Decide what you feed on when you make your character: blood, flesh, or emotions. Not choosing "They don't die" when you feed on someone means the MC decides their fate. You may only feed on humans, unless you take ***Adaptable Palate*** as a corruption advance.

Anyone who willingly enters your haven enters your web, but don't make your web an excuse to avoid taking action in the fiction; it's not much fun to sit at home while the other players engage the story. And remember that anyone who visits your haven knows where you live...

Indulging someone's vices to ***Keep Your Friends Close*** means offering them something they want, like drugs, sex, gambling, etc. You don't have to partake, but folks tend to be uncomfortable doing that kind of stuff while someone watches.

If someone ends up owing you a Debt as a result of an action that causes them to enter your web, you end up with two Debts. When a character comes to you looking for information, for example, they owe you one Debt and enter your web; they will end up owing you a second Debt if the information you provide is significant.

When you assign Debts at the start of play, consider selecting an NPC as the person that "bears responsibility for you becoming a vampire," especially if you're the oldest character in the game.

If you die or retire, you can declare any character—NPC or PC—as your end move target.

»Inspiration for The Vamp

- Books: *Fledgling* (Octavia Butler), *Salem's Lot* (Stephen King), Twilight series (Stephenie Meyer)
- Music: "Bring Me to Life" (Evanescence), "Enter Sandman" (Metallica), "Hot Blooded" (Foreigner), "House of the Rising Sun" (The Animals), "In a Lonely Place" (Joy Division), "No Church in the Wild" (Jay-Z & Kanye West)
- Movies: *Let the Right One In, Lost Boys, Near Dark*
- Television: *Angel, True Blood, Vampire Diaries*

THE WOLF

Primal, deadly, and awesome. There is little in the world that can match the werewolf's relentlessness or brute force. Those cursed by the wolf's bite or born into their bloodline carry a great fury within them. But fury, like all emotion, can be tempered…eventually.

NAME

(pick one)

Anders, Brenda, Carmen, Christian, Dana, Habib, Junot, Kareem, Lee, Lucia, Mani, Matt, Mel, Robin, Roxanne, Suze, Tori, Trent, Vanessa, Vic

LOOK

(pick as many as apply)

- Ambiguous, Female, Male, Transgressing
- Asian or South Asian, Black, Hispanic/Latino, Indigenous, Middle Eastern, White, __________
- Baggy Clothing, Concealing Clothing, Dark Clothing, Dirty Clothing

DEMEANOR

(pick one)

Aggressive, Excitable, Feral, Violent

CHARACTER STATS

(Add 1 to one of these)

Blood 1 Heart -1 Mind 0 Spirit 1

STARTING FACTIONS

(Add 1 to one of these)

Mortality 0 Night 1 Power -1 Wild 1

INTRO QUESTIONS

- Who are you?
- How long have you been in the city?
- What is the best part of the change?
- Who is the most important person in your territory?
- What do you desperately need?

GEAR

- A duffel bag with your personal belongings, a shitty cell phone
- 2 practical weapons
    - ☐ Snubnosed revolver (2-harm close loud reload concealable)
    - ☐ 9mm Beretta (2-harm close loud)
    - ☐ Butterfly knife (2-harm hand concealable)
    - ☐ Switchblade (2-harm hand concealable)
    - ☐ Baseball bat (2-harm hand)

THE TRANSFORMATION

By default, you change into your wolf form when the full moon rises; you gain natural weaponry (2-harm) and 1-armor; you can resist the change, but it's not easy; and you can only change back at sunrise.

Choose 2:

- ☐ You inflict +1 harm while transformed
- ☐ You gain armor+1 while transformed
- ☐ Your harm is armor piercing (ap)
- ☐ You transform every night, not just during the full moon
- ☐ Gain +1 ongoing to ***escape*** while transformed
- ☐ When battling groups, you fight like a small group
- ☐ You are all but immune to magical attacks while transformed

Choose 2:

- ☐ Silver weapons ignore your armor
- ☐ Sometimes you lose control while transformed
- ☐ When you transform, you ***keep your cool*** or declare a hunt
- ☐ You can't resist the change when it comes
- ☐ The transformation takes a while and causes you a lot of pain

YOUR TERRITORY

You've claimed an area of the city as your own. By default, your territory covers a city block or two and has the trouble: +crime.

Choose 2:

- ☐ Your territory spans several city blocks (add blessing: +influence)
- ☐ People here work hard to keep the streets safe (remove +crime)
- ☐ You are widely accepted as this place's protector (add blessing: +supported)
- ☐ Your territory includes grounds for you to roam and hunt (add blessing: +hunting ground)
- ☐ You've made a deal with someone, or something, to protect your territory when you're not around (add blessing: +guardian)

Choose 2:

- ☐ Your territory owes fealty to someone more powerful than you (add trouble: +obligations)
- ☐ Someone more powerful wants your territory and is working to get it (add trouble: +encroachment)
- ☐ Mortals in the area are actively trying to revitalize local businesses and infrastructure (add trouble: +upheaval)
- ☐ Your territory is plagued by a mystical or supernatural presence (add trouble: +haunted)
- ☐ You have offered protection within your territory to someone, and now their problems are yours (add trouble: +fealty)

DEBTS

- Someone is hiding you from someone, or something, powerful. You owe them a Debt.
- Someone hired you for a job and you fucked it up. You owe them 2 Debts.
- Someone lives in your territory, benefiting from your protection. They owe you a Debt.

WOLF MOVES

You get these two:

☑ **Comes with the Territory:** If you're actively patrolling your territory at the start of the session, roll with Blood. On a 10+, your territory is secure and trouble is at a minimum; take +1 ongoing to ***hitting the streets*** in your territory. On a 7-9, one of your troubles surfaces (your choice), but things are mostly stable. On a miss, or if you aren't attending to your territory, things go south and your troubles are fast and furious.

☑ **Bloodhound:** When you hunt someone, roll with Blood. On a hit, you know exactly where to find them and can follow their scent until you do. On a 10+, take +1 forward against them. On a miss, someone unpleasant finds you first.

And choose one more:

☐ **Regeneration:** When you ***let it out***, add this option to the list:
- Your wounds close; heal 1-harm

☐ **Alpha Dog:** When you ***persuade an NPC*** in your territory, roll with Blood instead of Heart.

☐ **From the Brink:** You can exit your wolf form at will. When you do, roll with Spirit. On a hit, you change back. On a 7-9, take 1-harm or mark corruption. On a miss, you change but the transformation is incomplete, lengthy, or painful.

☐ **Reckless:** If you jump right into danger without hedging your bets, you get armor+1. If you're leading a group, it gets armor+1 also.

DRAMA MOVES

»Wolf Corruption Move

When you begin a hunt for someone, mark corruption.

»Intimacy Move

When you share a moment of intimacy—physical or emotional—with another person, you create a primal bond with them; you always know where to find them and when they're in trouble. This bond lasts until the end of the next session.

»End Move

When you die or retire your character, anyone in the scene you wish to protect escapes and reaches safety, no matter the odds.

STANDARD ADVANCES

Advances available at beginning of play:

- ☐ +1 Blood (max +3)
- ☐ +1 Mind (max +3)
- ☐ +1 Spirit (max +3)
- ☐ A new Wolf move
- ☐ A new Wolf move
- ☐ Add 2 qualities to your transformation
- ☐ A move from another Archetype
- ☐ Change your Faction
- ☐ Join or lead a wolf pack

After 5 advances you may select:

- ☐ +1 to any stat (max +3)
- ☐ +1 any Faction (max +3)
- ☐ Erase a scar
- ☐ Resolve a trouble
- ☐ Erase a corruption advance
- ☐ Erase a corruption advance
- ☐ Advance 3 basic moves
- ☐ Advance 3 basic moves
- ☐ Retire your character to safety
- ☐ Change to a new Archetype

CORRUPTION ADVANCES

- ☐ Take a corruption move
- ☐ Take a corruption move
- ☐ Take a corruption move
- ☐ Take a corruption move from another Archetype
- ☐ Retire your character. They may return as a Threat

CORRUPTION MOVES

- ☐ **One with the Beast:** Mark corruption to add 2 more qualities to your transformation until the end of the session.
- ☐ **Force of Nature:** You get +1 Blood (max +4). Whenever you roll with Blood and roll a 12+, mark corruption.
- ☐ **Sun and Moon:** Mark corruption to transform into your wolf form at will.
- ☐ **Familiar Territory:** Mark corruption to know the source of the greatest danger to your territory, even if it has concealed itself with magic or misdirection.

PLAYING THE WOLF

Primal, unstoppable, brutal, unlucky. The Wolf is capable of transforming into a deadly werebeast when the moon rises into the sky. Little stands in their way, but they often find more trouble than they bargained for when they prowl the city's streets.

You might be a wild and uncontrollable beast, but your territory grounds you. You know the people who live there—their habits and problems, their lies and misdeeds—even if they don't regard you as their official protector. Generally, other supernaturals acknowledge your territory, unless they're making an explicit play to take it from you.

While other Archetypes might be wrestling with their position in society or the knowledge they bear, you're wrestling with yourself. The transformation feels real and true, the fucking rush you get from letting your true self run these streets. But will you find a way back from the unkillable monster? Will you manage to have some sort of life beyond the streets?

»Notes on Your Moves

You don't have to transform to use moves like ***Bloodhound***, ***Regeneration***, or ***Reckless***. Your werewolf nature is with you no matter what form you take.

Your wolf form is powerful, but barely within your control. If you try to resist the change, your MC might ask you to ***keep your cool*** one or more times. To transform into your wolf form at will without ***Sun and Moon***, you can try to ***let it out*** to "take definite hold of something vulnerable or exposed"—your weak, human body—but your transformation may leave your vulnerable or cause you to lose control.

Your territory's blessings are known and present: let your MC know if you want to call upon one of them during a session. Troubles show up less frequently, usually when you roll a 7-9 or miss on ***Comes with the Territory*** at the start of the session. A trouble might flare up in the middle of a session, but only if something demands that the MC bring it to bear.

You can have multiple primal bonds with other characters, provided you have multiple moments of intimacy.

You can use ***One with the Beast*** multiple times in a session—adding two more qualities each time—provided you mark corruption each time.

Force of Nature gives you +1 Blood and raises your max Blood to +4. If this move doesn't bring you to Blood +4, you can use standard advances to raise your Blood to +4 at a later time.

»Inspiration for The Wolf

- Books: Mercy Thompson series (Patricia Briggs), *The Wolfman* (Nicholas Pekearo), Twilight series (Stephenie Meyers)
- Music: "Howl" (Florence + The Machine), "Sacra" (Apocalyptica), "Hair of the Dog" (Nazareth), "Werewolves of London" (Warren Zevon), "Wolf Like Me" (TV on the Radio), "The Wolf of Velvet Fortune" (The Beau Brummels)
- Movies: *An American Werewolf in London, Ginger Snaps, Underworld*
- Television: *Being Human* (UK), *Hemlock Grove, Teen Wolf*

introducing power

THE ORACLE

The future is always in motion, like a great river dragging us all to our inevitable ends, lost in currents we cannot see. There are some who can swim against its strength, who can raise themselves above the surface to see what awaits us. They are the cursed, and they are the blessed.

NAME

(pick one)

Daniel, Dodona, Elijah, George, Hala, Humphrey, Joel, Jonathon, Joaquin, Kami, Khan, Malachi, Maria, Martha, Maximus, Olivia, Penelope, Pythia, Saira, Sonam

LOOK

(pick as many as apply)

- Ambiguous, Female, Male, Transgressing
- Asian or South Asian, Black, Hispanic/Latino, Indigenous, Middle Eastern, White, __________
- Dirty Clothing, Loose Clothing, Revealing Clothing, Warm Clothing

DEMEANOR

(pick one)

Distant, Paranoid, Soothing, Volatile

CHARACTER STATS

(Add 1 to one of these)

Blood 0 Heart -1 Mind 1 Spirit 1

STARTING FACTIONS

(Add 1 to one of these)

Mortality 0 Night -1 Power 1 Wild 1

INTRO QUESTIONS

- Who are you?
- How long have you been in the city?
- How do you cope with the visions?
- What are the nightmares like?
- What do you desperately need?

GEAR

- A simple apartment, a crappy car, a cell phone
- 1 set of unique items
    - ☐ Prophetic tools (e.g., tarot deck, crystal ball, runes, etc.)
    - ☐ Ritual objects (an athame, a pentacle, etc.)
    - ☐ Collection of tomes and grimoires

DEBTS

- Someone helps you understand your dreams and visions. You owe them 2 Debts.
- You've had a dire prophecy about someone, but you don't know how to help them...yet. You owe them a Debt.
- You are helping someone realize their true potential through your visions. They owe you a Debt.

ORACLE MOVES

You get this one:

☑ **Foretellings:** At the beginning of the session, roll with Spirit. On a 10+, hold 2. On a 7-9, hold 1. During the session, you can spend your hold to declare that something terrible is about to happen. You (and your allies) take +1 ongoing to avoid the impending disaster. On a miss, you foresee the death of someone important to you and take -1 to all rolls to prevent it.

And choose two more:

☐ **Psychometry:** Whenever you study and examine an interesting object, roll with Spirit. On a 10+, ask 3. On a 7-9, ask 1:

- What is the history of this object?
- What bans, wards, or limits are attached to this object?
- Where does this object belong?
- What secrets or mysteries has this object been privy to?
- What strong emotions have most recently been near this object?

On a miss, the emotion of the object overwhelms you and you take -1 ongoing for the scene.

☐ **Double Life:** Take Mortality as a second Faction. When someone rolls with or marks your Faction, tell them which one is most appropriate.

☐ **Conduit:** Advance ***let it out*** for all characters in your presence, including yourself.

☐ **Skim the Surface:** When you touch someone, you can read their surface thoughts. Roll with Spirit. On a 10+, ask 3. On a 7–9, ask 1:

- What is your character thinking about right now?
- Who are you protecting?
- Why are you keeping secrets?
- What is your character's hidden pain?

On a miss, you inflict 1-harm (ap) on them and yourself.

☐ **At Any Cost:** When you interfere with someone's plans or actions to prevent one of your visions from coming true, mark their Faction and take +1 forward.

DRAMA MOVES

»Oracle Corruption Move

When you give someone a false prophecy, mark corruption.

»Intimacy Move

When you share a moment of intimacy—physical or emotional—with another person, you gain a specific and clear vision about that person's future. You can ask up to 3 questions about the vision; mark corruption for each.

»End Move

When you die or retire your character, announce a proclamation upon the world that will reverberate in dreams worldwide. Detail the signs of its coming. The MC will make your prophecy come to pass, sooner rather than later.

STANDARD ADVANCES

Advances available at beginning of play:

- ☐ +1 Blood (max +3)
- ☐ +1 Heart (max +3)
- ☐ +1 Mind (max +3)
- ☐ +1 Spirit (max +3)
- ☐ A new Oracle move
- ☐ A new Oracle move
- ☐ A move from another Archetype
- ☐ A move from another Archetype
- ☐ Change your Faction

After 5 advances you may select:

- ☐ +1 to any stat (max +3)
- ☐ +1 any Faction (max +3)
- ☐ Erase a scar
- ☐ Get a sanctum
- ☐ Erase a corruption advance
- ☐ Erase a corruption advance
- ☐ Advance 3 basic moves
- ☐ Advance 3 basic moves
- ☐ Change to a new Archetype

CORRUPTION ADVANCES

- ☐ Take a corruption move
- ☐ Take a corruption move
- ☐ Take a corruption move
- ☐ Take a corruption move from another Archetype
- ☐ Retire your character. They may return as a Threat

CORRUPTION MOVES

- ☐ **Empath:** When you ***figure someone out***, ***Skim the Surface***, or use ***Psychometry***, mark corruption to ask any questions you'd like, not limited to the lists.
- ☐ **I, All-Seeing:** Mark corruption and suffer 1-harm (ap) to have a vision about the situation at hand. Ask the MC a question; they will answer it honestly.
- ☐ **Dark Fate:** Mark corruption when face to face with someone to pronounce a curse on them. Roll with Spirit. On a 10+, choose 2. On a 7-9, choose 1:
    - The curse lasts for a long time
    - You are not the obvious source of the curse
    - The effects of the curse are potent and obvious
- ☐ **Eyes That Burrow:** Mark corruption to lock eyes with someone and force them to be still for as long as you maintain the gaze.

PLAYING THE ORACLE

Prophetic, blessed, cursed, intense. The Oracle is a seer, mystic, or psychic, gifted with sight beyond sight. They can see beyond the present, beyond this reality, but they cannot turn away, no matter how terrible their visions become.

All around you is the truth—lying just out of reach of most mortals—but your attempts to warn off or persuade others about what's coming for them often land on deaf ears. After all, they aren't fools, ready to be bamboozled by the first "psychic" to walk in the door.

And so you must take matters into your own hands. If those around you won't avert the terrible future coming for them, you've got to get out there into the streets and make a new future, one that's just a little brighter, one in which your visions don't come to pass.

For that kind of work, you'll need friends and allies, other characters—PCs and NPCs—who are willing to hear you out and trust that what you're seeing is more than a weak premonition.

»Notes on Your Moves

When you spend hold from ***Foretellings***, you're not necessarily guaranteeing that thing will happen; you're giving yourself and your allies the chance to act before the thing comes to pass. If you're hiding from a vampire assassin, for example, you might spend your hold to say, "She's going to find me," and take a +1 ongoing to attempts to ***escape*** before she notices you or ***unleash an attack*** on her when she gets close.

You can always use ***let it out*** to extend your supernatural senses, but ***Psychometry*** and ***Skim the Surface*** allow you to ask specific questions without risking corruption. If none of the questions from either of those two moves work, you can use ***Empath*** or ***let it out*** to get your answers.

Choosing ***Double Life*** means that you maintain a mortal identity in addition to your known supernatural dealings. When someone rolls with or marks your Faction, you get to select which Faction you think is the right Faction for that situation.

The specifics—beyond the options you select—of a ***Dark Fate*** curse are up to the MC. You can't know for certain what kind of darkness you'll inflict on your victim until you actually lay the curse upon them.

»Inspiration for The Oracle

- Books: *The Dead Zone* (Stephen King), *The Fire Sermon* (Francesca Haig), *The Vision* (Dean R. Koontz)
- Music: "Killing Me Softly" (The Fugees), "Out of My Hands" (Dave Matthews Band), "You Ain't Seen Nothing Yet" (Bachman Turner Overdrive)
- Movies: *Fear, The Gift* (2000), *Ghost*
- Television: *Carnivale, Medium, Tru Calling, Penny Dreadful*

THE WIZARD

Mages are among the deadliest and most powerful of all humans. Their ability to re-shape the world around them grants them tremendous powers. Nothing corrupts quite like power.

NAME

(pick one)

Ailea, Alanna, Andrés, Brandon, Calvin, Christine, Desmond, Hugo, Jocelyn, June, Krista, Laura, Marlowe, Miranda, Randall, Vincent, Vivian, Wesley, Wraith, Zoha

LOOK

(pick as many as apply)

- Ambiguous, Female, Male, Transgressing
- Asian or South Asian, Black, Hispanic/Latino, Indigenous, Middle Eastern, White, ___________
- Archaic Clothing, Comfortable Clothing, Dark Clothing, Fancy Clothing

DEMEANOR

(pick one)

Detached, Disheveled, Ominous, Volatile

CHARACTER STATS

(Add 1 to one of these)

Blood -1 Heart 0 Mind 1 Spirit 1

STARTING FACTIONS

(Add 1 to one of these)

Mortality 1 Night -1 Power 1 Wild 0

INTRO QUESTIONS

- Who are you?
- How long have you been in the city?
- What keeps you up at night?
- What have you sacrificed for your power?
- What do you desperately need?

GEAR

- A nice apartment or simple house, a crappy car, a decent cell phone
- A mystical focus (detail) and sanctum (detail)
- 1 practical weapon
    - ☐ Snubnosed revolver (2-harm close loud reload concealable)
    - ☐ 9mm Glock (2-harm close loud)
    - ☐ Sword (3-harm hand messy)

SANCTUM

Choose and underline 4 features of your sanctum:

an extremely knowledgeable assistant, a testing ground, magical booby traps, a library of old tomes, a scattering of ancient relics, a mystical prison, magical wards, a portal to another dimension, a focus circle, an apothecary.

Choose and underline 2 downsides of your sanctum:

it attracts otherworldly attention, it contains many volatile substances, its location is known by many, it always lacks a key piece or ingredient, it's tough for you to access.

When you go into your sanctum to work on something, the MC tells you what it will take to complete your task, as if your sanctum was a mystical workspace.

FOCUS

You have a mystical focus item that helps you channel your magics. Without it, take -1 to ***Channeling***.

Choose a benefit your Focus grants you:
- ☐ Inflict +1 harm with your magics
- ☐ Gain armor+1 while you have hold from ***Channeling***
- ☐ Gain 1 additional hold when using ***Channeling***

DEBTS

- Someone is helping you keep your demons at bay. You owe them a Debt.
- Someone is your go-to when you get into trouble. You owe them 2 Debts.
- You are helping someone keep a dangerous secret. They owe you a Debt.

WIZARD MOVES

You get these two and your spells:

☑ **Channeling:** When you channel and collect your magics, roll with Spirit. On a 10+, hold 3. On a 7-9, hold 3 and choose 1 from the list below. On a miss, hold 1, but you cannot channel again this scene.

- Take -1 ongoing until you rest
- Suffer 1-harm (ap)
- Mark corruption

Your hold lasts until you spend it. You can spend it to cast any spell you have as per the spell's details.

☑ **Sanctum Sanctorum:** When you go to your sanctum for a spell ingredient, relic, or tome, roll with Spirit. On a 10+, you've got pretty much just the thing. On a 7-9, you've got something close, but it's flawed or lacking in some significant way. On a miss, you don't have what you're looking for, but you know someone who probably has it in stock.

SPELLS (CHOOSE 3)

☐ **Tracking:** Spend 1 hold to learn the location of someone. You must have a personal object that belongs to the target or recent leavings of their body (a lock of hair, fingernail clippings, their blood, etc.).

☐ **Elementalism:** You conjure the elements to strike out at your enemies. Spend 1 hold to use ***unleash an attack*** with your magic as a weapon (3-harm close or 2-harm close area).

☐ **Memory Wipe:** Spend 1 hold to cause a helpless target to forget some of their short-term memories, up to an entire hour's worth. You can spend an additional hold and mark corruption to put alternate memories in their place.

☐ **Shielding:** Spend 1 hold to provide armor+1 to yourself or someone nearby, or spend 2 holds to provide armor+1 to everyone in a small area, possibly including yourself. This armor lasts until the end of the scene. You can stack multiple uses of ***Shielding*** at once.

☐ **Veil:** Spend 1 hold to make yourself invisible from sight for a few moments.

☐ **Teleport:** Spend 1 hold to teleport yourself a short distance within a scene you're in.

☐ **Hex:** Spend 1 hold to inflict 1-harm (ap) on someone from any distance. You must have a sample of their hair, blood, or saliva to do so.

DRAMA MOVES

»Wizard Corruption Move

When you strike a deal with someone dark and powerful, mark corruption.

»Intimacy Move

When you share a moment of intimacy—physical or emotional—with another person, decide whether you care about them or not. If you don't, they go about their business as normal. If you do, they take -1 ongoing to ***escape*** until they get some intimacy somewhere else.

»End Move

When you die, you may place a devastating curse on someone nearby. Specify the effects of the curse and how they may end it.

STANDARD ADVANCES

Advances available at beginning of play:

- ☐ +1 Heart (max +3)
- ☐ +1 Mind (max +3)
- ☐ +1 Spirit (max +3)
- ☐ Add 2 features to your sanctum
- ☐ Take 3 more spells
- ☐ A move from another Archetype
- ☐ A move from another Archetype
- ☐ Change your Faction

After 5 advances you may select:

- ☐ +1 to any stat (max +3)
- ☐ +1 any Faction (max +3)
- ☐ Erase a scar
- ☐ Remove a downside from your sanctum
- ☐ Add a benefit to your focus
- ☐ Advance 3 basic moves
- ☐ Advance 3 basic moves
- ☐ Retire your character to safety
- ☐ Change to a new Archetype

CORRUPTION ADVANCES

- ☐ Take a corruption move
- ☐ Take a corruption move
- ☐ Take a corruption move
- ☐ Take a corruption move from another Archetype
- ☐ Retire your character. They may return as a Threat

CORRUPTION MOVES

- ☐ **The Dark Arts:** When you ***unleash an attack*** with magic or psychic energies, mark corruption to roll with Spirit instead of Blood for the rest of the scene.
- ☐ **Upon a Pale Horse:** Mark corruption and speak the true name of an NPC in the scene to inflict 3-harm (ap) on them.
- ☐ **Black Magic:** Mark corruption to ignore a requirement set by the MC when using your sanctum.
- ☐ **Warding:** Mark corruption to create a magical ward the size of a small room. The ward lasts for a month and a day or until you release it.

PLAYING THE WIZARD

Powerful, dedicated, hermetic, strange. The Wizard relies on years of training to channel intense magics. With enough preparation, these mages can move mountains...or turn them to dust. When caught alone and unprepared, they are still painfully mortal.

With great power...comes every damn problem in the world.

People think you've got what they need: the resources, contacts, and power to make things right. But all that power doesn't mean that you know how to solve any of their fucking problems. Or that the other wizards who live in the city are too keen on attempts to "fix" things with powerful magic. Your kind takes the long view.

But maybe you can do a little good. Maybe you can fix the things that really need fixing. Maybe you can take all that power and knowledge and training you've accrued and do something with it that someone will remember long after you're gone.

»Note on Your Moves

In order to cast spells, you first have to ***Channel*** and collect your magics. Each spell tells you how many hold you must spend to activate it. If you want to be ready for trouble, you might want to channel first.

You start with three spells, but you can gain more through standard advancements. Some notes on your spells:

- ***Elementalism*** creates an elemental weapon for a single attack. You still have to ***unleash*** to attack another character. You have to decide before the attack which type of weapon it is (3-harm close or 2-harm close area).
- ***Memory Wipe*** requires some time, intimacy, or physical contact with your target. It's likely to trigger your intimacy move when you use it.
- ***Veil*** and ***Teleport*** almost always give you the opportunity to ***escape***, so long as no one else can magically pierce your illusions or teleport to pursue you.
- Only one ***Hex*** can be cast on a target at a time. Additional hexes do not inflict additional harm.

When you use your sanctum to work on a problem, the MC may give you requirements that are extremely difficult to fulfill; you may need to turn to allies and cash in Debts to get what you need. You can only use ***Black Magic*** once per project, even if you're willing to mark additional corruption to ignore additional requirements.

Warding allows you to protect a location from whatever you like for a month and a day. You must declare what threat the ward is supposed to exclude when creating the ward.

»Inspiration for The Wizard

- Books: Hellblazer (DC Comics), The Dresden Files (Jim Butcher), The Harry Potter series (J.K. Rowling)
- Music: "The Grand East" (LABORS), "Uranus" (Gustav Holst), "Magic Man" (Heart), "Power" (Kanye West)
- Movies: *A Beautiful Mind, The Prestige, The Sorcerer's Apprentice*
- Television: *Bewitched, Charmed, Witches of East End*

introducing wild

THE FAE

Fickle and enigmatic, the Fae are impossible for a mortal to completely understand. Their ways are steeped in tradition, honor, and, above all else, bargains. They do not simply appreciate these virtues, they embody them.

NAME

(pick one)

Ava, Brianna, Cesar, Chiko, Chloe, Connor, Dylan, Elliot, Fahim, Fiona, Lucas, Maeve, Manuel, Nora, Roman, Salomé, Su-mi, Rachel, Vicente, Yaki

LOOK

(pick as many as apply)

- Ambiguous, Female, Male, Transgressing
- Asian or South Asian, Black, Hispanic/Latino, Indigenous, Middle Eastern, White, __________
- Colorful Clothing, Expensive Clothing, Messy Clothing, Revealing Clothing

DEMEANOR

(pick one)

Alien, Eccentric, Feral, Seductive

CHARACTER STATS

(Add 1 to one of these)

Blood -1 Heart 1 Mind 0 Spirit 1

STARTING FACTIONS

(Add 1 to one of these)

Mortality 0 Night -1 Power 1 Wild 1

INTRO QUESTIONS

- Who are you?
- How long have you been in the city?
- What do you love most about humanity?
- Who is your closest confidante in the city?
- What do you desperately need?

GEAR

- A nice house or apartment, a car, a smart phone
- A relic from your homelands
- A symbol of your court (sun, moon, storm, winter, spring, etc.)

DEBTS

- Someone broke an important promise to you and swore they would make it up to you. They owe you 2 Debts.
- You are keeping something hidden for someone. They owe you a Debt.
- You entrusted someone with a dangerous task. Ask them if they succeeded or failed. If they succeeded, you owe them a Debt. If they failed, they owe you 2 Debts.

FAE MOVES

You get this one:

☑ **Faerie Magic:** Whenever you use a faerie power, choose 1:

- Mark corruption
- You owe your monarch a Debt
- Suffer 1-harm (ap)

And choose two more:

☐ **A Dish Best Served Now:** When you commit to exact revenge on behalf of someone (including yourself), gain +1 to all rolls against the target of that vengeance. For every scene in which you do not pursue vengeance, suffer 1-harm (ap).

☐ **In Our Blood:** When you ***trick*** someone, roll with Heart instead of Mind.

☐ **Scales of Justice:** You may ***cash in a Debt*** with someone to use a power from ***faerie magic*** (including powers not normally available to you) on them at no cost.

☐ **Draw Back the Curtain:** When you ***escape***, add this option to the list:

- You escape to your homeland, for better or worse

☐ **Words Are Wind:** When someone breaks a promise to you or lies to you and you find out, they owe you a Debt and you take +1 forward against them.

FAERIE POWERS (CHOOSE 3)

☐ **Wild Fury:** You summon an element of nature capable of striking your enemies (2-harm close area or 3-harm close/far).

☐ **Nature's Caress:** Your touch heals 2-harm. You cannot use this power on yourself.

☐ **Wither:** You imbue your touch with the power to kill (3-harm intimate ap).

☐ **Glamours:** You create illusions to fool the senses. The effects don't last long.

☐ **Shape Change:** You can briefly change your shape into that of an animal.

☐ **Bedlam:** Touch a target to place them in a specific emotional state (your choice). Mark corruption to have that emotion directed toward a target of your choosing.

DRAMA MOVES

»Fae Corruption Move

When you break a promise or tell an outright lie, mark corruption.

»Intimacy Move

When you share a moment of intimacy—physical or emotional—with another person, demand a promise from them. If they refuse you or break the promise, they owe you 2 Debts.

»End Move

When you die or retire your character, choose a character and bestow the favor of your court upon them. They can choose either to take ***faerie magic*** and two of your faerie powers or to advance ***persuade an NPC***.

STANDARD ADVANCES

Advances available at beginning of play:

- ☐ +1 Blood (max +3)
- ☐ +1 Heart (max +3)
- ☐ +1 Mind (max +3)
- ☐ +1 Spirit (max +3)
- ☐ A new Fae move
- ☐ A new Fae move
- ☐ A move from another Archetype
- ☐ A move from another Archetype
- ☐ Change your Faction

After 5 advances you may select:

- ☐ +1 to any stat (max +3)
- ☐ +1 any Faction (max +3)
- ☐ Erase a scar
- ☐ Join or lead a faerie court
- ☐ Erase a corruption advance
- ☐ Advance 3 basic moves
- ☐ Advance 3 basic moves
- ☐ Retire your character to safety
- ☐ Change to a new Archetype

CORRUPTION ADVANCES

- ☐ Take a corruption move
- ☐ Take a corruption move
- ☐ Take a corruption move
- ☐ Take a corruption move from another Archetype
- ☐ Retire your character. They may return as a Threat

CORRUPTION MOVES

- ☐ **Gach Cumhacht:** You gain the remaining faerie powers. When you use ***faerie magic***, you may no longer choose to suffer harm.
- ☐ **Shrewd Negotiator:** When you roll a 10+ to ***refuse to honor a Debt***, mark corruption to cancel the original Debt and claim a Debt from the person you refused.
- ☐ **Unearthly Grace:** You get +1 Heart (max +4). Whenever you roll with Heart and roll a 12+, mark corruption.
- ☐ **Everyone's Got One:** Touch someone and mark corruption to declare one of their vulnerabilities. All damage from that source (fire, steel, iron, etc.) is treated as +1 harm and ap.

PLAYING THE FAE

Fickle, enigmatic, cold, illogical. The Fae is a being from beyond this world or the offspring of a creature with ties to distant realities. They are able to draw upon the logic of their native world, tying themselves to oaths and promises in exchange for great power.

To put it bluntly...*you aren't from here.* You're a visitor, an immigrant (or the child of immigrants), who has one foot in this world and one foot in another. No one—not the mortals of this world or the faeries of your homeland—will ever let you forget that you don't belong.

But "not belonging" has power. You walk in this world, but carry powerful magics and relics. You are bound by oaths and promises and gain power in return from those who would bind themselves to you. They might not understand the depth of their commitments, but their Debts spend just fine.

Ask for promises. Tell no lies. The Debts you collect will keep you safe and alive.

»Notes on Your Moves

The relic you carry from your homelands may hold magic powers, but remember that the more powerful it is the more likely that someone powerful is looking for it.

Faerie magic is always accessible to you, provided you're willing to pay the cost (corruption, Debt, or harm). Some notes on your powers:

- ***Wild Fury*** summons an elemental weapon, but you still need to ***unleash an attack*** with the weapon to harm others. Unlike The Wizard's ***Elementalism*** spell, you don't need to summon the weapon again each time you use it during a scene.
- ***Wither*** cannot be used on the same target more than once per day. You may need to ***keep your cool*** to get close to a resistant target.
- ***Glamours*** don't last long, but they are extremely effective. A generous MC might allow you to ***mislead, distract, or trick*** someone with your glamours as if you rolled a 10+.

In Our Blood requires that you do more than mislead or distract your target. It has to be a trick, an intentional falsehood that captures their full attention.

Scales of Justice can only be used if you have a Debt on the target of your magic. Remember that you can ***cash in a Debt*** with someone to transfer a Debt they have on someone else to you, so getting Debts on your chosen target shouldn't be too hard. Mark Faction whenever you use this move, as if you ***cashed in a Debt***.

When you escape to your homeland using ***Draw Back the Curtain***, the MC may decide that other characters who are also trying to flee end up in your homeland with you.

Whatever you declare as a vulnerability using ***Everyone's Got One*** does +1 harm (ap), even if the target wasn't previous vulnerable to that element. The vulnerability lasts until the end of the scene, but some damage has to occur to add the additional harm.

»Inspiration for The Fae

- Books: Fever series (Karen Marie Moning), The Iron Druid Chronicles (Kevin Hearne), The October Daye Novels (Seanan McGuire)
- Music: "Cold as Ice" (Foreigner), "Keep Ya Head Up" (2Pac), "You Got Your Hooks in Me" (Little Charlie & The Nightcats), "Where I End And You Begin" (Radiohead)
- Movies: *The Brothers Grimm, Labyrinth, Midsummer Night's Dream (1999), Pan's Labyrinth*
- Television: *Lost Girl, Once Upon a Time, True Blood*

THE TAINTED

You remember what it was like being human, or at least fully human. But that was before all this; before your soul ended up in the hands of demons and devils. Now you're something else, working jobs for a "patron" who is never satisfied, never done with you. It's the worst job you've ever had.

NAME

(pick one)

Alfred, Alma, Catarina, Dawa, Fahad, Father Luke, Iris, Jake, Jeremiah, Kaito, Kyo, Lana, Landon, Latifah, Nabhi, Nadia, Ophelia, Shiro, Tamali, Yuina

LOOK

(pick as many as apply)

- Ambiguous, Female, Male, Transgressing
- Asian or South Asian, Black, Hispanic/Latino, Indigenous, Middle Eastern, White, __________
- Dirty Clothing, Expensive Clothing, Formal Clothing, Trendy Clothing

DEMEANOR

(pick one)

Corporate, Detached, Paranoid, Volatile

CHARACTER STATS

(Add 1 to one of these)

Blood 1 Heart 1 Mind -1 Spirit 0

STARTING FACTIONS

(Add 1 to one of these)

Mortality 1 Night -1 Power 0 Wild 1

INTRO QUESTIONS

- Who are you?
- How long have you been in the city?
- Who would you die for?
- What is your daily release?
- What do you desperately need?

GEAR

- A house or apartment, a car, a smart phone
- 1 weapon of choice
    - ☐ Collapsible baton (2-harm hand)
    - ☐ 9mm Beretta (2-harm close loud)
    - ☐ Pump-action shotgun (3-harm close loud messy)
    - ☐ Sword (3-harm hand messy)

DEBTS

- You're protecting someone from a dark power. They owe you 2 Debts.
- Someone is trying to save you and keeps suffering for it. You owe them 2 Debts.
- You have a demon patron who holds the contract for your soul. You owe them 3 Debts.

TAINTED MOVES

You get this one:

☑ **The Devil Inside:** When you assume your demon form, roll with Blood. On a 10+, choose 2. On a 7-9, choose 1. On a miss, choose 1 and you owe your patron a Debt.

- Gain armor+1
- Heal 2-harm
- Inflict +1 harm
- +demonic weapon (3-harm hand or 2-harm close)
- +demonic movement (flight, flaming motorcycle, etc.)

If you're working a job for your patron, choose 1 more. If you mark corruption, choose 1 more.

And choose one more:

☐ **Invocation:** You may ***cash in a Debt*** with someone to appear in their presence. Others may ***cash in a Debt*** with you to have you appear as well.

☐ **Don't Look at Me:** When you ***mislead*** someone, roll with Heart instead of Mind.

☐ **Tendrils in the Dark:** When you seek the guidance of your patron through rituals and portents, roll with Spirit. On a hit, the signs and signals are laid out before you: take +1 forward if you follow the path. On a 7-9, you're drawn further into your patron's service; ***keep your cool*** to make your own way. On a miss, your patron has a job for you right now; assume your demon form and go to work or suffer 2-harm (ap).

☐ **Cold as Ice:** Take +1 Blood (max +3)

☐ **Tough as Nails:** You get 1-armor. Blessed or holy sources ignore your armor. Weapons designed to stun or impair you have no effect.

DEMON FORM

Since your patron claimed your soul, you have a new look: a demon form. Pick as many as apply from the lists below:

☐ **Head:** horns, flames, spikes, halo, smoke

☐ **Hands:** claws, bones, flames, pincers

☐ **Wings:** feathers, leather, none

☐ **Skin:** chitinous, rocklike, misty

☐ **Eyes:** glowing, burning, empty, smoky, none

DEMONIC JOBS

Your dark patron keeps you on Earth for a reason. Choose two jobs from the list below:

collecting souls, tracking down rogue demons, delivering threats and messages, guarding someone or something, assassinating your patron's enemies, brokering demonic contracts, hiding demonic contraband.

When you complete a job for your patron, mark Wild. Your patron owes you a Debt for every job completed.

You can ***cash in a Debt*** with your Patron in order to have them:

- Answer a question (honestly) about their Faction
- Introduce you to a powerful member of their Faction
- Give you a worthy and useful gift without cost
- Erase a Debt they hold on someone
- Give you a Debt they have on someone else
- Give you +3 to ***persuade*** them (choose before rolling)

Your patron may offer you the chance to buy your freedom, but Debts alone won't be enough.

DRAMA MOVES

»Tainted Corruption Move

When you persuade someone on your patron's behalf, mark corruption.

»Intimacy Move

When you share a moment of intimacy—physical or emotional—with another person, they give you a Debt they hold on someone else.

»End Move

When you die, cash in all the Debts your patron owes you to come back. If you have none, your patron will ask someone else to pay the Debt for you. If they refuse, time's up. It's been a good run.

STANDARD ADVANCES

Advances available at beginning of play:

- ☐ +1 Heart (max +3)
- ☐ +1 Mind (max +3)
- ☐ +1 Spirit (max +3)
- ☐ A new Tainted move
- ☐ A new Tainted move
- ☐ A move from another Archetype
- ☐ A move from another Archetype
- ☐ Change your Faction

After 5 advances you may select:

- ☐ +1 to any stat (max +3)
- ☐ +1 any Faction (max +3)
- ☐ Erase a scar
- ☐ Gain fiendish underlings
- ☐ Erase a job from your contract
- ☐ Erase a corruption advance
- ☐ Advance 3 basic moves
- ☐ Advance 3 basic moves
- ☐ Change to a new Archetype

CORRUPTION ADVANCES

- ☐ Take a corruption move
- ☐ Take a corruption move
- ☐ Take a corruption move
- ☐ Take a corruption move from another Archetype
- ☐ Retire your character. They may return as a Threat

CORRUPTION MOVES

☐ **Fringe Benefits:** Mark corruption to ***drop the name*** of your demonic patron as if you rolled a 10+. You don't have to have a Debt on your patron to use the move.

☐ **Just Below the Surface:** Mark corruption to assume your demon form without a roll and gain all the options listed.

☐ **Not to Be Denied:** When someone ***refuses to honor a Debt*** you've cashed in on them, mark corruption to make their result a miss (after they roll).

☐ **From Hell:** Mark corruption to have your patron send a gang of demons to work on your behalf for a scene (2-harm small group 2-armor demonic).

PLAYING THE TAINTED

Brutal, intense, callous, manipulative. The Tainted was a mortal who sold their soul in exchange for power, wealth, or security. They are of two worlds, torn between their human compassion and demonic obligations.

You made a fucking deal. Perhaps it was for some noble and good reason, but the results are the same: you spend your days racketeering for hell. Buy for one, sell for two. Profits, my friend. Profits.

But the hold your patron has on you is loose. You're not a fucking servant, doomed to follow orders without any free will. You've still got some humanity rattling around underneath those flaming horns and chitinous skin, some vestige of who you once were. Or at least that's what you tell yourself at the end of a long day.

It's easy to be the villain, the demonic muscle just doing your job. But what would you do to be free?

»Notes on Your Moves

You have two distinct forms: your normal human appearance and your monstrous demon form. Assuming your demon form is instantaneous, unless you decide you want it to take longer. Any benefits gained from your demon form—armor+1, inflict +1 harm, etc.—last until you return to your human form.

Invocation allows you—or might force you—to move great distances to appear before your creditors or debtors. Resisting an invocation is treated as ***refusing to honor a Debt***.

Tough as Nails provides both 1-armor and resistance to s-harm (see *Stun Harm* in **The Streets** on 152). If someone hits you with a baseball bat or lead pipe, you still take harm, but it can't knock you out or knock you off your feet.

From Hell requires that you let your demon patron know in advance that you want a gang of demons for a scene: you can't summon the demons to you just by marking corruption. If the job isn't finished by the end of the scene, you can mark corruption to make the gang stick around for the next scene as well.

If you die and your patron asks someone else to pay your Debt, your patron will ask one character—PC or NPC—for a single Debt to bring you back. The choice is entirely theirs to make. If they say no, that's it. You're done.

»Inspiration for The Tainted

- Books: *Lucifer* (DC Comics), *Ghost Rider* (Marvel Comics), Dante Valentine series (Lilith Saintcrow)
- Music: "99 Problems" (Jay-Z), "Born to Die" (Lana Del Rey), "Breaking Down" (Florence + The Machine), "Highway to Hell" (AC/DC)
- Movies: *Constantine, The Devil's Advocate, Hellboy*
- Television: *Angel, Brimstone, Millennium*

FIVE

THE STREETS

LIFE ON THE STREET

Characters in *Urban Shadows* are no strangers to violence. The supernatural world is like any community that focuses on illegal or illicit activity: violence is a substitute for all the other forms of communication that are excluded by the nature of the business. You can't, for example, sue another werewolf pack in municipal court for taking your territory or call the cops to tell them that an undead vampire lord murdered and ate your brother. You've got to handle all that shit on your own.

There are methods that help supernatural communities resolve conflicts without resorting to physical force—ancient faeries who serve as neutral arbiters, wizarding traditions for resolving territory disputes, or demonic contracts that magically enforce nonviolence—but they only delay the inevitable or shift the burden onto other parties. The language of the streets is violence. Always has been, always will be.

This chapter is devoted to explaining how violence works in *Urban Shadows*, including rules for dealing with harm and scars, constructing and wielding gear and weapons, and running battles between larger groups of characters.

HARM

When your character suffers injury and trauma, you take harm. If you take too much harm, you die.

The harm track consists of five boxes moving through three tiers: one faint, two grievous, and two critical. When your character suffers harm, check off a number of boxes on your harm track equal to the harm suffered. A weapon like a gun usually does 2-harm, so getting shot usually requires you to check off something like two boxes.

HARM **ARMOR** ☐

☐ **Faint**

☐☐ **Grievous**

☐☐ **Critical**

The different levels of harm reflect how badly your character is hurt, moving up from minor injuries to wounds that require immediate medical attention:

- **Faint harm** is relatively minor, like getting stabbed in a nonvital area or getting into a fist fight that doesn't last too long. Most characters can shrug off faint wounds by taking a day or two off and getting some rest.
- **Grievous harm** is serious stuff, like getting shot in the shoulder or hit by a car. If you suffer grievous harm, you need to get medical attention to keep things from getting worse, but you'll be back on your feet in a few days.
- **Critical harm** means that you're on the verge of dying, like getting shot in the stomach or beat repeatedly in the head with a metal baseball bat. If you don't get to a hospital—or find some magic to patch you up—you're going to die.

You always begin by marking harm in the faint tier and moving down the track into grievous and then critical. When you mark a box of harm in a new tier, write a short description of the injury on your sheet in the space beside the boxes to remind yourself what harm your character has suffered (and how best it might be treated later). If you ever need to mark harm and can't—because all your other boxes are full—you die (and probably trigger your end move).

HARM **ARMOR**

[x]	Faint	BLEEDING
[x] [ ]	Grievous	GUNSHOT WOUND
[ ] [ ]	Critical	

HARM RATINGS

Harm is a simple metric for evaluating how much physical damage an attack does, a rough approximation that differentiates throwing a punch from shooting a gun. Here are some ways to think about how harm shows up in the fiction:

- 1-harm is rough but blunt trauma: fists and baseball bats, punches thrown at a rock concert, the kind of thing people sleep off after a bad night.
- 2-harm is painful and obvious: a gunshot wound, a bad car wreck, wounds that are impossible to hide without bandages and slings.
- 3-harm is worse than all that: a bullet at point-blank range, a sword cleaving tendon and bone, a beating that leaves you unrecognizable for a week.
- 4-harm means instant death to a mortal human and weeks of pain and recovery for supernatural creatures: a grenade blast at close range, losing a limb or internal organ, falling off the top of a ten-story building.

You don't need to worry too much about measuring harm as a player. Each weapon lists a harm rating that helps to inform the conversation, and your MC will tell you how much harm you suffer whenever you suffer harm. Remember that when you ***unleash an attack*** on someone and choose *inflict terrible harm,* you step up the violence to the next level and inflict one more harm than normal.

Nathaniel, Derrick's Vamp, is trying to run down a fellow vampire, Rictus, who left him for dead at the bottom of an elevator shaft in the projects. When Nathaniel **hits the street**, *he gets word that Rictus is out hustling drugs on a local corner. Within a few moments, Nathaniel is sitting in his car, watching Rictus from a dark alley.*

"You see Rictus calling to cars rolling by, offering up something in his left hand, probably heroin. Do you get out and start shooting?" Mark, the MC, asks.

"Nah. I think I'll just hit him with my car."

Mark laughs. "Yeah, okay. That sounds like you're **unleashing** *on him with the car..."*

Derrick rolls an 8. "Oh, I **inflict terrible harm.** *I don't want to get put in a spot, though. I figure he's got corner boys around that might give me some trouble. I'll take* **they inflict harm on you**, *since I rolled the 7-9."*

"Right. You gun the engine and turn on the hi-beams, racing toward Rictus. He turns and bares his fangs, then withdraws a submachine gun from his jacket and opens fire. Usually it does 2-harm, but you're in a vehicle, so let's make it 1-harm from all the glass flying around from the broken windshield."

Derrick marks in the first box of his harm track on his sheet and writes "Glass Cuts" in the line next to the faint harm box.

Mark continues: "You don't slow down at all. Rictus realizes your plan too late and fails to jump out of the way in time. You catch him full on with the weight of the car, and he goes directly under. You hear bones crunch as he falls under the wheels of your ride. You skid to a stop, and throw the car into reverse, crushing him a second time under your wheels while his goons scatter. Let's call it 3-harm: 2-harm for the car and 1-harm for choosing **inflict terrible harm**.

"You're pretty sure that would have killed a mortal, but a vampire like Rictus might still be alive. Do you stop?"

"Nah. I think he'll remember me now. We're good."

HEALING HARM

If your character suffers only faint harm, it will heal naturally without any special treatment. But when your character suffers grievous harm, your injuries are serious enough to need special attention before they'll heal on their own. You might need to find a doctor who can patch you up, a wizard or faerie who can magically close your wounds, or—at the very least—a friend willing to pull bullets out of your back and bandage you up. Grievous wounds may even get worse if left untreated, but they probably won't kill you right away.

If your character suffers critical harm, on the other hand, your injuries are immediately life threatening. Grievous harm is broken bones and bullet wounds; critical harm is shattered skulls and sucking chest wounds. This kind of damage doesn't get better without serious medical intervention or magic. In fact, it's absolutely going to get worse. If you don't do something quickly, you're going to fucking die.

How long before your grievous or critical injuries worsen is entirely up to your MC. They make the decision based on the injuries you've sustained, the conditions in which you find yourself, and the dramatic tension of the scene. In other words, your MC will tell you when to mark another harm when your wounds get worse.

You heal from harm by receiving medical or supernatural aid—***hitting the streets*** is often useful for finding someone who can patch you up. Once you've gotten medical attention or magical assistance, healing happens slowly, generally removing one faint or grievous harm every couple of days and one critical harm every week. Your MC will tell you when you heal harm; mortals can't walk off a bullet wound in a day or two, but some supernatural creatures can bounce back a bit faster.

When you erase harm, you always begin with the harm in the faint tier and move down the track, removing the faint conditions before the grievous and critical conditions. This represents your less severe injuries healing first while the more severe take additional time. It's possible you sustain further faint harm while still healing from grievous and critical injuries.

Weakened and wounded, Colby is on the run from a hunter, Tiana, who believes that Colby's grown too close to her werewolf lover, Matt. As Colby tries to make a break for it, Tiana steps out of the shadows and shoots. Andrew, Colby's MC, says, "You feel a sharp pain in your back...and then you hit the ground. Hard. Take 2-harm."

"Hmm. That's it. Those are my last two boxes of harm." She marks in both critical boxes and writes "Shot in the Back" in the space to the right.

"You hear Tiana yell, 'I'm sorry, girl. You know how it is sometimes. It's not personal.' You half expect her to walk over and shoot you again, but instead you hear footsteps walking away. You think maybe she's leaving you here to die..."

"Fuck that. I took **Regeneration** *last session as an advance. All this time spent screwing my werewolf boyfriend has to count for something. I'd like to* **let it out**.*"*

Erica, Colby's player, rolls a 12 on **let it out**. *"Yes! I choose the new option* **Regeneration** *gives me:* **Your wounds close; heal 1-harm** *and I'm not going to mark corruption. Is that enough to keep me alive?"*

"Sure! You feel woozy for a moment, but then your flesh starts to knit back together. You feel the bullet push out of your body, and you hear the metal slug hit the asphalt. You're alive, but in bad shape. What do you do?"

Erica erases her faint harm box. She's still dying, but she's bought herself some time. "I call Matt. He and his pack aren't far, right? They should be able to get me."

Andrew says, "Yeah, that makes sense. Matt, I assume you'd take her to a hospital?" Matt's player nods. "Okay, cool. Let's skip forward in time a day or two. They've treated you—go ahead and heal 2-harm—but they definitely have some questions about who shot you. A few detectives who've been waiting patiently while you were going through surgery come into the room. What do you do?"

STUN HARM

Some weapons and situations inflict **s-harm**, a type of harm that incapacitates or disables characters. Tear gas, tasers, electric shocks, and concussive blasts may knock you off your feet and unconscious long before they kill you.

When you suffer s-harm, your MC will tell you what effect it has. Sometimes you may lose your footing or drop something you're holding or you may need to ***keep your cool*** in order to stay on your feet. Regardless, s-harm doesn't cause you to mark harm on your sheet, unless you fall down and hit your head while you're passing out.

Lianne and Gareth are breaking into an office complex when they trigger an active security system. Andrew, as MC, says, "The floor all around you crackles with electricity. You both take s-harm as the voltage runs up your legs into your body. You both need to **keep your cool** *to stay on your feet."*

Jana, Lianne's player, rolls with Spirit and comes up short: snake eyes. Even though Lianne has Spirit +3, she collapses to the ground. "Ouch."

Miguel smiles. He's recently picked up **Tough as Nails** *for Gareth. "It says here that 'Weapons designed to stun or impair you have no effect.' What happens to me?"*

Andrew says, "Nothing! The electricity surges over your body, but it has no effect. You see Lianne fall to the ground unconscious. What do you do?"

SCARS

When you suffer harm, you may always ignore that harm by marking a **scar**. Scars represent your character pushing through the immediate situation at some permanent cost, ignoring harm suffered by immediately reducing one of your main stats. In other words, you get to decide when your character dies from massive trauma by choosing (or not choosing) to negate lethal injuries before they happen (at a steep price).

Your character has four scars available:

- Shattered: (-1 Blood)
- Crushed: (-1 Heart)
- Fractured: (-1 Mind)
- Broken: (-1 Spirit)

Shattered means frightened, weakened, and overly cautious. Shattered characters hesitate when they should move, and their attempts to ***unleash an attack*** on someone or ***escape a situation*** often come up short.

Crushed means traumatized, timid, and uncertain. Crushed characters bear the full weight of the wounds they've suffered, and their attempts to ***persuade an NPC*** are inhibited by their reticent approach to conflict.

Fractured means confused, disoriented, and disjointed. Fractured characters are unstable and unsure, and their attempts to ***figure someone out*** or ***mislead, distract, or trick*** others are unfocused and imprecise.

Broken means hopeless, forlorn, and cowardly. Broken characters have lost their will to fight, and their attempts to ***keep their cool*** or ***let it out*** are often half-hearted and incomplete.

Despite her best efforts to hide in a dark alley, Veronica finds herself trapped by Okai, a vampire hunter intent on killing her to "save her immortal soul." Veronica is not fucking amused.

After a few exchanges, Veronica finds herself with only one box of harm left to mark. Okai has inflicted 4-harm on her, and she's near death. When she misses on her **unleash** *roll, Andrew, her MC, says, "Okai knocks you to the ground and pushes his stake into your chest. Given the close range here, I think you're taking 2-harm."*

Sophia sighs. That's enough to kill Veronica. "I'll mark a scar. I really don't want this guy to kill me."

Andrew asks, "Okay, which one?"

"Fractured. Veronica has been on edge the last few weeks anyway. It feels like everyone is out to get her. I think she's going to be a bit paranoid after this encounter."

Andrew nods. "Great. As Okai starts to drive the stake into your chest, the pain awakens something inside you, something feral and ugly. You roar and headbutt him, knocking him backward. You pull the stake out of your chest and stand up. Okai is scrambling backward, trying to get away. What do you do?"

If you're about to die...check off the scar, adjust the stat, and live to fight another day. Each scar cannot be selected more than once unless you've healed from that scar through standard advancement.

ARMOR

Characters wearing armor (a Kevlar vest, stab-vest, chainmail shirt, etc.) receive a layer of protection from most physical attacks. If they suffer harm from which their armor would protect them, they reduce the harm suffered by the rating of the armor.

Most armor is rated at 1-armor or 2-armor. 1-armor is typically lighter and less conspicuous—bulletproof vests, heavy leather jackets, etc.—whereas 2-armor is obvious to anyone who sees it—riot gear, plate mail, etc.—and bound to attract a great deal of attention; anyone who sees someone walking around the city with riot gear armor is probably going to call the fucking cops.

Archetype moves may grant your protagonist an armor bonus or rating without the need to wear actual armor. This armor is typically supernatural or situational in nature, and may not appear to the naked, mundane eye. That said, mortals will notice if someone unloads a full clip from a 9mm at close range and misses every shot.

If a character's armor would reduce the harm suffered to zero, the attack inflicts no harm at all; the armor has absorbed the damage, even if the attack was successful. At the same time, attacks that inflict no harm can still have consequences. If a faerie troll knocks you off a bridge while you're wearing riot gear, you might avoid damage from the blow, but you'll have to find your way back to the bridge before you can defend your friends.

When armor is listed, it's written in one of two ways: *x-armor* or *armor+x*. *X-armor* is the base value of a source of armor; *armor+x* is the value added to a character's base armor by a supplementary source. Thus, *x-armor* won't stack with another *x-armor*. Only *armor+x* can combine with other armor effects to increase the amount of armor a character is wearing.

Armor piercing (ap) weapons ignore armor when used. If your character is wearing a 2-armor bullet-proof vest and suffers 3-harm from a shotgun blast, you would normally reduce the harm to 1-harm instead of 3-harm. If you suffer 3-harm from an armor piercing sniper rifle, you suffer the entire 3 points of harm normally, even if the armor results from a supernatural source.

Liam and Olivia are trapped in a burning rowhouse, struggling to escape a demon who lured them to the abandoned building with a false prophecy. Olivia, stunned that her dream was a trap, opens fire on the demon and inflicts 2-harm. Andrew, as MC, tells her, "The rounds just glance off the demon's skin. It looks like his hide is made of magma. What do you do, Liam?"

Liam's player, Troi, thinks for a minute. "I still have Solomon's gun, right? Isn't it blessed?"

Andrew smiles. "Yup. That makes it armor piercing against demons."

Troi smiles back. "I think I'll **unleash** *on the demon with the gun, then."*

Liam inflicts 3-harm on the demon with Solomon's magnum, casting the demon back to hell. Olivia breathes a sigh of relief and the two of them start to look for any evidence the demon left behind.

WEAPONS AND TAGS

If your character starts play with a weapon—or acquires one during play—it will be listed with a harm rating and tags. **Tags** are descriptive words that can alter the mechanics of a weapon, assign constraints or limits to what a weapon can do, or offer cues to the players and MC about how that weapon should be treated in the fiction. Here's a starting list:

- **Anchored (cue):** This weapon is mystically anchored to you, such that it returns upon command or cannot be lost.
- **AP (mechanical):** armor piercing—this weapon ignores an opponent's armor rating, inflicting full harm.
- **Area (mechanical, cue):** this weapon affects an area with its fire. When used against a group, area ignores the group's size when determining harm inflicted, assuming the group is clustered together closely enough.
- **Autofire (mechanical, cue, constraint):** this weapon can be used as an +area weapon but doing so exhausts its ammunition, requiring the character to reload.

- **Close (constraint - range):** this weapon can only be used against someone within close range of you, somewhere between 2 to 10 meters.
- **Close/Far (constraint - range):** this weapon is considered able to affect targets within close or far range.
- **Concealable (cue):** this weapon is easy to keep out of sight, small enough to fit in a pocket of a jacket.
- **Far (constraint - range):** this weapon can only be used to target an opponent that is far off, more than 10 meters away; any closer and it's too unwieldy to bring to bear.
- **Fire (cue):** this weapon is fire-based. It will ignite combustibles nearby and cause serious burns on any targets it makes contact with. Supernatural creatures that are vulnerable to fire may take extra harm and/or flee when a fire weapon is used on them.
- **Hand (constraint - range):** this weapon can be used against someone within a meter or so of your reach, probably about the length of the weapon you're holding.
- **Hand/Close (constraint - range):** this weapon is considered able to affect targets within hand or close range.
- **Intimate (constraint - range):** this weapon can only be used up close and personal, closer than just a +hand weapon, up to the end of your arm.
- **Intimate/Hand (constraint - range):** this weapon is considered able to affect targets within both the intimate or hand range.
- **Loud (cue):** everyone nearby hears it, and can potentially identify what made the noise. It wakes up sleeping people, startles people who aren't expecting it, etc.
- **Messy (cue):** this weapon inflicts wounds that are severe and bloody or destroys the environment surrounding the target. These weapons are not suited to precision work.
- **Reload (cue):** this weapon has limited ammunition and needs to be reloaded often when used.
- **S-harm (cue):** instead of inflicting regular harm on a target, stun-harm weapons incapacitate their targets. Characters hit with an s-harm weapon may have to ***keep their cool*** to stay on their feet.
- **Silver/cold iron/holy (cue):** This weapon is made of a unique material or has been blessed by someone of great faith. Supernatural creatures may be especially vulnerable to these weapons, granting +ap when used against them or inflicting +1 harm.
- **Valuable (cue):** This object is rare and expensive; it may be a functional weapon, but it values style over substance.
- ***X*-harm (mechanical):** *X* is the amount of harm this weapon deals to an opponent, before armor is applied.

SAMPLE WEAPONS

Use these weapons as guidelines when giving stats to new weapons:

- 9mm (2-harm close loud)
- Assault rifle (3-harm close/far autofire loud)
- Brass knuckles (1-harm intimate concealable)
- Bolt action rifle (2-harm close/far loud)
- Cold iron katana (3-harm hand valuable cold iron)
- Grenades (3-harm hand area reload messy)
- Longbow (2-harm close/far)
- Shotgun (3-harm close messy loud)
- Submachine gun (2-harm close area loud)
- Spear (2-harm hand/close)
- Sniper rifle (3-harm far loud reload)

GROUPS

Much of the violence in *Urban Shadows* is personal and intimate, but on occasion conflicts spiral out of control until they involve gangs of people all fighting for what they want. We call these gangs of people **groups**, and the rules around violence work a bit differently when so many characters are engaging in the conflict.

GROUP SIZE

A group is treated as a single NPC when they fight as a unit; there's no need to take the time to resolve what each person does when there are a dozen or more people in the group. In general, larger groups can take more damage and inflict more damage; smaller groups tend to favor indirect confrontation or smaller opposition because they are weaker and more prone to serious harm.

There are four sizes of groups: small (fewer than 10 people), medium (10-20 people), large (20-30 people), and huge (30-40 people). A small or medium group might be able to operate without attracting too much attention, but large and huge groups almost always cause nearby civilians to notify the police, call the news, etc. Thirty or forty gun-wielding people are scary in an enclosed urban area!

GROUP HARM AND ARMOR

The harm a group inflicts is based on the weapons they wield, on average. A group of highly trained mercenaries bearing assault rifles (3-harm) is considerably more deadly than a group of bikers with baseball bats and chains (1-harm). Groups that aren't trained to use their weapons—corner boys wielding katanas (2-harm)—or groups with inconsistent weaponry—a street crew with only a few submachine guns and no other weapons (1-harm)—inflict one less harm than a group of trained folks with consistent weaponry.

Groups can be armored just like a character: provided that most of the group is wearing armor or is protected in some similar way, they gain the armor value of that armor. The aforementioned mercenaries probably have advanced military armor (2-armor) while the bikers probably have little more than matching leather jackets and a few bullet-proof vests (1-armor).

When a group inflicts harm on a person or another group, compare the size of the attacking group to the receiving group or individual. For every size category greater the attacking group is than the defending group, increase the harm inflicted by 1. Conversely, reduce all harm inflicted by the smaller group on the larger group by one for each size category. As always, armor soaks up harm, one for one.

LEADING A GROUP INTO BATTLE

If your character is leading a group against one or two people, you can roll to ***unleash an attack*** against your target using the group's harm and armor: the group is essentially a weapon you can wield, including harm rating and tags. Any harm your opponents inflict on you is applied both to you and the group (see *Suffering Harm as a Group*, 160). Of course, if your group is spread out or unable to focus their attention on your target, you can't use the group as a weapon.

If your character is leading a group against another group, however, a special battle move comes into play. Unlike when you roll ***unleash*** on your own, your group *trades harm* with the opposition as established when you ***lead a group into battle against another group***; In an all-out brawl, both groups suffer the harm the other group is capable of inflicting. There's little chance that your side (or their side) is going to walk away unharmed.

When you ***lead a group into battle against another group***, roll with Blood. On a hit, trade harm as established. On a 10+, choose 3. On a 7-9, choose 2.

- Your group suffers little harm
- Your group inflicts terrible harm
- Your group seizes a vital position
- Your group avoids collateral damage

Suffering little harm means that your group fights defensively, reducing the amount of harm suffered by 1-harm in addition to their armor. This might limit your group's effectiveness, but it does keep them alive in the face of grave danger.

Inflicting terrible harm means that your group goes for the throat, punishing the opposition with brutal violence and inflicting 1-harm more than they would otherwise inflict. Remember that this is more than just adding 1-harm to the attack; inflicting terrible harm is painful and scarring.

Seizing a vital position means that your group takes the high ground or occupies a chokepoint. The opposition will be at a disadvantage until they can force you to move or give up your holding.

Avoiding collateral damage means that no bystanders are hurt and no property is permanently damaged. If you do not pick this option, the MC has the right to harm other people and objects in the area as a result of your group's attack.

If you're leading a group, you suffer the same harm the group does, unless the group is doing something to protect or cover you. After all, you're getting fucking shot same as them, even if there are a lot of you.

> *Roxy leads her pack of werewolves (2-harm small group 1-armor messy) against a rival faction of fae besetting her allies. As the leader of the group, Roxy rolls Blood to* **lead a group into battle** *against a group of trolls that they find in a downtown park after dark. She succeeds with a 7-9 and chooses to* **seize a vital position** *and* **avoid collateral damage**.
>
> *The group of trolls (2-harm medium group 0-armor) and the werewolves exchange harm as established to start; the trolls suffer 1-harm (2 for the werewolf pack's harm rating minus 1 for the size difference in their favor). Roxy's wolves, including Roxy herself, suffer 2-harm (2 for the fae's harm rating plus 1 for the size difference, minus 1 for the wolves' armor). Roxy's wolves are a bit outmatched by the trolls!*
>
> *Mark, as the MC, tells Roxy's player, "You're taking 2-harm, but you force the trolls back to the edge of the park. It looks like you've spread out enough to keep them scattered; they're trying to get to a nest of trees in the center, but you've pushed them off that position. So long as you can hold it, your pack will get armor+1.*
>
> *"You also manage to keep your pack from tearing into a group of teenagers that was caught in the crossfire. Zach moves to go after one who's running away, but a quick snarl from you gets him back on track. What do you do?"*

If you're not leading the group—say some other PC or NPC is actually leading the charge—you don't make the battle move. The MC will have you make moves as normal, avoiding or inflicting harm to individuals while the two groups battle.

SUFFERING HARM AS A GROUP

Groups can suffer up to 6-harm, regardless of their size. The MC and the nature of the group determine how much harm they will endure before retreating or surrendering. Mindless undead are likely to fight and die to the last, while a pack of human hunters will probably cut their losses and flee after a few fatalities. Groups with strong leaders, especially player characters, are more likely to keep fighting.

Any group that suffers six (or more) harm is broken and unable to fight. At that point, the group dissolves; there are simply too many injured and dead to keep fighting. Characters who are leading groups that take six or more harm cannot lead those groups into battle any longer, even if they themselves still have the capacity to keep fighting.

When a group suffers harm, you can use the following guidelines to translate the damage.

- **1-2 harm:** some injuries, a few minor to moderate, no fatalities
- **3-4 harm:** many injuries, several serious, possibly a couple of fatalities
- **5-6 harm:** widespread serious injuries, many fatalities

Groups aren't just faceless weapons to inflict upon your enemies. They're made up of people with their own lives, motivations, and agendas. Abuse a group too often and you may find yourself with more trouble than you bargained for from them. Trying to get a group to fight for you isn't a foregone conclusion; you must spur them into action somehow: bully them, bribe them, insult them, whatever will work. When they suffer fatalities, the remaining members will certainly hold you responsible for what happened.

After several more rolls, Roxy's pack kills enough of the trolls to break them (4-harm). They scatter, and Roxy howls for her pack to regroup. Yet...not all her wolves answer her call (4-harm). Despite her best efforts to keep him safe, Zach's broken body lies at the edge of the park, a painful reminder that Roxy's alliances have cost them dearly. The pack, wounded and broken, gathers around his body.

Mark says, "Aliah is heartbroken. She lifts Zach's body up and sobs into it, as if her grief could bring him back. She turns to you, and shouts, 'We told you this was going to happen! He told you! Why wouldn't you listen? Why are we fighting for bloodsuckers?' What do you do, Roxy?"

SIX

THE LONG GAME

ADVANCEMENT

Characters in *Urban Shadows* aren't static: changes that happen in the fiction affect your sheet and changes that happen on your sheet affect the fiction. The two have to work together, hand in hand.

Sometimes you make changes to your sheet because you actually accomplish something in the fiction:

> *Roxy's wolf pack frees another pack held captive by a wizard from the east side of town. Without a territory to protect, a number of wolves start hanging out with Roxy's crew. Mark, her MC, tells Roxy's player to change the pack from small to medium. A stronger pack, but more mouths to feed.*
>
> *Solomon gets Liam to make him a new sniper rifle in Liam's workspace so that Solomon can offer cover fire at a distance. Andrew, his MC, stats up the rifle and tells Solomon's player to write the rifle down on Solomon's sheet. The gun is his now.*

And sometimes things go to shit in the fiction and you have to pay the price:

> *After he* **unleashes an attack** *on an intruder in his sanctum using* **Elementalism**, *Wesley's whole apartment burns down, destroying his collection of relics. Mark, his MC, tells Wesley's player to cross his sanctum off his sheet. Tough break.*
>
> *Gareth's fiendish underlings are all killed in a battle against another crew of demons. Andrew, his MC, tells Gareth's player to erase the group from his sheet. Everyone's dead.*

Advancement works the other direction: you make changes to your sheet, and the fiction catches up with you. Most of the time, you need to work with your MC to make the advancement make sense.

> *Pythia, The Oracle, advances and selects* **Get a sanctum**. *She works out with her MC that her collection of tomes and relics has grown to the point that her tarot shop is functioning as a full sanctum. She grabs a copy of The Wizard Archetype to get all the sanctum rules.*
>
> *Veronica, The Vamp, advances and selects* **A new Vamp move** *from the list of advancements. She chooses* **Haven**, *since she's getting tired of trying to find a safe place to sleep during the day. She works out with her MC that she's found a little club downtown she likes, and that she's already got her claws in the owner.*

MARKING FACTION

In order to advance, you've got to mark all four Factions. There isn't any particular order in which you need to mark the Factions, but you can't mark a Faction again until you've marked all of them once; if you ***hit the streets*** with Mortality when you've already got Mortality marked, you can't mark it.

Here are all the ways that you can mark Faction:

- make a Faction move
- trigger an intimacy move
- cash in a Debt
- honor a Debt
- make a move that tells you to mark Faction

Successfully ***refusing to honor a Debt*** means that you don't mark Faction for that Debt. You have to actually be true to your word to mark Faction for honoring your Debts. On the other hand, the person ***cashing in the Debt*** gets to mark Faction even if their debtor ***refuses to honor the Debt***.

Once you've marked all the Factions once, erase all your Faction marks and take your advancement: choose one of the options under "Standard Advances" in your Archetype playbook. You can only take each of these advancements once, but you're free to mark Factions again as soon as you erase the last set of marks and advance.

It's possible to gain multiple advancements in a single session, especially if you're making a lot of Faction moves and spending Debts. In other words, the pace of your character's advancement is entirely within your hands.

STANDARD ADVANCES

Most of the advances available are self-explanatory: add +1 to a stat raises a stat by one, taking a move from your Archetype gets you a new move, etc. Here are some notes and clarifications for stuff that might not be obvious.

»Stat Boosts

- ☐ +1 [stat] (max +3)
- ☐ +1 to any stat (max +3)
- ☐ +1 any Faction (max +3)

If you've got a stat at +3 already, you can't take these improvements for that stat. Otherwise, choosing this advancement raises the stat in question by 1. Note that raising your Faction stat effectively raises the total of your Faction stats by 1, allowing you to maintain stronger ties to multiple communities.

»New Moves

- ☐ A new [Archetype] move
- ☐ A move from another Archetype

Taking *a move from another Archetype* doesn't entitle you to their extras; you can't take ***Channeling*** to get The Wizard's spells or ***The Devil Inside*** to get The Tainted's demon form. Anything that relies on an extra can only be acquired via advancement by fully switching over to that Archetype; you've got to go all the way if you want access to the big stuff. Of course, your MC might give you an extra from another playbook if the fiction demands it.

»Changing Factions

- ☐ Change your Faction

If you find your alliances and relationships in other Factions more appealing, you can switch your Faction. Tell the MC what it looks like for you to reject your existing Faction and adopt a new community. Raise your score in that Faction by 1 and reduce your score in your old Faction by 1.

From that point on, everyone in the city regards you as part of a different community, including when someone ***lends a hand*** to or ***gets in the way*** of your actions. Also, when others mark Faction with you, as the result of an intimacy move or cashing in a Debt, they mark your new Faction and you get to ask an additional question of members in your new Faction when you try to ***figure them out***.

Beyond the mechanical changes, though, changing your Faction is huge. You become the wizard that cares more about the street (Night) than the politics of the city or the demon that has chosen to protect mortals (Mortality) instead of honoring their contract. Even some folks in your new community might not trust you until you prove yourself...

»Erasing Scars and Corruption

- ☐ Erase a scar
- ☐ Erase a corruption advance

The struggles of the street leave marks on all of us, but you can walk away from the sins and wounds of the past. Taking either of these advancements means that your character is engaged in some healing; tell the MC what you do to make things right for yourself. Is it a religious conversion? A new project for the community? Or just letting go of your old ways?

»Location, Location, Location

- ☐ Get a workspace (The Hunter)
- ☐ Get a sanctum (The Oracle)

A few playbooks have the option of adding a workspace or sanctum to their Archetype. If you choose one of these, go ahead and pull the move from The Veteran (workspace) or The Wizard (sanctum) whole cloth.

»Special Features

- ☐ Add 2 more features to your workspace (The Veteran)
- ☐ Add 2 qualities to your transformation (The Wolf)
- ☐ Add 2 features to your sanctum (The Wizard)
- ☐ Take 3 more spells (The Wizard)
- ☐ Add a benefit to your focus (The Wizard)

A few playbooks can select additional options for their existing extras. Tell the MC how you acquire these new features, either by some training or through some other magical means. These new features probably don't arrive instantaneously, but it might make sense for them to show up between sessions.

- ☐ Resolve a trouble from your territory (The Wolf)
- ☐ Remove a downside from your sanctum (The Wizard)
- ☐ Erase a job from your contract (The Tainted)

In contrast, a few advances allow you to resolve problems with your extras, such that a previous issue is put to rest. Sometimes these make natural sense in the story—your character may have already put in some effort to settling a trouble or removing a downside—but some action might occur between sessions as well. Work with your MC to make the resolution work, such that it makes sense that the trouble won't ever return.

»Ending Your Story

- ☐ Retire your character to safety
- ☐ Move on through to the other side
- ☐ Change to a new Archetype

Sooner or later, everything ends. When you select these options, your character's current story arc ends. In the case of retiring your character (or moving through to the other side), you get to describe what safety looks like—you might return to Arcadia, leave the city forever, or just give up the game completely. No matter what you decide, the MC can't use your character as a Threat or put you into danger from this point out. Safety means safety, even on these dark streets.

Changing to a new Archetype, however, keeps you in the game. You shift from one Archetype to another, gaining everything that comes with that new Archetype and leaving behind your old life. Maybe your Hunter finally gets bitten by a vampire to become The Vamp or your Fae makes a deal with a devil to become The Tainted. Urban fantasy is filled with heroes and villains who used to be one kind of supernatural creature and are now something entirely different.

When you change Archetypes, follow these steps:

- Keep everything associated with your old Archetype: Your moves, your main and Faction stats, your Debts, your gear—they are all still yours.
- Get rid of everything lost in the transformation: You've got to give up everything you lose in the fiction. If a werewolf gives up her territory to become The Veteran, no fair keeping your territory.
- Take everything belonging to your new Archetype: New moves, new gear, new extras—anything that you would normally get for starting a new character, you get.

If there is some confusion, the MC will tell you what stuff you keep and what stuff you lose.

GROUP ADVANCEMENTS

Several playbooks list a group that the character can join or lead as an advancement. By the time most characters get around to these advancements, they've usually got a reputation in the city that would draw other characters to them, but you and the MC might need to work out a bit of backstory to square the circle.

> *Justin chooses* **Join or lead a watcher's society** *for his character, Rashid. Mark as his MC asks, "Do you want to start up a neighborhood watch kind of thing with the hunters you met last session or are you interested in joining a secret society a bit larger than your current network?"*
>
> *Justin thinks for a moment. He likes the idea of a street-ready crew of folks who might also be willing to back him up in a tough situation, but he also wants to expand the game into ancient conspiracies and clandestine meetings. "I think I'll go with the secret society."*
>
> *Mark says, "Cool. You don't know a lot of folks in that line of work, so let's have them reach out to you. Rashid gets a letter in the mail: no postmark, no return address. Instead there's just a single letter stamped on the seal: a handdrawn 'Q' in dark red ink. You think for a minute it might be blood...but that's ridiculous, right? What do you do?"*

The group advancements are tied to specific Archetypes, so they aren't available to everyone. Some come with a gang or crew of characters that your character recruits; others are more like an informal network or family that might put demands on you as well. Moves associated with group advancements are treated as Faction moves for the purposes of advancement.

»The Aware: Watcher's Society

A **watcher's society** is a group of mortals who have banded together to fight against the influence of the supernatural in the city. The oldest and most traditional of these organizations are secret societies with ties to Ivy League schools and wealthy scions, but recent years have seen an explosion in street-level watcher groups that concern themselves with a block of the projects or a particular corner. Regardless, they know about the supernatural, and they're eager to share common cause with people who fight for humanity.

☐ Join or lead a watcher's society

When you select this advancement, determine with the MC what kind of society you're joining or leading. The society won't fight for you unless there are some extraordinary circumstances, but you gain access to the move ***Thick as Thieves*** so long as you remain in good standing with the organization.

☐ **Thick as Thieves:** When you go to your watcher's society for intel, roll with Mortality. On a hit, someone in the society knows something significant and is willing to share what they know. On a 7-9, what they tell you raises more questions than it answers or places you in serious danger, your choice. On a miss, your inquiries reveal that the society is already involved in the situation you're asking about, working for the wrong side.

Thick as Thieves bears some resemblance to ***hit the streets***, but you should note that the watcher's society gives out information for free, even on a 7-9.

»The Fae: Faerie Court

A **faerie court** is a collection of fae who swear fealty directly to you, instead of answering to a fae higher up in the hierarchy, like your monarch. Most fae who gain such a following take on an honorific—Duke or Duchess, maybe—but some fae are more modest, preferring to keep their budding royalty quiet for the time.

☐ Gain a faerie court

When you select this advancement, work with the MC to name a few of the NPC fae who make up your court and determine why they've sworn fealty to you and the conditions of your oaths. These can be broad—fealty for a year and a day in exchange for protection—or specific—killing a mortal a month for a drop of your blood—but each court member must have a defined oath to you that compels you to act.

Your court won't fight for you as a group, but their fealty gives you leverage to ***persuade*** them without seduction, promises, threats, or Debts unless a task is truly dire or dangerous. So long as you maintain your oaths to the court, you gain access to ***Debutante***.

☐ **Debutante:** When you present a mortal to your court, roll with Wild. On a hit, you bestow a faerie power upon them, provided the mortal publicly swears an oath and holds it true. On a 7-9, the power permanently marks the mortal in accordance with your court, even if they give up the oath at a later time. On a miss, a member of your court reveals that a powerful faerie from another court already holds power over this mortal, precluding your claim.

Presenting a mortal usually requires a formal ritual; work one out with your MC. You can draw the faerie power from the list of faerie magic or create something new with your MC's permission.

»The Spectre: Body of Ghosts

Not all ghosts are fully trapped on this side of reality; some exist in a half-life state, their corpus displaced between the two worlds, bridges from this life to the next. A **body of ghosts** is a colony of such unfortunate souls, bound to a location or object that anchors their corpus halfway between realities.

☐ Join or lead a body of ghosts

When you select this advancement, work with the MC to describe the body of ghosts. Where do they reside? How did you meet them? Why are they drawn to you? What object or location anchors their existence? Treat whatever object or location you determine as a ***Link***, even if you don't have the move; you also gain access to ***Thin Walls***, provided that the object or location is safe.

☐ **Thin Walls:** When you bring a supernatural object to your body of ghosts, roll with Night. On a hit, ask the congregation questions and they will answer honestly. On a 10+, ask 2. On a 7-9, ask 1.

- Who created or birthed this object?
- Who could be reached on the other side through this object?
- How could a ghost make special use of this object?
- What do those on the other side whisper about this object?
- When will this object end its journey?

Treat a miss as though you ***let it out*** to touch the other side and missed on the roll.

You might be able to determine some of this information with ***let it out***, but ***Thin Walls*** doesn't risk corruption and gets you more specific answers.

»The Tainted: Fiendish Underlings

Demons that work their contracts eventually get promoted, perhaps even to... middle management. **Fiendish underlings** are a gang of demons sent from hell to do your bidding, so long as the "senior partners" deem you worthy of their assistance.

- ☐ Gain fiendish underlings

By default, your minions are a small gang of 5-10 demons (2-harm small group 2-armor vulnerabilities: unruly demonic) who work for you because they also serve your dark patron. When you choose this advancement, you get ***Middle Manager*** and choose 1:

- ☐ Your underlings consist of 10-20 demons. Medium instead of small
- ☐ You have a hold over your underlings, supernatural or otherwise. Remove +unruly
- ☐ You recruited your underlings from hell yourself. They get +loyal
- ☐ Your underlings are imbued with demon forms of their own. +1 harm

And choose 2:

- ☐ Your underlings revel in some vice unavailable in hell. Vulnerability: addicted
- ☐ Your underlings disdain—and alter—an aspect of their human forms. Vulnerability: unnerving
- ☐ Your underlings attract the attention of mortal hunters. Vulnerability: hunted
- ☐ Your underlings are working some secret plan for your dark patron. Vulnerability: nefarious
- ☐ Your underlings are vicious and aggressive monsters. Vulnerability: savage

Miguel chooses fiendish underlings for his character Gareth's next advancement, so Gareth gets a gang of demons sent by his dark patron. Miguel chooses **You recruited your underlings from hell yourself** *and adds* **+loyal** *to Gareth's minions. He also chooses* **Your underlings disdain—and alter—an aspect of their human forms** *and* **Your underlings are working some secret plan for your dark patron**. *Miguel adds the vulnerabilities* **unnerving** *and* **nefarious** *to his group as well: 2-harm loyal small group 2-armor vulnerabilities: unnerving unruly nefarious.*

Andrew, his MC, asks him, "What do those vulnerabilities look like?"

Miguel says, "I think my demons don't like their human faces. They are constantly scarring and altering them in creepy ways. I'm not sure what they're up to, but I sometimes catch them talking about Liam, The Veteran. I think they might be trying to get revenge for something Liam did to my dark patron back in the day."

- ☐ **Middle Manager:** When you order your fiendish underlings to solve a problem for you, roll with Wild. On a 10+, they follow your instructions precisely and no one can trace them back to you. On a 7-9, either things get messy or you're clearly to blame, your choice. On a miss, they do exactly as they are told and it leads to disaster.

Note that rolling a 10+ here doesn't avoid consequences that result from a bad plan; it's just assured that they will follow the plan and no one can trace it back to you. On a miss, even a good plan leads to some terrible outcome.

»The Vamp: Vampire Clan

A **vampire clan** is a family network, a group of vampires bound by blood and kinship spread throughout the city. New vampires don't get immediate access to these resources, but eventually the sire of a clan will deem a new vampire worthy of full membership. Like any worthy criminal enterprise, a vampire clan brings in new business and makes a few demands on your immortal time.

☐ Join or lead a vampire clan

By default, your clan is a distributed network of vampires who keep in contact on a regular basis. When you select this advancement, take ***Eyes Everywhere*** and choose 2 areas of expertise for your clan:

- ☐ bars and clubs
- ☐ gambling (legal and illegal)
- ☐ high fashion
- ☐ illegal drugs
- ☐ music/performance
- ☐ prostitution
- ☐ smuggling

- ☐ **Eyes Everywhere:** When you tell your clanmates to keep an eye out for someone in the city, roll with Night. On a hit, someone spots your target without alerting them to the hunt. On a 10+, word comes quick: if you move right now, your prey is in your grasp, vulnerable and exposed. On a miss, your clan's lusts get the best of them before you have a chance to intervene and someone gets hurt.

Your clan's area of expertise determines what kind of word you get back, but your clan is distributed enough throughout the city to spot nearly anyone. On a 10+, you're guaranteed to catch up to your target, provided you head to the location straight away without too many distractions. If you miss, the person who gets hurt isn't necessarily your target, but you don't put a whole vampire clan onto someone without breaking a few eggs.

If you're leading the clan, your clan mates will expect you to take care of their problems, especially any disputes that arise between vampires; if you're not leading, then you can expect the head of the clan to come to you when your services are needed...

»The Wolf: Wolf Pack

Holding territory as a lone wolf is tough; most werewolves seek out a full pack to keep their territory secure. A **wolf pack** is a group of werewolves large enough to be considered a full pack—at least five werewolves—that has chosen to defend a particular territory.

☐ Join or lead a wolf pack

By default, your pack is collection of 5-10 ferocious werewolves (3-harm small group 1-armor savage urge: to hunt) who live in your existing territory. So long as you're alpha of the pack, you get ***Pack Alpha***. When you select this advancement, choose 1:

- ☐ Your pack is trained in efficient and effective pack tactics. Remove savage
- ☐ Your pack constructs makeshift armor for their wolf forms. +1 armor
- ☐ Your pack has a number of seers or mystics. It gets +traditional
- ☐ Your pack is fiercely territorial and coordinated. Urge: to protect

And choose 2:

- ☐ Your pack is young and inexperienced, and a bit clumsy in a fight. -1 harm
- ☐ Your pack eats what it kills, even when it hunts humans. Urge: to consume
- ☐ Your pack is loose-knit, members coming and going as they please. Urge: to wander
- ☐ Your pack serves a spirit or guardian of your territory. Urge: to serve
- ☐ Your pack owns you more than you own them. Add +zealous

☐ **Pack Alpha:** When you try to impose your will on your wolf pack, roll with Night. On a 10+, get all 3. On a 7–9, choose 1:

- They do what you want
- They don't fight back about it
- You don't have to make an example of one of them

On a miss, someone in your pack makes a dedicated bid to replace you for alpha.

You don't need to make this move every time you ask your pack to follow your lead; you're the pack alpha, so they should take orders from you no fucking problem. But if you want them to do something against their instincts or exceptionally dangerous, you might need to flex some muscle. Note the combinations here on a 7-9:

- They do what you want, but they fight with you about it *and* you have to make an example of one of them.

- They don't do what you want, but you avoid a fight by making an example of one of them.
- They don't do what you want, but you avoid making an example out of one by getting in a fight.

If you get in a fight, it means that some portion of your pack actually gets in a scrap with you that causes harm; making an example of someone means putting them all the way to the ground, dominance and all. On a miss, someone's going to challenge your position as alpha, but it might take them some time to build up the courage to make a move. It's not like they're going to be stupid about it, though; they won't endanger the pack to get what they want.

If you're not alpha, then the pack alpha runs things. We hope you two get along.

ADVANCING YOUR MOVES

Advancing moves adds some new rules that trigger when you hit a 12+. Otherwise, the move remains the same: if you roll a 10+, 7-9, or miss, the move works as normal. On a 12+, you find some outcome even stronger than a 10+.

☐ Advance 3 basic moves

Advanced moves give you new options or allow you to select more options off the existing list than you can get for a 10+. The Hunter is the only Archetype that can advance all the moves; everyone else can only advance six out of the seven, so choose wisely when you select this improvement. You can't go back later and change your mind about which moves you advance.

Here are some notes on the advanced moves:

»Unleash an Attack

When you ***unleash an attack*** on someone, roll with Blood. On a hit, you inflict harm as established and choose 1:

- Inflict terrible harm
- Take something from them

On a 7-9, choose 1 from below as well:

- They inflict harm on you
- You find yourself in a bad spot

On a 12+, your target chooses: surrender completely or you incapacitate them.

Advancing ***unleash an attack*** fundamentally changes the way the move works. On a 12+, you inflict harm (and choose an option off the top list) as normal and give your opposition a tough choice: surrender or suffer enough additional harm to incapacitate them completely. It's still their choice what happens, but you're so utterly terrifying that they're out of the conflict, one way or another.

When you ***unleash an attack*** on another player's character with this move, remind them that you've advanced it before you roll. If you hit the 12+ and they refuse to surrender, you can either knock them unconscious for the scene or inflict 5-harm (ap) no matter your weapon, your choice.

»Escape a Situation

When you take advantage of an opening to ***escape a situation***, roll with Blood. On a hit, you get away. On a 10+, choose 1. On a 7-9, choose 2:

- You suffer harm during your escape
- You end up in another dangerous situation
- You leave something important behind
- You owe someone a Debt for your escape
- You give in to your base nature and mark corruption

On a 12+, you get away and make an important discovery.

Advancing this move is the only way to get out of danger without strings attached. If you hit the 12+, you not only exit the scene without bearing any costs—you don't have to choose any options off the list—but the MC will also give you some information that's definitely useful to the situation at hand. If the information doesn't seem immediately useful, let the MC know.

»Persuade an NPC

When you ***persuade an NPC*** through seduction, promises, or threats, roll with Heart. On a hit, they do what you ask. On a 7-9, they modify the terms or demand a Debt.

If you ***cash in a Debt*** you have with them before rolling, you may add +3 to your roll.

On a 12+, they do what you ask and help you see it through to its end.

Advancing this move allows you to build alliances with NPCs that last longer than a single Debt. *Helping you see it through to its end* means that the NPC is in for the long haul, investing in your vision of the future long enough to see the job done right. If you threaten a vampire smuggler to get information about a missing child, for example, a 12+ on the roll means that the typically disinterested merchant is sufficiently scared of you to help look for the kid without needing any further persuasion.

»Figure Someone Out

When you try to ***figure someone out***, roll with Mind. On a hit, hold 2. On a 7-9, they hold 1 on you as well. While you're interacting with them, spend your hold 1-for-1 to ask their player a question:

- Who's pulling your character's strings?
- What's your character's beef with ______?
- What's your character hoping to get from ____?
- How could I get your character to ____?
- What does your character worry might happen?
- How could I put your character in my Debt?

If you're in their Faction, ask an additional question, even on a miss.

On a 12+, you can ask any question you like, not limited to the list.

Yup. Ask any question you like, even "Are you telling the truth?" Your target is an open book.

»Mislead, Distract, or Trick

When you try to ***mislead, distract, or trick*** someone, roll with Mind. On a hit, they are fooled, at least for a moment. On a 10+, pick 3. On a 7-9, pick 2:

- You create an opportunity
- You expose a weakness or flaw
- You confuse them for some time
- You avoid further entanglement

On a 12+, you get all 4 and choose 1 for double effect.

Creating a double opportunity can mean two opportunities or an opportunity so generous you can't believe the MC is giving it to you.

Exposing a double weakness or flaw can mean that you spot two weaknesses or that the MC gives you a flaw that you can act upon in some immediate, profound way.

Doubly confusing them for some time means that whatever you were attempting to convince them of becomes the absolute truth to the character. Even close friends and family aren't able to convince them they have been duped.

Doubly avoiding further entanglement means that you escape the scene or change your position without a roll. As far as your opposition is concerned, you don't exist.

»Keep Your Cool

When things get real and you ***keep your cool***, tell the MC what situation you want to avoid and roll with Spirit. On a 10+, all's well. On a 7–9, the MC will tell you what it's gonna cost you.

On a 12+, your opposition's cool is compromised. Tell them what it will cost to maintain their current course of action.

Rolling a 12+ here means that the usual 7-9 formula is reversed: you get to tell the MC what it's going to cost your opposition to keep pressuring you. For example, you might say, "If they want to keep shooting at me, they have to take harm because I'm shooting back" or "If they want to keep driving the truck at me, they'll wreck it because I'll take cover at the last moment." What they do is up to them, but they'll pay the cost to do it.

That said, you've got to follow the fiction when you set the costs for the opposition. You can't say, "If they want to keep shooting at me, they have to die because they get eaten by giant rats" unless controlling giant rats is somehow associated with your character.

»Let It Out

When you ***let out the power within you***, roll with Spirit. On a hit, choose 1 and mark corruption. On a 10+, ignore the corruption or choose another from the list.

- Take +1 forward on your next roll
- Extend your senses, supernatural or otherwise
- Frighten, intimidate, or impress your opposition
- Take definite hold of something vulnerable or exposed

On a 12+, your powers or abilities manifest in an unexpectedly useful way. Mark corruption to make that manifestation permanent.

The MC will tell you how your powers or abilities manifest; sometimes they're in keeping with other moves from your Archetype, but your MC might give you something unique to your character. *Marking corruption to make that manifestation permanent* means that you get to keep it. The MC will give you a new move, existing or custom, to represent that new power.

CORRUPTION

The darkness of the city's streets isn't just about shadows and monsters; it lives in your heart, burrowing its way deeper into your psyche each time you take a step toward your darkest self, each time you look for salvation in the worst parts of your soul.

Corruption.

A whisper in the dark when you aren't expecting it. A sudden flush of lust and greed in a vulnerable moment. A feeling—all too certain—that you're better than all this, that you should be ruling this city of weak-willed sycophants. Corruption eats at you when you're alone, promising power in exchange for just a bit more control. And it's there when you desperately need an out, ready to trade you everything you need for just a little piece of your soul.

Until one day, you wake up to find there's nothing left to give it. The darkness already has it all; it's gobbled you up a piece at a time. And now *you're* the danger and the darkness.

CORRUPTION ADVANCES

Corruption is a bit like an advancement system. When you're told to mark corruption, check off a box in the corruption track; when you've checked off all five boxes, you unlock a corruption advance and clear your corruption track to start anew. These corruption advances, like standard advances, offer your character new powers and abilities, but they usually come at a high price: more corruption.

There are only a few ways to mark corruption:

- Triggering your Archetype's corruption move
- A move tells you to mark corruption
- The MC tells you to mark corruption

The main way Archetypes gain corruption is through their primary **corruption move**. Each of these moves is a unique trigger that represents your character stepping further away from a normal mortal life or giving in to their supernatural nature. In other words, corruption represents their slide toward inhumanity and darkness.

> *Nathaniel, the Vamp, decides to feed on one of the men bartending at his club to heal his wounds after a fight with Elora, The Hunter. He lures the man up to his haven for some drugs and proceeds to feed on him while he's passed out.*
>
> *Mark, his MC, says, "Yeah, I think that triggers your corruption move. He's an unwilling victim."*

Nathaniel's player, Derrick, argues a bit: "He knows I'm a vampire! And I took him up to my haven."

"Yeah, but you didn't ask his permission. No consent. Mark the corruption."

Several of the basic moves (***escape a situation*** and ***let it out***) offer opportunities to mark corruption as well.

»Additional Corruption Moves

Corruption advances are simple: they allow you to unlock additional corruption moves from your own Archetype or to take corruption moves from other Archetypes:

- ☐ Take a corruption move
- ☐ Take a corruption move from another Archetype

Corruption moves are powerful, but they also generate additional corruption points when you use them, a downward cycle that pushes your character further down the dark path. Whenever you use one of these moves, your character has to pay the price.

Maeve lies to a loved one about her whereabouts the previous night. Since she's The Fae, she marks corruption, her fifth. Her player decides to take **Shrewd Negotiator** *as her corruption advance. Now when Maeve* **refuses to honor a Debt** *on a 10+, her player can mark corruption to cancel the Debt and claim a Debt from the person she refused. Clever girl.*

Olivia tells her brother that he has to leave town because she's seen his death, a false prophecy. Since she's The Oracle, she marks corruption, her fifth. Her player decides to take a corruption move from another Archetype as her corruption advance: **Telekinesis** *from The Spectre. Now she can move small objects with her mind, and larger objects if she marks corruption.*

»Retiring as a Threat

Eventually, your character will no longer have any more corruption advances to take that unlock additional moves. Instead, you'll be left with only one, ugly option:

- ☐ Retire your character. They may return as a Threat

If you unlock this advance, your character is no longer yours; they now belong to the MC. Unlike *retiring to safety*, *retiring as a Threat* means that the MC can now use your character like a weapon against the other players' characters. You slipped over the edge, grew too close to the darkness, and your friends and allies will pay the price.

Karl—furious that Tiana almost killed Colby—starts a hunt, triggering his Wolf's corruption move and marking his fifth corruption. He's already marked off all of his other corruption advances, so the only option left is to **retire his character**. *He hands his Archetype over to his MC, Andrew. Now Matt, Karl's Wolf, is an NPC, a dangerous werewolf who is seeking revenge on those who have harmed his loved ones. Andrew can do what he likes with Matt, but one thing is clear: Matt is a Threat to the city.*

»Changing Archetypes and Corruption

Note that changing your Archetype through advancement doesn't delay this choice. Whenever you change Archetypes, everything essential to the character comes with you, including your existing corruption advances. You get to keep the corruption moves you've already gained, and you must mark off the same number of corruption advances on your new Archetype. If you want to get rid of corruption, you have to use up an advance *erasing a corruption advance.*

CORRUPTION IN PLAY

There's no hard and fast rule about what it looks like for your character to fall to darkness. Your new moves will drive you toward marking more corruption, but that doesn't mean that you have to give in all at once; some characters fight the darkness, hoping to save themselves and the city all at once.

But some characters revel in the thrill of what they've acquired, the sharp rush of power beyond anything else available. They mark corruption whenever they can, and they rush toward the cliff, hoping to accomplish as much as they can before the fall. Judge not lest you be judged; as Lucifer himself once said, "It's better to reign in hell than serve in heaven."

SEVEN

THE MASTER OF CEREMONIES

THE MC

Can we tell you a secret? Of course, we can. You're good folk. Trustworthy.

All of this, every word in the book to this point, every bit of design that we've packed into these pages...it wasn't for the players. They'll read it, of course, maybe even master it. They'll point out a passage you missed that changes a rules call or pushes you in a different direction during a session or they'll come up with some interesting trick from another Archetype, but none of that makes it *for them.*

It was always for you. The Master of Ceremonies. The MC.

You see, *Urban Shadows* divides up authority in a pretty traditional way for a roleplaying game. Your players tell you who they are and what they do in the city, what goals they pursue and what they feel. They make decisions about how their characters advance and how much corruption they're willing to accept to get what they want.

And you're going to tell them *everything else.*

We think that's the best part of the game, the slow unfolding of the consequences of their decisions, the blank looks on their faces when they realize that the city *has them now,* the moments in which they turn against each other because there's no other way forward. The dark, beating heart of the city pounding in their ear drums as you lay out how their choices built all of this: the pain and the promise of heroes in a world that promises nothing but corruption.

And you've got a ringside seat to all that drama, constantly spinning them around until the only thing they can do is give in to the madness—and logic!—of the city's dark streets. You've got your bloody fingerprints all over everything, pushing and pulling and adjusting and moving it all into place. Not forcing it before it's ripe, but always on the fucking lookout for the next perfect move.

This is how you run *Urban Shadows.* This way and no other.

USING THIS CHAPTER

We assume at this point that you've read Chapters 1-6, and that you've had some time to look over the Archetypes. Although the previous chapters are all directed toward the players, there's lots of information in there for you as well, including advice about character creation, rules clarifications about specific moves, and systems for harm, advancement, and groups. We put those rules in front of the players so that you and they are on the same page.

This chapter contains the agendas, principles, and moves that act as the rules systems for your side of the conversation. **Agendas**—your overall goals—point you toward the kind of play that works best for *Urban Shadows*; **principles** give you the best practices we've learned running the game; **moves** are specific actions to take in response to the players' choices. Together, these systems make MCing a taut, directed experience that productively structures running the game.

In addition to presenting agendas, principles, and moves in this chapter, we also cover managing NPCs (209), tips on running the game for specific Archetypes (216), and advice for exploring adult and mature themes in *Urban Shadows* (221). Don't get overwhelmed, though; you don't have to learn all of this before you run your first session! You'll likely return to this chapter a few times, digging in deeper as you master the art of MCing *Urban Shadows*. Good luck!

AGENDAS

At the highest level, your job is to balance three **agendas** when you MC:

- Make the city feel political and dark.
- Keep the characters' lives out of control and evolving.
- Play to find out what happens.

It's your job to bring the city to life—whichever city you pick—and make it a convincing world of shadows and intrigue, a seething metropolis of rival Factions and umbral mysteries that keeps the players' characters off balance and engaged. The rest of this chapter is dedicated to giving you the tools you need to accomplish these goals.

It's important to remember that it's *not* your job to run the players through a preplanned plot or to mess with their heads or to beat them at every turn or to introduce a pet NPC that solves all their problems. All of that is bullshit here, the kind of crap that will make your players throw their hands up in the air and stop caring about the city you've built together. All of that *betrays these agendas.* Leave that shit at the door.

We talked in **The Basics** about the discipline it takes to play *Urban Shadows* (25); all of that goes double for you. You have to commit to the moment you're in and follow the fictional logic of the situation at hand, caring deeply about the outcome but giving yourself the room to find out what happens; you have to learn to stop demanding the story go your way and trust that the story is going somewhere interesting. And in that moment—when the dice hit the table and you don't know what's coming next—you will find the heart of the city, bloody and perfect.

ALWAYS SAY...

When you MC *Urban Shadows*, you might sometimes find yourself without a clear path forward, caught between multiple agendas without a clear sense of balance. When that happens, always say:

- ...what the principles demand (as follows).
- ...what the rules demand.
- ...what the city demands.
- ...what honesty demands.

The principles and the rules of the game are your backbone, the steel inside your story that never bends or breaks. If a move says that a character takes harm, inflict it; if a roll comes up short, accept it. Say what the principles and the rules demand, no matter how it breaks your heart. Discipline, first and foremost.

The city has its own ruthless discipline too. *It doesn't care what's just or right or fair; it cares about who has power and who doesn't.* If a powerful NPC is betrayed by your players' characters, let the NPC take revenge; if a weak and greedy NPC has an opportunity to take advantage of your players' characters, make sure the NPC seizes the moment. The game's the game, no matter how it breaks your heart. Power, first and foremost.

But the players only know what you tell them, so be generous with the truth. Don't hide the ball or play cute with the facts; the players don't have an external point of reference for what a room looks like or how another character holds their head during a conversation. They only know what you tell them. If an NPC is head over heels in love with a player's character, make it obvious; if an NPC is getting ready to sell them out, tell them it's coming. The world has to be clear and direct, no matter how it breaks your heart. Honesty, first and foremost.

THE PRINCIPLES

The agendas are your goals, but the principles lay out a path forward toward those goals. These are rules too—like the agendas and moves—but they operate like best practices, guidelines for you to follow that produce the best possible fiction within the system. Do these things, and you'll find the system working for you instead of against you. Break these rules, and your game will flounder.

- Display the city, from skyscrapers to slums.
- Address yourself to the characters, not the players.
- Push the characters together, even across boundaries.
- Put the characters at the center of conflicts, political and personal.
- Cloak your moves in darkness.

- Name everyone, give them all drives.
- Treat everyone according to their station.
- Ask loads of questions and build on the answers.
- Be a fan of the players' characters.
- Give the players the chance to weigh in (time to think).
- Dirty the hands of all involved.
- Give everything a price, even friendship.

DISPLAY THE CITY, FROM SKYSCRAPERS TO SLUMS

Your city isn't a wasteland of nightclubs and office buildings; your story shouldn't be either. Look for opportunities to showcase the insanely wealthy and the desperately impoverished, the highest highs and the lowest lows. And don't forget the supernatural elements either. Werewolf bars, vampiric blood banks, wizard movie theaters, ghostly cemeteries. All of them are opportunities to present new facets of the city, new political elements and groups that are plotting and scheming for their piece of the pie.

Push the characters out of their natural environments as well. Give Father Davis a reason to leave his low-income parish and journey uptown for information; find a justification to demand that Volund head out to the docks to complete a deal before time runs out. At every opportunity, narrate the city in grim and vivid detail and remind the players that there's no way to take it all in, no way to say, "Yes, I've seen the whole fucking city and there's nothing left to see."

ADDRESS YOURSELF TO THE CHARACTERS, NOT THE PLAYERS

Your players aren't the ones stuck in an elevator with a ravenous demon or caught in the middle of a turf war between a gang of drug-dealing vampires and territorial werewolves. The players' characters are the ones who have to deal with all that shit, so *talk directly to them.* Say "Maeve, where are you hiding from the vampires?" instead of "Tristan, where do you think Maeve would hide from the vampires?" Calling them by their characters' names pushes the players into thinking and talking and acting like their characters.

Don't mess around with what the characters see or hear, either: "Olivia, the man who scheduled the tarot reading is sweating bullets; *it's obvious* he's here about his cheating wife." Give the information as if the player was standing in the room, as if you were *right fucking there* pointing out things that are obvious to anyone. And if their Archetype gives them greater access to obvious information—the kind that comes with a wizard's magical sight or a werewolf's sense of smell—give that information to them too. Fucking gratis.

PUSH THE CHARACTERS TOGETHER, EVEN ACROSS BOUNDARIES

Cities have millions of people, obsessed with their own busy lives and petty bullshit. The players' characters are no different, and they sometimes feel an urge to tell their own separate stories—apart from other characters—veering off into things that interest them and ignoring each other. Encourage players to embrace their characters' lives and explore them, but you need to ensure they don't spend too much time alone.

Urban Shadows is most interesting when the players' characters interact. Give them secrets, conspiracies, and threats that concern each other, common gossip that drives them together instead of further apart. When you find a barrier between characters—a wizard and fae on different sides of a conflict, a vampire and werewolf who claim territory in different parts of town—find ways to bring them together, common threads that get them talking. Frame scenes that drive them together (physically and emotionally), cash in Debts to get them to work on the same side, and connect them through their NPC relationships until they're all hopelessly mired in each other's lives.

PUT THE CHARACTERS AT THE CENTER OF CONFLICTS, POLITICAL AND PERSONAL

The city is filled with institutions and organizations that make demands on the players' characters; use those relationships, political and professional, to put the characters in the position to be pivotal to the city's future. No single character can wake up one day and just decide to change the course of history, but someone has to tilt the balance, right? Someone has to be in the right place at the right time to thwart the powers that be or crush a rebellion before it starts. Make sure the players' characters end up in those positions, even when they try to escape their responsibilities or run from their problems.

Placing them at the center of conflicts won't make things easy for the players' characters. Institutions and organizations *want things*; they have their own agendas, their own plots and plans that have taken years—decades or centuries even in the case of vampires, wizards, and faeries—and they won't like it when the characters muck things up by disobeying orders, especially if the reasoning for the betrayal is rooted in personal shit. When a hunter organization tells Elora that she's been selected as the avatar of a ritual that will empower her to kill every wizard in the city right after she finally ties the knot with her wizard girlfriend, what's she going to do?

CLOAK YOUR MOVES IN DARKNESS

When you make a move—we'll talk in a minute about your moves—don't directly call out the name of the move to the players. Don't say something dumb like, "Okay, I guess I'll ***put someone in danger***" and look around the table for someone to hammer with "danger" or point at one player and say "I'm going to ***activate your stuff's downside***." You've got to do a little magic trick to make it seem real, a little misdirection to keep their eyes on your left hand while your right hand picks their pocket.

Your moves need to look like they're coming directly from the fiction, like there's a fictional cause for the fictional effect you're about to drop on the players. When you ***activate their stuff's downside***, you say something like "Aw, shit. It's been forever since you've fed, Nathaniel. You feel that gnawing hunger pulling at your insides, that thirst for blood leaving you light headed and grouchy. You aren't going to be able to hold off for long." When you ***put someone in danger***, you say something like, "Your first shot goes wild, Solomon. You're trying to reload your bow when one of the vampires sprints toward you, leaping over three lanes of traffic to land on the hood of your car." Make it look like the fiction is choosing the move—not you—and that you're just relaying what's obviously true about the world.

NAME EVERYONE, GIVE THEM ALL DRIVES

The city's got a million stories, but the players only care about the NPCs that end up in front of them. The fastest way to make those NPCs seem real is to give them all names. We give you a list of names on the MC worksheet (and space to track NPCs by Faction), and you can pull more names from any of the unused Archetypes. All the name lists are filled with a diverse set of names from cultures all over the world.

Names and details help the players connect to the NPCs. It's not "a werewolf bartender who might help you out in a fight." It's "Joaquin, the werewolf bartender with a nasty scar over his right eye and a mean left hook." If a character in the story gets lines and spotlight—even for a few moments—give them a name and explain a few quick obvious things about their look.

This principle has a nice synergy with ***put a name to a face***. When you introduce new characters to the fiction, the players' characters will try to remember if they know them, and you'll get a bunch of rich history to draw on depending on their rolls. If the players miss on their rolls, claim Debts on them for the NPCs whenever you can make it fit the existing fiction. Each Debt has the potential to push the characters to action or complicate a difficult situation.

Every character gets a name, but that doesn't mean that they need to be special snowflakes with unique motivations. In fact, it's best if they *aren't* particularly complicated. Peter is a demon who wants to find a way to stay in this dimension; Lakisha is a hunter who hates vampires for killing her sister. These NPCs pursue their passions, attack their targets, and advance their agendas without thinking too hard about their own motivations. We call these motivations **drives**, and we've given you a list on the MC worksheet to help you generate ideas for new NPCs. See 210 for more on using drives in your game.

TREAT EVERYONE ACCORDING TO THEIR STATION

Cities demand hierarchy, official and unofficial. When the spotlight falls on a particular NPC, location, or feature of the city, ask yourself, "What station does this hold?" Important things are protected—not by you, of course, but by the city itself—and weak things, things that hold no station, are exposed and vulnerable. If the players' characters come for Watanabe, the evil vampire lord, he'll have guards, allies, and Debts to use against them; if they come for one of his minions, that character may have no protection at all.

Don't mix these stations up. Protecting the minion—or failing to protect Watanabe—feels inauthentic. The players need to know that the city isn't run by your capricious wishes, that the order and structure of the city is a knowable thing, even if they don't quite understand it yet. Fucking with people like Watanabe should have dire consequences, but there can only be a few like him in any city. The rest, the vast masses of minions and goons, can't enjoy those kinds of narrative protections; when the spotlight falls on them, they're in the crosshairs.

Of course, this principle goes for the players' characters as well. Use every opportunity to reflect their station back at them through NPCs: "Sorry, Nathaniel, we don't allow vampires here on Council grounds" or "Really, Gareth? You expect us to just fucking accept that you're too good for demonic rituals now?" or "Rashid, you're Iraqi. The last place you need to be seen is outside a federal courthouse building when a bomb might go off." The rest of the city has a specific view of these characters, where they belong, what they ought to be doing with their time. Don't ever let them forget.

ASK LOADS OF QUESTIONS AND BUILD ON THE ANSWERS

From the moment the players introduce their characters to the end of your last session, ask probing and provocative questions. "Why did you move to the city?" or "Where did you learn to control your foresight?" are great starting questions, but take it further by asking leading questions: "Who did you have to kill to complete your training?" or "What emotion is dead to you since you became a vampire?" Push the players with your questions, then grab the answers, trust them, and use them to build up a city more interesting than you could build on your own.

Building on players' answers starts by reincorporating what they give you into the fiction. It's not enough to ask, get an answer, and then drop the topic; you've got to actively use the stuff your players give you to flesh out the city. Sometimes this is easy—the players tell you that mortal hunters control a specific neighborhood—but you often need to dig deeper with them to determine why they think a contribution is valuable. Don't hesitate to ask followup questions to figure out what the players mean by "demons come and go here" or "the faeries ask everyone for tribute." Get something useful before you move on to the next player.

As you ask questions, add details to their contributions as well, building upon them so that they feel like they've always belonged in the city. If Liam's player talks about an old hunter organization that fell apart when he retired from the game, introduce some characters who are trying to build it back up and want Liam to return to lead it; if Pythia's player talks about an old mentor who taught her about the supernatural, make that person a central figure to other characters aligned with Power as well. Let it influence your own vision of the city.

For specific advice on asking questions as the MC, see *Using Questions* in **The First Session** on 227.

BE A FAN OF THE PLAYERS' CHARACTERS

"Keep the characters' lives out of control and evolving" doesn't mean "make the characters' lives worse." No one—not you, not the players—wants to see the characters suffer at every turn. It's predictable, boring, and dull. Being a fan means you want to see them do their thing, to be excellent at something, but also to struggle and maybe even triumph in the face of adversity.

Thus, it's your job to introduce difficult situations that challenge the players' characters in meaningful ways. You have to put real stakes on the line—endangering people and places the characters hold dear—but you do so in order to watch them rise above the bullshit or fall to their own worst selves. It's never to watch them suffer just for the sake of suffering.

The worst way to try to keep the characters' lives out of control is to mindlessly take away their stuff or break what makes them interesting. If The Tainted is trying to keep custody of his kid, don't kill the kid or resolve the custody battle without exploring the issue first. Those moves make his life *less* interesting; his responsibilities become easier to balance because he no longer has to contend with the mortal world. Same goes for his demonic form: take that away and he's just another goon in a city filled with replaceable muscle. These moves aren't totally illegitimate—imagine how awesome it would be for The Tainted to get his demon form back after an absence—but avoid sloppily punishing the character for being interesting.

Same goes for dealing with their successes. If Nathaniel kills the demon that's been plaguing the city with a dark ritual, don't take that away from him by bringing that demon back. Make his success *matter*. Now he's got a target on his back: every demon that owed fealty to the one he killed wants a piece of him, and every vampire in the city wants to use his reputation to build up their own kingdom. Evaluate the politics and the Factions when the characters succeed. There's always more drama when power rushes in to fill a void or old conflicts resurface between former allies.

GIVE THE PLAYERS THE CHANCE TO WEIGH IN (TIME TO THINK)

Always look to the players for where to go next, what to do next. Follow them—whenever possible—instead of trying to push them down some magical road of plot and story. When they display an interest in a thing, spend more time with it, incorporate it into what you're already doing and draw connections that previously weren't there. If a player wants to go to a bar to look for information, fill the bar with opportunities and move the action there instead of trying to get them to go somewhere else that matters more or feels right to you.

When a player gets stuck or stymied, jump cut the action to someone else. Give each player time to think about their next move, especially in situations where their choices have a huge impact on the fiction. It makes sense for their character to be rushed and hurried, but the players themselves don't get any benefit out of you steamrolling or ignoring their contributions. Take the time to make their interests a priority in the fiction.

DIRTY THE HANDS OF ALL INVOLVED

The city is compromise writ large, a land with no easy outs. No matter where the players' characters go, no matter which options they pursue, there are no clean solutions. Destroying a nest of demons in the projects means that the nearby vampires are going to get more aggressive—after all, it was the demons that kept them at bay—but leaving the demons where they are means the demons are likely to finish that ritual they've been planning for the last year. No easy outs.

This goes for their personal relationships too. Show that evil monsters have loved ones and projects they care about in the city; complicate the noble and good characters by highlighting the ways they fail to live up to their own ideals. Make it clear that shades of grey dominate the city, that there are no easy outs even when it comes to deciding on who is an ally and who is an enemy. Never let them get comfortable with the idea that anything is black and white.

Note here that *no easy outs* doesn't mean *no outs at all*. If the forces in the city can't be stopped, can't be bargained with, can't be interrupted...why are we playing? You've got to give your players options, give them the hope that this time things will work out, even if the solutions might be messy and flawed. And—sometimes—let them get lucky: the costs for whatever deal they struck don't fall on them or the people they love. (It sure as shit falls on someone else, though. Make note of who suffers; they might want to get back into the game as a result.)

But let it go cleanly only occasionally, just enough to let them live in hope. The rest of the time, you've got to make it clear that there's no fucking way they are living on Easy Street. No fucking way.

GIVE EVERYTHING A PRICE, EVEN FRIENDSHIP

Nothing is free in the shadows. Money doesn't mean much—especially to wizards who can turn lead to gold, or demons with bank accounts dating back a hundred years—but Debts and favors make the world go round. Don't miss an opportunity to charge for something, and don't feel shy about letting the players know that an NPC is looking to get paid: "Alfonso seems reluctant to say much at this point; you can tell he'd be a little more interested in spilling his guts if he got something for his troubles."

Friendship works the same way, but in reverse. Friends are walking obligations, people the players' characters care about enough that they can get them involved in their messes for free. Of course, this doesn't mean that all relationships are transactional; some characters really do fall in love or awaken a deep friendship that's mutually fulfilling. But the price for relationships ought to be clear in the obligations they demand from the players' characters; people in the city have problems and the players' characters sure look like solutions.

YOUR MOVES

Principles are the broad guidelines for your MCing; the **MC moves** are the blow by blow actions you take during the game when you make a contribution to the fiction. The players hit the ball to you by taking actions and making moves, and your job is to hit the ball back to them in ways that reinforce the city, the setting, and the system, turning their moves into opportunities for them to make more moves.

Often, the players (and their moves) drive the fiction forward and you don't have to do a damn thing. They make moves, they hit (rolling 7+ on the dice) on those moves, and you interpret what happens in the fiction according to whatever their moves tell you to do. Easy peasy.

But there are times when the player moves aren't enough, when just working through their side of the conversations isn't sufficient. The players still say what they do, but your job is to tell how the world reacts to their actions, and your contributions are modified and modulated by agendas and principles. In other words, *you make an MC move* to keep the fiction moving.

SOFT MOVES VS. HARD MOVES

Not all moves have the same impact on the fiction: when the game calls for you to make a move, you have to decide on how hard a move to make. **Softer moves** focus on setting characters up for future moves—threats, opportunities, and foreshadowing—while **harder moves** focus on irrevocable changes in the fiction that force the characters to react to keep the situation from escalating further. Moves lie on a spectrum, from softest to hardest:

- **Softest:** You hear your mentor has an old conflict with a dangerous adversary.
- **Softer:** You hear that your mentor is in grave danger right now.
- **Harder:** You find out that your mentor was kidnapped.
- **Hardest:** You find out that your mentor has been killed.

There's no rule for how hard a move you ought to make in a given situation, but remember your principles and agendas. You aren't **being a fan of the players' characters** when you make crippling hard moves every time they roll a miss; you aren't **dirtying the hands of all involved** if you let them walk away from golden opportunities without having to make some tough choices. There's got to be a balance, one that you manage scene by scene, move by move. Death, for example, is the hardest move of all.

»Soft Move Examples:

As you're sneaking through Rilaya's sanctum, you feel a sharp wind blow through the hall, cold and menacing. You look around, but you don't see anyone. A low growl starts to emerge from one of the darker corners of the room. Perhaps you've awakened a spirit guardian. What do you do?

The negotiation isn't going well. Rico says, "I don't know, cabrón. *Maybe we just kill you and take the drugs you say you've got with you. How about that?" He pulls out a 9mm from his jacket and casually gestures with it for you to get out the drugs. It's a ploy for sure, but you worry he might get more dangerous if you don't make the deal soon. What do you do?*

Michael has been distant for weeks, but he's uncharacteristically straightforward when you confront him about his lengthy absences from work. "This marriage doesn't work for me anymore. I started seeing someone. It's not serious, but I'm tired of hiding it from you." He looks down at his wedding ring as if he's ashamed to be wearing it. What do you do?

»Hard Move Examples:

As you're sneaking through Rilaya's sanctum, you feel a sharp wind blow through the hall, cold and menacing. Suddenly something is on you, digging claws into your flesh and scratching at your face. You can't make out what it is, but you assume it's a spirit guardian bound to this place by Rilaya herself. Take 2-harm. What do you do?

The negotiation isn't going well. Rico says, "I don't know, cabrón. *Maybe we just kill you and take the drugs." His gang starts to nod. "Yeah, I like that option." He take out his gun from his jacket—a 9mm that looks like it's seen some use—and shoots you in the leg. "Search him," he says to his pack. What do you do?*

Michael has been distant for weeks, but the note he left you is uncharacteristically straightforward: "This marriage doesn't work for me anymore. I'm leaving you. My bags are packed. The kids are already staying with your mother." His wedding ring sits on the counter, nothing more than a paperweight for the note underneath it. What do you do?

MAKE A MOVE WHEN...

You make a move—as hard or soft as you like—when:

- ...there's a lull in the action.
- ...a player misses a roll.
- ...a player hands you a golden opportunity.

It's your job to keep the story moving. If the fiction ever stalls out, gets boring, or drags, it's time for you to make a move. Generally, moves you make when there's a lull in the action are softer moves, designed to get the characters moving and push the story forward, but you might need harder moves to get the characters to stand up and take action.

It's your job to interpret misses. If a player misses a roll, it's time for you to make a move. The moves you make in response to misses should always flow from the fiction—a fictional result rooted in a fictional cause—such that the player can understand the fictional source of the fictional outcome. If the move tells you what to do on a miss, then follow through on that promise, but otherwise you're set to make a move, as hard or soft as you like.

It's your job to represent the city. If a player gives you a golden opportunity—ignoring an immediate problem, opening themselves up to a dangerous foe, or generally acting without regard to their social or emotional security—it's time for you to make a move. Golden opportunities usually demand hard moves: if the characters ignore the city's dangers, the city gets to act upon them with impunity.

BASIC MOVES FOR THE MC

Here is the list of basic moves for the MC, followed by some information and advice about using these moves in play:

- Surface a conflict, ancient or modern.
- Put someone in danger.
- Inflict (or trade) harm.
- Offer an opportunity with a cost.
- Reveal a deal done in their absence.
- Turn a move back on them.
- Offer or claim a Debt owed.
- Mobilize resources to shift the odds.
- Warn someone of impending danger.
- Lock down, exploit, or claim a place of power.
- Tell the consequences and ask.
- Activate their stuff's downside.
- Make a Threat or Faction move.
- After every move: "What do you do?"

»Surface a conflict, ancient or modern

Cities are rife with conflicts, filled with communities that clash over resources and strong-willed individuals who make bids for power against entrenched opposition. Look for opportunities to push these conflicts onto the players' characters, especially when they go looking for useful resources or solutions to their problems. Alternate between old and new, serious and trivial, deadly and merely annoying. Diversity in everything.

> *You cast the bones on the floor of your store, gently chanting Watanabe's name. The visions rush through your mind, almost too fast to comprehend. He's an* old *vampire. Only one thing is certain: he's the one that closed the gates to Arcadia a hundred years ago. What do you do?*

> *Outside the club, Abby leans in close to you. Her blood is racing, you can hear it pounding in her veins. "Rico wants Elora dead. She's become a problem for our pack. Maybe we can come to a deal?" What do you do?*

»Put someone in danger

Above all others, this is your go-to move for raising the tension in a scene. You can put the players' characters in danger directly or threaten NPCs they care about onscreen and offscreen. The city is a dangerous place; bring that danger to bear directly and give the players' characters a chance to react accordingly.

> *You land softly in the alley, close enough to the feeding vampire to smell the victim's blood. You ready a stake when you hear laughter behind you. Four*

more vamps, all armed, wearing the same gang colors as the one you were hunting. Looks like this was a trap. What do you do?

When you call home to check on the babysitter, fucking Sabrina *answers the phone. "Everyone's fine here, darling. Just don't do anything stupid, and everyone will be fine." What do you do?*

»Inflict (or trade) harm

Harm is a versatile tool for raising the stakes. You can inflict it against people close to the players' characters—allies, loved ones, enemies—or directly against the players themselves. The amount of harm is completely up to you, but the weapons and situation should provide guidance. See *NPC Harm and Healing* on 213 for more on how NPCs deal with harm.

You hear the crack of a sniper rifle from a nearby apartment complex. You turn to look for the source when Kozlov's head snaps back and he crumples to the ground. Shit. You can tell right away that he's not breathing. What do you do?

As it leaps at you, you level the shotgun at the first demon, inflicting 3-harm. The blast rips through its chest knocking it to the ground. A second demon grabs your shoulder and lifts you off your feet, throwing you into the wall across the room with superhuman strength. Mark 2-harm. The demon starts to march toward you, undeterred by your shotgun. What do you do?

»Offer an opportunity with a cost

If the players seem stuck or frustrated by a problem, leap in with NPCs that promise to solve the problem...at a cost. Be honest and direct with your offers: don't wait for the players to exhaust themselves when you've got a city full of people ready and willing to make a deal to get something done. Same goes for narrative opportunities—tell the players what they see or hear in a scene, how they can take advantage of those opportunities, and what costs they will bear.

The dark wizard grins, his smile a sharp cluster of knives: "It's a simple offer. Bring me one of your friend's personal possessions, and I'll do the resurrection ritual. No one should have to bury a child." What do you do?

You can close the gap between here and Elena, but you'll have to leave Lianne to fight that elemental alone. Wanna risk it?

»Reveal a deal done in their absence

The city moves all around the players' characters, striking deals and solving problems. Think about what your NPCs are doing offscreen sometimes, and look for opportunities to relay to the players' characters that they face active and determined opposition. Make this stuff obvious; it's a great moment when an ally reveals a betrayal or a villain monologues about their plans. Remember that if your players don't know that a deal has been struck, it's like the deal was never struck at all.

"I'd love to help you, my friend. I really would. It's just that Rico came by earlier. He made it clear that you're on your own in his territory. Best of luck. Nothing personal, you know."

The Queen of Winter laughs. "You want me to side with you? I've been the one trying to kill you, love. And once I finish the job for Watanabe, I'll finally be able to stop worrying about what I owe him." What do you do?

»Turn a move back on them

Sometimes the best move is to let the players have everything they want and more. Much more. A miss isn't a failure, right? It's your chance to make a move and a great way to remind the players' characters that their choices have real impact. Give them an unexpected consequence that results from their move, and make it clear to them how their actions are driving the fiction.

You tap your inner wolf, looking for enough strength to shrug off these chains and get out of here. But your wolf isn't satisfied with a taste of freedom; it wants the whole meal. Your body shifts and warps, changing completely into your wolf form. Those that imprisoned you must pay. Mark a corruption. Are you ready to hurt them?

The demons nod when you lie to them about Wong; she's not to blame, but better to put them on her trail than yours. The demon in charge—Vasquez, you think—smiles and gestures at the demons near the van. "It's good to know that someone is to blame for all this." The van door opens, revealing Wong, already captured by these demon fuckups. What do you do?

»Offer or claim a Debt owed

Debt is the central economy of the game. Claim Debts whenever a character does a favor for another and offer Debts when you need the players' characters to get moving. Remember that both parties need to agree that a Debt is owed, though, so you need your players buy in to claim a Debt from them. Make it obvious why they owe.

> *"I need to eat, man. I'll...owe you." Looks like Kreider needs blood badly enough to offer you a Debt to get it. You cool with that?*
>
> ---
>
> *The fae who saved you from the burning wreckage carries you to his car. He says, "Don't move. You've got burns all over your body. Stay still." You're groggy, but you'll fucking live. You definitely owe him a Debt. What do you do?*

»Mobilize resources to shift the odds

The city isn't static; the odds are constantly shifting as powerful forces move resources around to deal with problems and secure their holdings. When things get too easy or too dire, look for an opportunity to change the odds. Allies may send support, enemies may send resistance, or the situation within a scene might change as NPCs activate supernatural powers.

> *Your first shot glances off the werewolf. Looks like silver bullets don't do dick. He rears his head back and howls. You reload. You know you don't have much time before the rest of the pack is here. What do you do?*
>
> ---
>
> *As'ad isn't deterred by the forces you've brought to bear against him. "Is this all you have? You should have stayed away." He starts to chant, his skin growing harder and more resilient as magic reinforces his fragile human form. What do you do?*

»Warn someone of impending danger

Be clear, early and often, about the dangers the players' characters face. Talk about the small details—the fragments of bone they find outside a monster's lair or the cold gunmetal glint of a corner boy's 9mm—and the violent politics—a werewolf pack on a hunt or the deadly machinations of a vengeful fae. Before you ***put someone in danger*** or ***inflict harm***, make it brutally, painfully clear that danger lurks around every corner of the city.

> *The call from Anya is short. "Get the fuck out of town. Razor is looking for you and he's not pleased. I didn't tell you any of this."* **click** *What do you do?*
>
> ---
>
> *By the time you get to Roger's place, you know something's wrong: the door is ajar and you smell blood. No one's home, though. Instead there's just a symbol on the wall. Riker's symbol. Drawn in Roger's blood. What do you do?*

»Lock down, exploit, or claim a place of power

Use this move to change the status quo of a place that matters to the players' characters, perhaps because they care about it or want to threaten it themselves. Locking down a place of power makes entry to it more difficult: added security, locked and reinforced entry points, political pressure to stay out, etc. Exploiting a place of power means revealing a weakness in it or striking at someone inside who might have thought they were safe. Claiming a place of power means someone or something takes possession of the place somehow, claiming it as their own.

The city planning office said this building was abandoned, but the wizards who are squatting here don't seem to have gotten the memo. They're tapping a ley line here. Hard. You can feel it from a block away. What do you do?

The faeries don't take kindly to your threats. The Queen of Summer rises to her feet. "All doors to Arcadia are closed. By my order. Let us see how the mortals deal with an absence of wonder in the world." What do you do?

»Tell the consequences and ask

Whenever the players' characters try to get something, make it clear what it's going to cost them. Sometimes that cost is direct, like taking gunfire when you wade into a battle or marking corruption to complete a terrible act, but often it's about risk and uncertainty: tell them what it might cost them and then go to the moves to see what comes of their choices. If you tell them the cost of something outright, though, let it stand; don't double back to make things easier on them later.

You can tell that the werewolves aren't interested in storming your position. Too much chaos. They all want to live. If you make a run for your truck, though, you're exposed and vulnerable. What do you do?

When you get everything together for the banishment ritual, you remember that this kind of ritual requires dark magics your mentor warned you not to touch. You'll have to mark corruption if you complete it. You still want to go forward with it?

»Activate their stuff's downside

The fictional positioning around each character gives you an infinite number of opportunities to turn their own bodies, powers, relationships, and resources against the players' characters. Whether it's the limitation on a weapon, the cost of supernatural power, or an ally's selfish desire, turning something the players see as useful into a problem or complication drives home how vulnerable the characters are to the city's dangers.

> *Your knees can't take this shit, old man. There's a reason you got out of the game. You'll have to walk from here on out. Unfortunately, you can hear the ghost that was knocking around downstairs moving this direction. What do you do?*
>
> ...
>
> *You try to strike the demon with your sword, but she's too quick for you. She gets in close, teeth bared, and goes for your throat. At this range, the sword is useless. What do you do?*

»Make a Threat or Faction move

In addition to your basic moves, you can use Threat moves (254) and Faction moves (198) to diversify your responses to players. Rely on these moves when you want to emphasize a particular Threat or Faction in the fiction. Examples of each are listed in their respective sections of the text.

»After every move: "What do you do?"

Each time you move, put the focus firmly back on a player by asking, "What do you do?" Make it clear who gets to act next and what conditions they face. Pass the ball back to them with purpose and direction. Do this enough times, and your players will start to be ready to take the narrative and run with it as soon as you hand it to them.

FACTION MOVES

In addition to your basic moves, each of the Factions in the city has a set of additional MC moves associated with the Faction. If that Faction is in play—the agents and minions of that Faction are working to accomplish some goal or the players' characters are investigating the holdings or politics of that Faction—then these **Faction moves** are available for you to use whenever you could use a basic MC move. Using Faction moves helps to differentiate communities from each other by adding variety and specificity keyed to their core values and conflicts.

Mortality:

- Adapt to the changing circumstances
- Gather in numbers to confront a threat
- Discover information that puts someone in danger
- Remind someone of their mundane obligations

Night:

- Display an aggressive show of force
- Threaten someone's interests or holdings
- Claim territory from the weak or foolish
- Make the best of a difficult situation

Power:

- Prioritize the long-term consequences
- Mystically foreshadow a coming Storm
- Act in opposition to chaos or change
- Snap up resources vulnerable or exposed

Wild:

- Reveal the diversity of cultures alien and unique
- Offer power for a promise or a pledge
- Pull something from one realm into another
- Escalate conflict for reasons mysterious or opaque

»Mortality: Adapt to the changing circumstances

The only true resource that humans have in the face of the supernatural is their adaptability and cunning. Mortals move quickly to change tactics or invent new technologies that even the odds with supernatural creatures, including the players' characters.

The crew of hunters you dealt with earlier swings around the corner in their truck. It looks like they've patched up the front end you destroyed and they've mounted some kind of crossbow on the back. What do you do?

You swear that you left Akai tied up here in the closet, but she's gone now. Looks like she managed to cut herself loose on some of the metal grating. There's blood everywhere, but she's free. What do you do?

»Mortality: Gather in numbers to confront a threat

Mortals have one other advantage on supernatural creatures: numbers. Simply put, there are more mortals in the city—more cops, more hunters, more mundanes—than there are vampires, werewolves, demons, wizards, and ghosts. And when mortals form a mob, they can even the odds quite quickly.

Talia isn't stupid. You caught her off guard before, but she's brought eight or so additional hunters this time. You spot them through the window, loading their guns and securing their gear before coming into the building. What do you do?

You thought the vote before the school board would go smoothly, but it looks like a community organization has mobilized residents of the apartment building against you. One of the local leaders, Rashida, stands up to the mic: "We don't want people like him"—she points directly at you—"telling us how to raise our children." How do you respond?

»Mortality: Discover information that puts someone in danger

The worst part about mortals, however, is their incessant curiosity. Investigators, landlords, doctors, all kinds of people may learn things about the city or the players' characters that they would be better off never knowing.

When you get home, you find your hunter gear strewn all over the living room. In the bedroom, your wife is packing a bag, your infant son already wrapped up in his coat. "I don't know what you've been keeping from me. But it looks awful," she says. What do you do?

The books you've come to the library to get—tomes of magic that no mortal should possess—are gone. The librarian says, "A high school student checked them out last week." What do you do?

»Mortality: Remind someone of their mundane obligations

It's easy to forget that Mortality still runs the world, still collects taxes, still processes paperwork. Other Factions lay claim to territory and ancient rights, but mortal authorities track ownership via legal documents. The same goes for personal obligations: your boss doesn't care that you're a faerie prince from Arcadia when your quarterly reports are due.

Your sister calls: "Mike got in an accident. I'm still out of the country and the boys are at home with my mom, but she's leaving for work in an hour. When can you be there?"

The superintendent for the building doesn't even bother looking apologetic. He says, "This whole area is contaminated with asbestos. I'm afraid that you'll have to leave your apartment until we get it sorted out." What do you do?

»Night: Display an aggressive show of force

Night is filled with predators and exploiters, people changed into something dark and hard to recognize. They know the power in violence and prefer to gain the upper hand by throwing their weight around in tense situations.

The other bar patrons laugh at your joke, but Masika doesn't think you're fucking funny. You try to explain, but she's on you too quickly, her vampiric canines descending as she tries to get close to your neck. What do you do?

Your search for the ring in the sewers is cut short by a body of ghosts shouting and cursing at you. They're flooding through the walls, as if your presence has disturbed their eternal rest. One of them knocks the flashlight out of your hand, blanketing the room with darkness. What do you do?

»Night: Threaten someone's interests or holdings

Threats come naturally to Night; violence is the language of the street. They focus on veiled threats and direct impositions, openly placing forces in preparation for an attack, anything they can do to intimidate others from the darkness.

Watanabe is unimpressed by your show of force. He says, "Any further intrusion on my property will cost you a digit; any further destruction of my property will cost you a limb. Are we clear?" How do you respond?

You park your car on the street, the soft click of the lock echoing in the darkness. As if on cue, you hear a low growl emerge from the alley. A pack of werewolves trying to scare you off from this place. What do you do?

»Night: Claim territory from the weak or foolish

When territory lies in the hands of those who show signs of weakness, Night will move in to claim it with surprising force. They prefer to lie in wait until the perfect opportunity arises to spread their influence in the city, avoiding conflicts with powerful foes if possible.

As you leave the bar, you see Rico and his werewolf pack standing around your car. One of his wolves already has the door open and finishes hotwiring the car as you walk up. "Thanks for the car," Rico laughs. What do you do?

You came looking for Anita, your faerie contact, but there aren't any faeries here at all. In fact, it looks to you like this whole bar turned over in the last week: it's all vampires as far as you can tell. What do you do?

»Night: Make the best of a difficult situation

Mortality thrives in the face of adversity, but Night is slow to learn new tactics and adjust. Instead, they tend to openly negotiate for what they can achieve in the moment, striking sudden compromises or violently settling for less than they could get.

Bleeding and broken, Martinez grabs the briefcase of money and flees, abandoning his plan to kill you before collecting his reward. He leaps up to climb the wall of the building, using some vampiric ability to scale the wall with ease. What do you do?

When the ghost realizes it can't scare you away, it manifests directly. Its voice is hollow and cold, little more than a whisper: "Do you want to get the boy who is trapped here? Maybe then you'll leave? I give you help...then you leave?"

»Power: Prioritize the long-term consequences

Power looks at events in the grand scheme, considering both the short and long-term ramifications of their actions. Power views the trials and sacrifices needed to achieve greatness as temporary—even when other communities are drowning and dying.

The head of the Wizard's Council cracks his gavel, interrupting your impassioned speech. "The answer is 'no.' Our interests lie elsewhere at this time, no matter how much power Rico gains in the short-term. He's not of consequence." What do you do?

You hear a shot ring out and feel a sharp pain; the world starts to blur and you fall to the ground. Mark 2-harm. Ezekiel is standing over you. "I'm sorry," he says, "this is the way that ends up with the fewest deaths. I'm sorry." What do you?

»Power: Mystically foreshadow a coming Storm

The magical burden carried by members of the Power Faction shows them the shape of things to come. Prophecies, divination, and rituals all give cryptic clues about the coming Storms and Threats that the players' characters will soon face. (See 247 for more on Storms and Threats.)

"There's something coming," Sudarat says, her voice a candle in the darkness. "It will upend everything. You have to stop it. Go to the corner of 4th and Edelson tonight. Late. You'll see. It will become clear there." What do you do?

Mikael's face falls as he helps you complete the ritual. "Did you see it?" he asks. "The darkness on the other side of the veil. You must stop what you've started here!" He grabs you by your jacket. "Do you hear me? It must be stopped!" What do you do?

»Power: Act in opposition to chaos or change

Power likes the status quo; after all, they tend to be the ones in control. Order and consistency are their preferred way of life, not anarchy and restlessness, and they often intercede to prevent radical change or inhibit the reckless abandon of others.

The two gangs charge at each other, a brawl that's sure to leave a number of them dead. Before they can really injure each other, a wave of magical energy floods the area, freezing them in place. A shadowy figure emerges from the alley nearby: "Well...we can't have them killing each other, can we?" What do you do?

"I'd love to tell you that you can kill Watanabe. He's an evil creature, warped by centuries of parasitic existence. But right now that would destabilize the vampire power structure, and thrust the city into chaos. Better to serve the devil you know when there are so many devils around." What do you do?

»Power: Snap up resources vulnerable or exposed

Power doesn't care much for territory, but they keep a close eye on resources that might be turned to a greater cause. When an opening presents itself, Power quickly seizes whatever useful thing they can get their hands on, even if their claim is obvious and brazen.

There's a sizzle of blue lightning, and your whole library crackles with ethereal energy. As you reach out to try to hold onto it, the whole thing vanishes in a flash. You stumble backward, stunned by the blow. Every book. Gone. What do you do?

"I'm telling you, the fucking palm reader lifted the amulet. It was there when I went into the shop, and now it's gone. I say we get it back before she does something stupid with it." What do you do?

»Wild: Reveal the diversity of cultures alien and unique

Wild is a Faction of outsiders, creatures from outside our world who prioritize things others would consider meaningless or have customs that seem to make no sense to mortals. They often turn to strange traditions, rules, passions, or drives when pressured or threatened.

The demon princess Eronth begins the negotiation in the traditional way: she cuts off her assistant's tongue and presents it to you. The red flesh squirms and moves on the plate, the black blood dripping off the edges to the ground. What do you do?

It doesn't matter where you look in the city, you can't find any *faeries. It's like they all took a fucking holiday today, as if they all took a trip home for some important event. What do you do?*

»Wild: Offer power for a promise or a pledge

Promises and pledges matter to all members of the Wild Faction; they are bound by word and contract. They wield power from worlds beyond this one, granting this power to others, provided that promises are made and oaths sworn.

"Oh, I can help you. I just need an ounce of your flesh and bone. One ounce. Not too much to ask, is it?" The faerie looks at you with hungry eyes. What do you do?

The demon sits at the table next to you, uninvited. He's got a cup of ice cream and a smile. "I hear you're looking for some help with Draxen. He's a tough bastard. I'd be willing to lend my skills to you if you help me out a bit with a little contract dispute. What do you say?"

»Wild: Pull something from one realm into another

Members of Wild can often travel between realms, sometimes taking others with them. They can sometimes bring things from their native worlds into our own, both wondrous and frightening.

As you grab hold of the Queen of Winter, you feel her weight shift. There's a sharp pain in your stomach, and you're falling, crashing into ice and snow instead of to the floor of the hotel. You look up...and find yourself far from the city, alone in a winter wasteland. What do you do?

As'ad smiles. He expected you to come with more allies. "I can assure you that we have contingency contracts." He spits some demonic phrase, and there's a crack of brimstone and flash of smoke. A twelve-foot tall, horned beast rises out of the haze. What do you do?

»Wild: Escalate conflict for reasons mysterious or opaque

Wild is fickle and enigmatic; their ways are unclear to outsiders. They take offense at incidental slights and react unexpectedly towards offenders. They are prone to escalate a conflict suddenly and without warning when unspoken lines are crossed.

> *"I was willing to do business with you...until you brought that* thing *in here," Constance shrieks, pointing at the corsage you are wearing. "I cannot believe you would disrespect me and my house in such a manner." He withdraws a knife from his jacket. What do you do?*

> *The demons, previously uninterested in your comings and goings in Chinatown, stop and stare at you. You can feel them watching you enter the building, their eyes like needles running up and down your spine. In the reflection of the glass, you see them getting closer. What do you do?*

CITY MOVES

When you select a city for your game, think of a few **city moves** you can make that are specific to that urban environment. Use these moves whenever you want to reinforce the nature of your chosen city for your players, reminding them that they are in a specific urban environment instead of a generic set of city blocks.

Here are a few examples:

- **Baltimore:** Escalate a racial tension in a marginalized community.
- **Chicago:** Delay a city service at the behest of a powerful union.
- **Denver:** Disgorge a danger from the nearby wilderness.
- **Houston:** Strand someone on the wrong side of town.
- **Seattle:** Herald an oncoming Storm with rain and shadows.

If you're interested in more city moves, check out *Dark Streets*, a collection of city guides funded by the *Urban Shadows* Kickstarter. You can learn more at www.magpiegames.com/darkstreets.

MOVES UPON MOVES

Moves in *Urban Shadows* are designed to snowball, the outcomes from any move bleeding into more moves and more drama. This is especially true in the 7-9 range of most moves, where the opposition gets a chance to act or the consequences for the move are more direct and severe, requiring a serious reaction from the character who made the move in the first place. Often, you'll have moves upon moves, a back and forth between characters that only results in some resolution once both sides have had plenty of chances to act.

It's your job to modulate the pace of the snowballing chain reaction. At the beginning of a scene, create drama, giving answers to questions that lead to more questions or putting people into danger in a broad way that encourages action. As scenes reach their peak, change tack, confirming existing information and bringing threats to bear quickly in order to make the players make hard choices.

SESSION MOVES

A good example of snowballing moves can be found in the start of session move. The whole purpose of this move is to set up conflicts and drama that can be explored during the session, so the move does nothing but snowball, regardless of which outcome the player gets on the roll.

»Start of Session Example

In this example, Andrew is MCing *Urban Shadows* set in Seattle for a new group of players—an Aware named Colby, an Oracle named Olivia, and a Vamp named Veronica. They've already established their Debts and relationships, so they're ready to play.

Andrew starts by asking Colby's player to read the start of session move:

At the beginning of every session, announce which character your character trusts the least; their player will spotlight a Faction for your character (that isn't already marked). Mark that Faction. Tell the MC about a rumor or conflict that you've heard about that Faction, building on previous established information if you'd like, and roll with the Faction.

On a 10+, you're prepared for the conflict you laid out: you've got a Debt on someone in that Faction or a useful piece of information or equipment, your choice. On a 7-9, you're neck deep in it: you owe someone in that Faction a Debt, and someone in that Faction owes a Debt to you. On a miss, you're caught flat-footed, unprepared, or unaware: the MC will tell you who is coming at you.

If you start a session in the middle of a chaotic situation or with plenty going on already, the MC might decide to skip this move.

"Great. Thanks! Let's start with you, Colby. Which character do you trust the least?" Andrew asks.

"I think it's Olivia. I'm leveraging dirt I have on her to get her to look into the downtown murders with me, and I don't think she likes me very much."

Andrew nods. "Olivia, which Faction do you want to highlight for Colby?"

"I think I'll highlight Power," says Olivia's player. "I want to see her deal with my people."

Andrew says, "Great! Colby, what rumor or conflict have you heard about the Power Faction?"

"Hmmm. How about this? The Power Faction is looking into the murders that I'm looking into as well. They are worried they're part of a ritual."

Andrew smiles. He hadn't planned that, but it fits perfectly. "Go ahead and roll with Power, then. You have a +1 in Power, so add 1 to whatever you roll." Colby's player rolls and gets a total of 9. "On a 9, you owe someone a Debt and someone owes you a Debt. I'm gonna say that Ahmed, an oracle who lives over on Bainbridge Island, owes you. What did you do for him?" Andrew is **asking loads of questions and building on the answers**.

"Maybe I gave him some information about the downtown murders? I don't think Power knows much about this situation yet.

"And why do you owe him?" It doesn't have to be the same person, but Andrew is **pushing the characters together**, *tying Colby tightly to Ahmed so they have reason to do business.*

"I think he tipped me off to the investigation in the first place. We used to date, and so he wanted me to know that the Power Faction might approach me soon. I definitely owe him for the heads up."

"How about you, Olivia? Who do you trust the least?"

"Veronica. For sure." Veronica highlights Olivia's Power as well. Olivia's player says, "I think I've caught wind of the same investigation. I know they're onto the case, and I'm worried I won't get the killer before the Council gets a hold of him." Olivia rolls her Power +2, and comes up with a 12.

"You get a Debt or a piece of useful information or equipment. Which one do you want?"

"I'll take the useful information or equipment."

"Cool. You learn from Akua—the wizard from which you're keeping your relationship with Colby secret—that the Council thinks Colby is the killer. They're planning on ordering their archons to capture her before there's another murder." Andrew is **pushing the characters together, even across a boundary**.

"Ah! I need to warn her!"

"Yes! But first we've got to get Veronica's start of session move done. Who do you trust the least?"

"I think both of these folks are too trusting...but I think Colby is more likely to screw me over." Colby's player highlights Night for Veronica. She wants to see Veronica deal with her own people. "Night, huh? Okay. I think I've heard that two street crews of vampires in my neighborhood are going to war. I don't want to get caught in the middle."

Veronica rolls with Night +2, but comes up with snake eyes. Ouch. "Uh oh. Who's coming at me? Both gangs?"

Andrew smiles. "Let's get started with our first scene and find out..."

When your players use other moves during the game, try to think of ways to push the fiction forward in the same way that the start of session helps to frame new conflicts and introduce new NPCs. Look for places to give out information, complicate relationships, and claim Debts. When the time comes to bring things full circle—when the plot reaches a peak moment of drama and uncertainty—you want to make sure that you've laid the groundwork for the hard moves you're going to make.

PLAYER VS. PLAYER

Players and MCs new to *Urban Shadows* sometimes doubt that the system can handle extensive player vs. player fiction. It's certainly the case that the game is more interesting if the players have opposition from the Factions and NPCs that run the city, but the system is perfectly capable of handling occasions when two players try to hurt or dominate each other.

»Sharing Spotlight

When PCs go at each other, it's important that you share the spotlight between them. One PC may start the conflict—***unleashing an attack*** or ***letting it out*** —but the action must pass around the table so everyone gets time in the spotlight. This doesn't meant that everyone gets *equal time*; it's your job to keep the focus on whatever is interesting in the conflict until the spotlight needs to shift. Remember to **be a fan of the players' characters**: no PC should stomp over all the others with impunity, but some PCs may get more of the spotlight. It's your call.

»Aiding and Interfering

Lending a hand and ***getting in the way*** become crucial moves for players engaged in player vs. player conflict. If one character attacks the other, then the target of the attack can only respond by ***getting in the way*** until the move is resolved. It doesn't matter if they're trying to distract the target, hit back hard, or run away; all attempts to reduce the effectiveness of the attack is rolled up into ***get in the way***. Only once the move is resolved can the targeted player follow through on that action and make a move of their own.

»Multiple Misses

Player vs. player conflict often involves misses, as the players ***get in the way*** of each other's actions and take risks they normally avoid. Take advantage of these moments to flip a move around—"Since you missed on your ***unleash an attack*** move, I'm going to give that to the other player as if she hit a 10+ on ***unleash an attack***. Which options do you want?"—or introduce external threats that push the players back together if things are too hot. Nothing ends an argument like a werewolf pack crashing the party!

»Player vs. Player Example

In this example, two characters (Veronica and Colby) have come to blows. Colby is convinced that Veronica is responsible for the downtown murders, and Veronica is unwilling to be taken to the Wizard's Council to be tried for the crime. Colby tried to ***cash in a Debt***, but Veronica successfully refused, leaving Colby with few options.

> *"Time to come with me, Veronica," Colby's player says. "I take out my gun and point it at her."*
>
> *Andrew looks at Veronica's player. "How do you react to that, Veronica?" Always* **asking loads of questions***!*
>
> *"I'm pissed. I didn't kill anyone. I want to* **let it out** *by baring my fangs." Andrew nods. Veronica's player rolls and hits on a 10. "I think I'll take* +1 forward *and* frighten, intimidate, or impress my opposition.*"*
>
> *"Hold on," says Colby's player. "I want to* **get in the way** *by shooting my gun into the ceiling and saying 'I'm not fucking around here.'" She rolls with Night +0 and comes up with a 10+, imposing a -2 on Veronica's roll.*
>
> *"The sound of the gunshot catches you off guard, Veronica. You're stunned a bit. Colby looks like a real threat," says Andrew. "Looks like you only get one option off the list and you'll have to mark corruption." Veronica's player sighs, takes* +1 forward*, and marks a corruption. Andrew doesn't need to do much here, since the two of them are going at it pretty hard. He's* **being a fan of the characters** *by just staying out of the way!*
>
> *"I leap at her," Veronica's player says. Andrew and Colby's player both nod, and Veronica rolls. With her Blood +3, Veronica gets a 13 on her roll. Too high for Colby to interfere. Veronica chooses* take something from her.
>
> *"The vampire catches you off guard, Colby, moving faster than any human you've ever seen. You take 1-harm as your head bounces against the carpet, dazing you just long enough for Veronica to snatch the gun from your hand. What do you do?" Now that Veronica has gotten in a hit, Andrew is* **sharing the spotlight** *with Colby.*

"I punch her in the face!" Colby rolls to **unleash an attack**, *but only gets a 4. Veronica doesn't even need to interfere here to make Colby fail.*

"Okay, Veronica. I'm going to give you the move as if you rolled a 10+ if you want it," **turning their move back on them**.

"Fuck yeah. I'll take inflict terrible harm. *I still have the gun, right? I shoot her in the head."*

Andrew winces. Rough. "Yeah, that's 3-harm at close range, plus 1-harm more for inflicting terrible harm. *Veronica unloads two rounds directly into your head. Combined with the harm you took earlier, Colby, that puts you up to critical. What do you do?"*

"Ouch. I think I'm out at this point." Colby's player looks at her sheet. "Yeah, full up on harm." Andrew nods and looks over at Veronica, **sharing the spotlight** *again.*

"I'm done here. I drop the gun on the floor and walk away. She started this, but I don't need to finish it. Let the Council put her back together if they want."

These moments—when the drama of the story pushes the characters up against each other hard—are some of the best moments you could ask for in a story. That said, we've never seen a conflict go to the point described above; players generally stay on the same side of the fight, like characters on a television show who snipe at each other but never really go the distance. If it happens, though, you'll be fucking ready.

USING NPCS IN PLAY

Creating and using NPCs in *Urban Shadows* is simple: when you want to introduce a new character, pick a Faction, give them a name, and describe them a bit to the players. That's it. No character sheets, no elaborate forms, no stress. To create an NPC, invent them fictionally and everything else will follow.

Andrew decides he needs a new antagonist after the PCs stop a few necromancers from performing an elaborate ritual. He decides that a faerie would be interesting, especially since Ryan's Fae, Volund, hasn't spent much time dealing with other courts. He names this new faerie the Queen of Winter, and decides that she looks like a beautiful, older woman with frost blue hair and a blindingly white dress. Right now, Andrew's not too worried about how much harm she can inflict or suffer; he can figure that out if she comes to blows with any of the PCs.

As you create more NPCs, you can start to think about how they relate to each other, who is enemies with whom, what other resources they can bring to bear. Think offscreen about their activities, and ***reveal deals done between them*** to the PCs to get them to engage the city's politics.

NPC DRIVES

In addition to selecting a name, Faction, and look for your NPCs, give them **drives**, core motivations that move the NPCs to simple, self-interested action. A vampire hunter probably has a drive like *avenge my sister* or *protect the weak*; a demon might have a drive like *find a way to stay on Earth* or *move up the corporate ladder*. Drives can be custom, created for each NPC you create, but there's also a list of common drives on the MC Worksheet.

When an NPC is presented with a challenge, think about how it impacts their drive. If the challenge opposes it, the NPC moves hard and fast against the opposition, hoping to knock it down and solve the problem. But if the challenge isn't directly opposed, the NPC might ask a few questions or bide their time to look for opportunities to make the best of whatever situation the challenge might create. Clever NPCs might even manipulate the PCs into helping the NPCs fulfill their drives...

NPC GOONS

Some NPCs are **goons**, replaceable muscle or minions that don't merit the same level of detail as important NPCs. Give them names, but characters shouldn't be able to ***put a name to a face*** with some minion who doesn't really have a reputation in the city. Goons aren't mechanically different from regular NPCs in any other way; they can still earn Debts, suffer and inflict harm as normal—although they may not be able to take as much harm—and build relationships with the PCs if they show up multiple times. Goons all have the same drive—*to serve the powerful*.

Using goons helps to avoid your players ***putting a name to a face*** with a bunch of important NPCs at the same time or trying to track too many important NPCs from scene to scene. Introduce important NPCs one at a time, each with their own set of minions and lackeys, and your players can follow what's going on in a bustling city without breaking out a database for NPCs. Later, once those NPCs are established, they can all show up in the same scene without overwhelming your players.

Some goons might move up to being important NPCs during play, especially if the NPCs they serve come to harm. This usually happens fairly naturally in the fiction—the same NPC starts showing up more often—but it might mean that a PC who hasn't met the goon before might actually be able to ***put a name to a face*** with the NPC.

PC-NPC-PC TRIANGLES

NPCs pursue their drives with abandon, but that doesn't make them one-dimensional. Take some time to show different PCs different sides of the NPCs, creating PC-NPC-PC triangles where two (or more) PCs have fundamentally different relationships with the same NPC.

Say the Queen of Winter wants to *conquer the city*, but she thinks of Olivia as a potential convert and Solomon as an existential threat. She's likely to extend an olive branch to Olivia, hoping to turn her against her friends, while simultaneously sending a few troll enforcers to kill Solomon before he figures out what's happening. The Queen doesn't see Olivia and Solomon's relationship as anything more than an obstacle to her drive, one that needs to be broken apart for her to achieve her goals. Now the two PCs have to deal both with the Queen's machinations *and* their own feelings about their out-of-control, evolving relationship with the powerful NPC.

NPC DEBTS

NPCs often acquire Debts from the PCs. You need to track these Debts separately for each NPC; a Debt gained by one NPC can't be ***cashed in*** by a different NPC even though you control both characters. We've given you space on the MC Worksheet to track NPCs and Debts, but we predict you'll need additional space as your story unfolds over several sessions.

Here's a few ways that NPCs gain Debts on PCs:

- a PC ***escapes*** a scene and chooses to owe someone a Debt
- a PC rolls a 7-9 while ***persuading an NPC***
- an NPC does a favor for a character without recompense
- a PC rolls a 7-9 or miss while ***refusing to honor a Debt*** to an NPC

If they hold Debts from the PCs, NPCs can ***cash in Debts*** with those characters per the Debt moves on 64. Players can ***refuse to honor a Debt*** if they don't want to honor the Debt, same as if a PC cashed in the Debt with them.

Remember your principles and moves when your NPCs ***cash in Debts***. Ask the PCs to do things they're good at doing—**be a fan of the characters**—but make the consequences of those things obviously complicated and messy—**dirty the hands of all involved** and ***put the characters in danger***. Point the PCs at each other, ask uncomfortable questions, and push the characters toward situations that demand more interesting moves to resolve completely.

WHEN NPCS ATTACK

Eventually, some of your NPCs will decide that the only way to deal with the PCs is to hurt or kill them. Since one of your moves is ***inflict harm***, you're free to hit the PCs with harm whenever it's appropriate in the fiction, even to the point that the NPCs kill the PCs. That said, you want to set up the punch before you follow through with harm; no player should ever be surprised that an NPC is stomping on their character's face.

The best way to set up harm is to make a soft move and let the PCs decide how to respond: "Solomon, two of the four vamps that trapped you in the alley run at you. One of them has a metal baseball bat; the other has a chain. What do you do?" No harm yet, but plenty of pressure.

If Solomon tries to get out of the way, he's ***keeping his cool***—and he'll probably say something like "I'm trying to avoid getting hurt"—and he'll roll to see what happens. He avoids their blows on a hit, but a miss means you can ***inflict harm*** as established (probably 1- or 2-harm, depending on how hard a move you want to make). Or he might try to ***persuade*** them to back down, ***trick*** them into thinking he's the wrong target, or ***cash in a Debt*** to stay their hand. All up to him.

Once he's dealt with your move, he can try to seize the moment and ***unleash an attack*** on them. If he tries to attack them without getting out of the way or just ignores them completely, you can ***inflict harm*** with impunity. You gave him a chance and he blew it. Vampires with bats and chains don't fuck around.

Conflicts move fluidly between characters. One side makes a move; the other side responds. This isn't a hard and fast back and forth, though. Sometimes you might make several moves before the PCs get to react, especially if they're hitting on 7-9s and making tough choices.

> *Liam, played by Troi, has found himself in a rough spot with a group of hunters that are enthralled to an elder vampire. He managed to get out of their safehouse with a 9mm before they killed him, but they're hot on his tail.*
>
> *Andrew, his MC, says, "As you run toward your car, you see the headlights of their truck round the corner. The driver guns the engine and they drive right toward you." These goons are* serving their master, *hard and direct.*
>
> *Troi says, "Ah, crap. Okay, I start shooting at the driver."*
>
> *"At this distance, you probably can't hit them with the 9mm. If you wait until they're close enough, the momentum of the truck will probably carry them into you, even if you do shoot the driver. You want to chance it?" Andrew's*

telling the consequences and asking; *he wants to make the costs of moving forward really clear to Troi before she commits in the fiction.*

"Dammit. No, I don't want to get hit. I'll try to dive out of the way and get in a better position. I guess that's **keeping my cool**, *since I want to avoid getting hit." Andrew nods, and Troi rolls a 7, barely a hit.*

"In order to move quickly enough, you'll telegraph your position. No chance they don't see where you take cover. They'll have the advantage when they roll up. Still want to move?"

"Yeah, I want to get to some cover."

"Okay. The truck barrels toward you, but you move quickly, throwing yourself to the ground behind a fire hydrant. They open fire on your position, the bullets striking the concrete all around you. What do you do?" Andrew's **putting someone in danger**, *but not yet* **inflicting harm**.

"I want to fire back! Can I **unleash an attack** *now?"*

Andrew **tells the consequences and asks** *again: "They've got you pretty solidly in their sights. If you stand up and fire, I think you're going to take full harm. Still wanna?" Andrew's* **saying what the city demands**, *keeping the pressure up on Liam.*

"Fuck no. Maybe I can shoot out one of their headlights by shooting wildly?"

"Yeah, that sounds like **distract** *to me. Go ahead and roll. If you make it, you might* create an opportunity *to do some damage."*

Remember that groups have special rules for inflicting and suffering harm. See *Groups* on 157 for more on groups, but the general rule is thus: groups inflict +1-harm and suffer -1-harm for every size larger they are than the opposition. A medium group (10-20 people) deals +2-harm and suffers -2-harm when dealing with a single individual.

NPC HARM AND HEALING

For the most part, NPCs take harm like PCs (see *Harm* on 148): they suffer damage equal to the harm of a weapon minus their armor, modified by move choices like *inflict terrible harm* or other special circumstances. If a PC shoots a cop wearing a bulletproof vest (1-armor) with a 9mm (2-harm close loud), it's probably 1-harm: 2-harm–1-armor. All of that math is pretty much the same as if a PC shot another PC.

Unlike PCs, however, mortal NPCs can't take nearly as much harm before they die. A gunshot (2-harm) tends to be fairly crippling, and a blast from an assault rifle (3-harm) is almost always fatal. Armor can help a bit, but few mortals walk around in bulletproof vests (1-armor), let alone riot gear (2-armor). A few might have some supernatural trinkets that offer protection, but it's rare to find a mortal who knows where to find that kind of stuff.

If a mortal NPC survives an attack, getting them to medical attention is crucial. Mortals who have suffered 2- or 3-harm might live for a short while after the injury, but they won't last long. Assuming they get to medical care (or receive magical healing), they recover harm at the rate of 1- or 2-harm per session. A mortal NPC who suffers a gunshot wound and lives probably spends a session or two in the hospital before they're back on their feet.

But mortals aren't the only opposition in *Urban Shadows*. The PCs might also face vampires, demons, ghosts, or any number of monsters that aren't as fragile as mortals. In these cases, it's good to have some guidelines for how supernatural NPCs suffer harm.

»Fictional Positioning Matters

Some creatures are simply invulnerable to certain kinds of damage. Ghosts, for example, might not have enough physical corpus to suffer harm from traditional weapons. In these cases, push characters toward other ways of dealing with these foes, using blessed or magic items or magical powers (***let it out***, rituals, etc.). "Invulnerable" opposition is a great excuse for The Veteran to head back to their workspace to build the weapons characters need to triumph.

»Resistances Act as Armor

If a particular kind of creature is resistant to damage (or to a particular type of attack), treat that as armor. Vampires, for example, may not suffer much harm from bullet wounds—they don't really have internal organs—so they get 1-armor even when they're naked. Armor is nasty business, though; a creature with 3-armor can't be harmed by a handgun, even when players select *inflict terrible harm*. Armor piercing weapons still inflict harm as normal, of course, even if the armor is supernatural in nature.

»Vulnerabilities Increase Harm

By the same token, anything that strikes at a creature's vulnerability either increases the harm done by 1-harm or makes the harm armor piercing (ap). Minor vulnerabilities (cold iron used against faeries) tend to do +1-harm; major vulnerabilities (blessed weapons used against demons or fire used against vampires) tend to be armor piercing or +2-harm, whichever does more damage.

»Surviving More Harm

Finally, supernatural NPCs can take more harm than mortal NPCs: it might take 4-harm to drop a vampire or 6-harm to bring down a werewolf. Let the fiction guide your hand when you establish how much harm an NPC can take; a demon that dies from a single gunshot wound isn't really threatening to the PCs, while a faerie that can take 8-harm is *terrifying*. Supernatural NPCs hate suffering injuries as much as anyone else, though; many flee when they catch a shotgun blast to the chest, even if they might be able to take another one before they die. Like mortal NPCs, supernatural NPCs heal harm in between sessions, but at a much faster rate (2- or 3-harm per session) and might be able to regrow lost limbs or recover from near-fatal injuries.

MANAGING NPCS

Managing NPCs in *Urban Shadows* can sometimes feel overwhelming: cities with millions of people have an infinite number of potential characters for your players to engage. Here are a few tips for keeping the list under control and manageable:

»Track NPCs by Faction

Each NPC has a Faction, the community with which they are most associated. Track the NPCs by their Faction so you know when they might come up. Generally, Night characters hang around on street corners and seedy bars; a trip to the penthouse suite of a downtown skyscraper is much more likely to involve Power or Wild. Keeping your notes by Faction lets you reach for the NPCs you need based on location and mood, instead of shuffling through a huge list of random names.

»Reincorporate, Recycle, and Reuse

When the players ***hit the streets*** to look for resources or have an opportunity to add an NPC to their backstories, encourage them to reincorporate existing NPCs. Felix, that vampire who helped Roxy find that missing girl last summer? He's the same one that Fahad goes to when he needs information about the Night Faction. And if Pythia has a vision about a vampire who might play a pivotal role in the coming conflict against a demon...Felix. After all, how many vampires are there in one city?

»Kill Them Off

Game's the game. Don't be afraid to off your NPCs and replace them with up-and-comers who are hungry for an opportunity to take the stage. If you look at your list of NPCs and it's gotten too long, start a war or ritual or conflict that will pare the list down to something more manageable. Elder vampire lords and ancient wizards have a lot of defenses, but even they end up on the wrong end of a fight sometimes.

BEHIND THE ARCHETYPES

Pay close attention to the Archetypes your players select at the start of the game. Your players are telling you what conflicts are interesting to them, what Factions draw their attention, without you having to ask them a single question. Frame scenes that play to those interests and conflicts: look for opportunities to present magical mysteries to The Wizard, long-forgotten conflicts and mysteries to The Veteran, and demonic politics and intrigue to The Tainted. At the same time, remember to **play to find out what happens**, following the characters where they want to go once they actually start talking to NPCs and engaging each other.

Also pay attention to the specific moves and extras they select, which offer additional information about how your players want to engage the fiction. A good rule of thumb is to try to give each character at least one opportunity to use their moves and extras each session. That's not possible for every move on every playbook, but it's not hard to look at the faerie powers The Fae took and envision a situation that might call for healing, glamours, and emotional manipulation (a bar fight would probably do it) or to present The Oracle with magical items if they select ***Psychometry***. Again, you're not scripting or planning the plot of the session; you're priming yourself to push the story in ways that let you **be a fan of the characters** that the players have created.

Finally, don't be afraid to say yes to the players when they propose details about the culture or physiology of their characters. Why can't the vampires in your city get their blood from a mobile blood bank service—we're sure you can't think of any way for *that* to go awry—or the wizards live forever once they've mastered some basic aging spells? All fictional positions have weaknesses, areas of conflict and nuance, places where the status quo can be upended with just a little push. Let the players say as much as they want about how the city lives and breathes, and then look for places to drink their milkshake, knock over their sand castle, and leave them scrambling to climb back on top.

Cloak your moves in darkness but always go for the throat. They'll love you for it.

On that note, here are some tips on running *Urban Shadows* for each Archetype:

MORTALITY ARCHETYPES

Mortality Archetypes stress the boundary between the supernatural and mundane; ask your players who select Mortality Archetypes lots of questions about their connection to the mortal world and look for places where their mundane obligations are going to put them (or the people they care about) in grave danger.

»The Aware

The Aware is a character in transition, caught between both worlds more than any other Archetype and forced to choose to which they truly belong. All of the other Factions in the city have a special interest in the outcome of that choice; The Aware represents untapped potential, a free agent who could eventually play for any team. Give them lots of supernatural relationships to reflect that potential, connections that offer seductive power and constant erotic tension. If The Aware takes ***Hard-Boiled***, give them lots of actual mysteries to work on as well, cases in which the mortal world needs The Aware to intervene before the supernatural villains escape without consequence. As the game goes on, remember to push on The Aware's mortal responsibilities—especially when it's least convenient for The Aware's supernatural relationships—and to introduce other mortal NPCs who can lay the groundwork for The Aware to join or lead a watcher's society.

»The Hunter

Some hunters are single-target killing machines, methodically stalking a specific type of supernatural; others are moralists, focusing on supernatural creatures that have done something immoral, which pretty much makes them vigilantes who happen to focus on supernatural monsters. Regardless, get specific with your Hunter about what they hunt, and give them a hunt *right away*; it can be tough to squeeze it in later when the other PCs get involved in the plot. While The Hunter is on a hunt, consistently put mortals in danger, but only injure them—triggering The Hunter's corruption move—when The Hunter willfully ignores the consequences of the hunt. Avoid taking away The Hunter's weapons and gear; it's easy to forget that The Hunter's cool stuff is a big part of what makes them a threat to their prey. The Hunter's ***Safe House***, for example, is truly safe, beyond your reach unless something crazy happens and that safety is intentionally violated.

»The Veteran

The Veteran has a slightly more narrow character arc than most of the other Archetypes; be clear about why they retired and what being retired means, but **being a fan** of The Veteran absolutely means dragging them back into the shit. Threaten them, attack them, harass them, cash in Debts...whatever it takes to get them to risk it all and get back into the game. That said, The Veteran works best with other characters to support, mentor, and assist; use their workspace as a reason for the characters to come together by presenting challenges that require specific technology or tools and establish requirements to earn that tech that require the assistance of the other characters. When The Veteran finishes a project in their workspace, remember that it's off limits to you; your NPCs can't take it, break it, or otherwise make it useless.

NIGHT ARCHETYPES

The Night Archetypes—for all their supernatural fangs and fur—are fundamentally mired in the day-to-day of the street: drugs, money, sex, guns, and territory. They're the closest to the violence inherent in the system, but you have to remind them that they aren't immune to the politics of the broader city.

»The Spectre

The Spectre can go virtually anywhere and touch nearly everything; no place is safe from their grasp except the occasional warded sanctum. Give them scenes of victimization and horror when they snoop, abusive relationships on display when the abusers think no one is watching. On occasion, confront The Spectre with dangerous spirits and ghosts. After all, they aren't the only one who haunts the night. Always clearly flag, however, when something is capable of harming them when they aren't ***Manifest***; The Spectre often becomes a bit cavalier about dying by the second or third session. If The Spectre chooses ***Link***, put the link in danger once every other session so they get a chance to defend it without constantly worrying about it.

Several of The Spectre's corruption moves put them at an advantage over mortals (***Possession***, ***Nightmare***, ***Siphon***). Never shortchange The Spectre when they use these moves; marking corruption is a high price to pay to get what they want. Make them terrifying and effective.

»The Vamp

No Archetype in the game comes with as much baggage as The Vamp: make sure that any player who chooses it understands what the Archetype is designed to do, i.e., entrap people into co-dependent relationships based around their vices and dark desires. That said, be generous when the players define The Vamp within those boundaries. Ghouls attached to The Vamp's haven, for example, can be any sort of undead or thrall that suits The Vamp's aesthetic and the larger vampire culture might have the typical fealty-based, lords of the night politics.

Since The Vamp often exploits and abuses other characters, remember to **push characters together, even across boundaries**. The Vamp is pure muscle, terrifying and feral when trapped, and they have connections to the vampire ecosystem that no other character can really match. Make those resources useful, such that other characters need The Vamp's skills. Don't let The Vamp get comfortable sitting in their haven while the rest of the characters chase down interesting plot threads.

»The Wolf

The Vamp may be muscle, but The Wolf is a stone cold killer; little in the city is as dangerous as a transformed werewolf on a hunt. The Wolf's territory, though, is a kind of leash, focusing their energy onto a specific set of troubles and blessings they've selected at character creation. Make these troubles and blessings central to The Wolf's story, and move hard against them when they trigger a trouble through ***Comes with the Territory*** with sticky social situations and nasty opponents that let them show off their killer claws. It's important to the Archetype that the wolf not be able to transform at will—***Sun and Moon*** is a useless corruption advance if The Wolf starts the game able to control their transformation—but you might be generous and let The Wolf transform in a crisis by using ***let it out***.

POWER ARCHETYPES

Power Archetypes believe they hold all the cards: they have the foresight to know what trouble lies ahead for the city and the mystical skills to change the course of things all on their own. The only problem, of course, is that all the other Factions always muck things up...

»The Oracle

The Oracle is a strange Archetype; visions that predict the future tend to interfere with **playing to find out what happens**. ***Foretellings*** avoids this problem by letting the player retroactively declare they foresaw something *as it's happening*. Play it up when The Oracle spends their ***Foretellings*** hold; move hard and fast against them so that their prediction feels both imminent and important. Conversely, give them specific opportunities to offer false prophecies to get out of trouble until they get in the habit of offering them without prompting, and provide plenty of objects and mysterious people about which they can divine psychic information. When you give information to The Oracle, speak boldly and incompletely; you can always figure out later how the visions fit together.

Like The Veteran, The Oracle works best when there are other PCs to bounce off of, both for moves like ***Conduit*** that directly affect other PCs and because visions that place other PCs in danger are much more interesting than visions that affect only NPCs. If you're playing a game with only one or two PCs, push your players toward other Archetypes.

»The Wizard

The Wizard has a number of powerful problem solving tools (spells, ***let it out***, their sanctum), but few ways to determine which problems should take priority. Throw mysteries in front of them—murders, mystical wards, missing people—and use their blindspots to catch them in the middle of messy PC-NPC-PC triangles and complex multi-Faction politics, situations in which they will struggle to find a good way forward in a mess of bad options. Offer the information (and additional resources) they need through dark and powerful NPCs to see how far The Wizard is willing to go to save everyone. The answer might surprise you.

On occasion, remind The Wizard how mortal they are by sending a crew from the Night or Wild faction directly at them, before The Wizard has time to prepare. The Wizard shines brightest when their back is up against the wall, improvising their way out of a dangerous situation.

WILD ARCHETYPES

Archetypes from the Wild Faction are immigrants, strangers in a strange land with deep connections to their home communities. Remind them often how different they are from everyone else, and how much power their masters still hold over them.

»The Fae

Promises are central to The Fae, so give them plenty of NPCs who are willing to make promises—both foolish and calculating—to get close to The Fae or get what they want. Make the NPCs' attention occasionally fickle; NPCs are enthralled by The Fae at first, but the connection grows weaker over time. If the Fae has taken ***A Dish Best Served Now*** or ***Words Are Wind***, have the NPCs make big promises and break them often. Call out promises that PCs make too; those all can trigger moves for The Fae as well.

Court politics are central to The Fae's relationship to their homeland. Most Fae who live in the city are exiled, but they might have free rein to go back and forth. Either way, use the Debts they give to their monarch through ***Faerie Magic*** to force The Fae to help consolidate the monarch's power. Courtly intrigue is about appearance and lies, glamours and illusions, much more than violence and intimidation.

If another PC takes ***Scales of Justice***, they gain access to ***Faerie Magic*** without switching Archetype, although the magic itself is probably reskinned to hedge magic, blood magic, or some other Archetype appropriate theme. It's got a high price—each use of magic costs a Debt—so it shouldn't step too much on The Fae's toes.

»The Tainted

Like The Wolf, The Tainted is a walking killing machine tethered by relationships and obligations. Only thing is...they are tethered by and obligated to something far worse than they are themselves—a dark patron. Give The Tainted plenty of jobs that let them use their demonic powers before you drop the hammer and put The Tainted in direct conflict with the PCs. Let them think they can do the devil's dirty work without too many sacrifices, then put The Tainted on a crash course with the other PCs and watch the fireworks.

If The Tainted dies without Debts on their dark patron, consider sending the dark patron to an NPC they care about—instead of another PC—with an offer to bring them back. Once the dark patron has their hooks into The Tainted's spouse, sibling, friend, or child, the tension between service and rebellion goes up a notch. You want The Tainted to be constantly torn, caught between the deals they've signed and the people they care about in the mortal world.

DANGEROUS CONTENT

Urban Shadows is a game about supernatural politics, but it's got one foot firmly rooted in the modern-day realities of urban life. As we discussed in **The Preface**, your players' characters live at the intersection of many identities, caught in a world that wants to not only do terrible things to them, but also wants them to do terrible things to others. All of that pathos and drama can be incredible, especially when the heroes triumph over the villains, but it's also ripe for creating problems at your table.

IDENTITY POLITICS

For many characters, their race, gender, sexual identity, or class are central to their experience within the city. It can be a struggle, however, to portray the systems of oppression that define urban life with grace and sensitivity, and you probably don't have time to read a few books on race or gender before you play! Here are some tips on honoring the diverse communities of the city that don't depend on you getting a college degree in urban or ethnic studies:

»Explore Communities Deeply

It's true that the West Baltimore drug trade is primarily run by people of color. It's also true, however, that the majority of social workers, community organizers, and political activists within that community *are also* people of color. It's not enough to show one face of a community—even a supernatural community—and expect your players to know the depth of what that community has to offer. Instead, you've got to show the community as it truly is, filled with different perspectives (even mutually exclusive perspectives!) on what makes their community special. If you introduce only one woman, one queer, one Latino, that person has to stand in for everyone else; don't make them carry that burden.

»Vary the Tone

A world without racism, sexism, and bigotry would be ideal, but it's not the world in which *Urban Shadows* is set. Black vampires in Harlem have an intersectional identity: they are both undead creatures of the night *and* the target of an ongoing campaign of police violence against people of color. You do the character a disservice if you forget that they are black when engaging with systems of power. At the same time, not every interaction should be viewed through a single lens: vary the tone by making issues like race or gender central to the fiction at times and incidental at other crucial moments. Make it clear what kind of obstacles the characters have to overcome, but give them opportunities to rise above all that hate and oppression to triumph.

»Defy Stereotypes

Whenever possible, defy stereotypes. If you introduce a Hispanic gangbanger from Los Angeles as a contact for a character, immediately reveal what makes him stand out from the stereotype of a Mexican thug. Is he going to community college for economics? Is he a devoted father? Does he abhor violence? This isn't just about avoiding offensive content; all of your NPCs are richer when you find ways to defy the players' expectations about what they have to offer. This counts for white male NPCs as much as everyone else; they may perform whiteness to conform to a dominant culture that rewards them for their performance, but they have differences, secrets, and complications all their own.

MATURE THEMES

In addition to identity issues, *Urban Shadows* often runs headfirst into mature content around violence, sex, drugs, and crime. The presence of the supernatural helps to make these issues more abstract, but it's inevitable that terrible things happen to many characters in the course of your story. Here are some ways to stay true to your agendas and principles while recognizing that not everyone has the same tolerance for these kinds of themes.

»Lean on the X-Card

If you introduce the X-Card, following the procedure on 24, you can modulate your moves based on the feedback your players give you. The X-Card isn't foolproof—some players are unwilling to say they're uncomfortable even when you give them an explicit tool—but it's a good method of immediate feedback that can keep a game from falling apart. Use the X-Card yourself early in the session to demonstrate that it's safe for players to use, and make sure to honor the system when a player does invoke it, even if you think what they're flagging is a perfectly reasonable addition to the fiction.

»Avoid Defaultism

Be wary of falling into defaultism when engaging mature content—your brain has been baked in racist, sexist, homophobic media that bubbles up when you least expect it, pushing messages that you might not even realize that you're sending. Switch things up whenever possible—instead of introducing a murderous serial killer who rapes young women before eating them, create a murderous vampire who harvests the brains of male scientists for some supernatural experiment on the nature of human intelligence. Swapping around a few cultural signifiers gets you the same (or better!) creepy punch without falling into boring clichés or dredging up uncomfortable history for people at your table.

»Elide the Crucial Moment

We often think of the moment of tragedy as the *most important* thing to show your players; after all, what else can drive home the darkness of the streets? But in reality, those moments are fleeting, barely remembered in retrospect by the survivors. It's *all the other moments* that stick with them forever—the heartbreak of a missing child, the blood soaked into the carpet, the phantom pain of a missing limb. When you push your players with adult content, think about ways to emphasize the consequences, the results, the remains in order to drive home the true costs of the violence and loss that surround them.

WHEN YOU'RE NOT BUSY...

Everything you need to run the game is in the principles and moves; stick to your guns and pull the trigger when the players are in your sights. Beyond that, we've got a few tips and tricks that make games of *Urban Shadows* really shine. When you've got a moment in between moves:

...linger on the details. Paint a picture for the players. Tell them in loving detail about a renovated building or a captivating dress or a perfect meal or a rotting body. Talk in color, sounds, smells, flavors. Make them believe they're right there, attending the mayor's fundraiser, watching the new construction on Broad Street, finishing the murder victim's autopsy. Bring the city to life and grab them by the throat, the ear, and the tongue, whatever seems like it will get their attention.

...make maps. Pull out scraps of paper, index cards, newspapers and draw all over them. Sketch out high stakes situations, especially violent encounters, and encourage your players to draw on the maps too. Be honest with your players; if there's a place they can take cover from incoming fire or get a bead on the opposition, draw it on the map and give them what they earned if they take that position. Clarify, clarify, clarify. The choices they make only matter if they are clear.

...show them pictures. Get online and find pictures of faces and places that fit your story. Print them out, big enough to hold up to the whole group and diverse enough to be your city. Show your players what Dominguez—the Mexican vampire who owns the nightclub on 7th Street—looks like by putting a picture in front of them and they'll never forget his name. Match that to a picture of his nightclub glittering in the midnight hour—a line of people waiting outside the door—and they'll be dying to meet him.

...share some history. Do some research about your city and share it with your players. Tell them all about the waterfront development that happened back in '86, the shooting that led to a race riot back in '65, the men who came back from the war in '48. The players' characters live in this fucking city; they ought to know that stuff. But don't let your prep work sit in a folder or notebook, unused. Any prep you do—any story you dig up—that doesn't jump off the page into your players' ears is *wasted.*

...ask about the past. The official record ain't all that matters. Ask your players to fill in the gaps, especially around the supernatural: "How did Watanabe come to power over the vampire clans?" or "How long has the Queen of Winter held the docks down here?" Build on their answers, even if they're incomplete or contradictory. Rumors are stronger than truth sometimes, especially when it comes to the supernatural underbelly of these dark streets.

...jump forward in time. If you're bored, say, "A week passes..." or "A few days later..." Time slips away from people, and your players' characters are no different. Ask them, "What have you been up to in that time?" if it makes them feel better, but manage the pace proactively, look for places where you can skip ahead to what matters. Take your time with the story when it's interesting, and pull back when the fiction needs room to develop.

...share the spotlight. Move the camera around the table, especially when a character hasn't been on screen for a while: "What have you been up to, Olivia?" If a scene gets tense or interesting, cut back and forth between another tense and interesting scene to keep the drama up; if a scene gets slow, wrap it up and move to a different player, a different conflict. You're the director, working the cameras to keep things moving, shifting the audience's focus to where it needs to be at this moment.

...zoom in and out. Vary the pace and length of conflicts by zeroing in and pulling back at the right times. Moves are flexible and fractal; you can resolve a whole battle with a single ***lead a group into battle*** roll or you might spell out each and every move that the players make, beat by fucking beat. Find the point of drama and dig in hard. Push the players to make choices, but be willing to step back to see the long-term consequences.

...take a fucking break. If you're stuck, take a break and think about your principles and moves. Your players will probably appreciate the time to think too, and everyone will come back to the table refreshed. When you get to a stopping point for the session, call it. Better to leave them wanting more—and give yourself time to do end of session moves—than it is to drag things on too long. Same goes with whole story arcs and campaigns; give yourself space so that you can stay excited about the rules and the material.

EIGHT
THE FIRST SESSION

BEFORE THE FIRST SESSION

This is it. This is where the magic happens. The first session.

The players have a pretty straightforward start to their work: they pick Archetypes and fill them out. You've got things a bit harder; you've got to design a **dark and political city**, an ecosystem of Debt and corruption that will **keep the characters' lives out of control and evolving** while **playing to find out what happens**. It's a lot to balance, and you haven't even met the characters yet.

Here's the trick: while the players get themselves set up with characters, you're going to build out the city, put them in tough spots, and MC the hell out of the start of the story like you had everything planned out—all without planning a damn thing.

MATERIALS AND PREP

Print out all the Archetypes you're going to offer to the players, and familiarize yourself with their moves and extras. You don't have to offer every Archetype—maybe you want to stay focused on street-level politics, so you don't offer The Wizard or The Fae—but take the time to learn the ones you make available. Also print out enough basic moves sheets for each player (and a copy of the MC worksheet and basic moves for yourself), and gather up some index cards, pencils, and dice, enough for everyone to have a set of materials in front of them during the session.

(You can find all the Archetypes and other printed materials at www.magpiegames.com/urbanshadows.)

Before folks show up to play, read this whole book. You can skim **The Archetypes** (79) and **The Long Game** (161), but be ready to reference them if needed. Glance through **The Storm** (247) to get familiar with Storms and Threats, but don't create a Storm yet. You need more information about the players' characters before you can set them up for real trouble.

Pick a city (or work with your players to pick a city). Think up a few city moves (204) that you can use to make the city feel real, and maybe even do some research on the city's history and pull down some pictures from the web to show your players. See 23 for more on researching your city and bringing that research to your first session.

STARTING THE FIRST SESSION

Once everyone's sitting around the table, start character creation. Go over the Archetypes, give a quick pitch for each one, and get your players rolling on filling out their playbooks. Answer questions when they come up, but give the players time to think and read, especially if they're unfamiliar with *Urban Shadows* or this style of play. See **The Characters** (27) for more in-depth information on creating characters; since your players probably haven't read the book, you might need to guide them through the process step by step.

Tell your players to pay close attention to the drama moves for the Archetype they select. Corruption, intimacy, and end moves all say quite a bit about the way the Archetype is structured, and can give players hints about how they might want to play the character. Generally, each Archetype is keyed to one or two stats, so point those out as well—"The Hunter is a high Blood and Mind Archetype, so your character would be good at fighting, escaping, and outsmarting their opposition. Does that sound like fun?"

Once mostly everyone—you might have one or two slowpokes—is ready to introduce their character to the other players, go ahead and start. The stragglers will catch up before it's their turn.

ASKING PROBING QUESTIONS

When the players are introducing their characters, jump in to ask probing questions. Try to alternate between questions directly about the characters and questions that are really about the city. The whole setting—your city, your characters, and your story—is radically open at the start; take advantage of the blank slate by pressing the players to fill in the holes.

Ryan's just finished creating his Fae, Volund (28). After he describes his character, his MC, Andrew, jumps in with a few **probing questions**.

"Tell me more about this crime you didn't commit, Volund. What happened?"

"Hmmm. My king thought I stole a necklace from him."

"Why did he think you stole it?"

"Actually, I think he gave it to me and then forgot. He saw me wearing it, and he banished me for my 'theft,' despite my protests."

Andrew thinks that's an odd answer: "Does the faerie king forget stuff like this often? Or was this surprising?"

"Oh, totally surprising. I still don't know what happened there."

Andrew nods. Good stuff. He can see that necklace—and the mystery around the king's accusations—making an appearance soon.

"Where do you live in the city, Volund? Hi-rise apartment downtown? At the edge of the suburbs?"

"It says on my Archetype that I get a simple apartment, so let's say that it's a few miles from downtown."

Andrew points at an area of the map he printed before the session. Ryan nods, and Andrew writes "Volund's apartment" directly onto the map. "What's that neighborhood like, Volund?"

"It's pretty rough. It was a good neighborhood when I moved in fifty years ago, but it's fallen to drugs and crime."

Andrew thinks that a rough neighborhood is a good chance to **explore a community deeply** *to avoid falling into stereotypes. "There's something that makes you stay there, though? Something beautiful. What is it?"*

"Oh, easy. The people that live in the area are really vibrant and active. They have block parties and street fairs, and I get to watch them surprise me often."

Since all these characters are people with families and history and culture, ask them about where they came from and how they ended up in the city. If someone comes from an immigrant family, ask them why they moved from their home country; if someone is "from the city," ask them why their family stayed all these years. And don't just ask questions like these of minority characters. Make characters that look white also explain where they're from and what their family cares about. Destroy the idea that any of them are just "living here" without reference to the people and events that brought them to this moment. No one is neutral. No one.

WHEN PROBING QUESTIONS FAIL

Don't be dissuaded if the initial answers players give to your questions feel flat or dry. Some players are great at adding interesting fiction to the city, but most players need a little help getting there. Look for **unspecified nouns and verbs**, **fat words**, and **generalities** to explore when things come up short.

»Getting Specific

Players who are stuck often put forward a lot of unspecified nouns and verbs in their initial answers. Dig into those unspecified words for specifics, and you might find that players have a lot of interesting ideas just below the surface.

If you ask, "Who owns this territory?":

> *"A gang of werewolves."*
>
> **"Which werewolves? A specific pack?"**
> *"Yeah, a pack of werewolves."*
>
> **"Whose pack?"**
> *"Uh...Rico's pack."*
>
> **"How do people know it's their territory?"**
> *"They are always around, patrolling and stuff."*
>
> **"How do they patrol, specifically?"**
> *"They drive around in cars, giving people a tough time if they don't like them."*

This kind of information is ripe for building upon. A pack of werewolves who drive around in cars looking for people to harass? That's an MC move waiting to happen!

»Unpacking Fat Words

In addition to vague nouns and verbs, players tend to use a lot of fat words that seem to convey meaning but actually hide the action, words like *love* and *patriotism* or even *fear* and *hate*. These words are fat with meaning, but it's often unexplored and undefined. We all know what you mean when you say "a 9mm," but two players might have very different ideas what "fear" looks like in the fiction.

If you ask, "How did Rico get this territory?":

> *"Rico is tough and stuff."*
>
> **"How does everyone know that Rico is tough?"**
> *"When he took the territory, he killed the whole pack* by himself. *When it was over, everyone was afraid of him."*
>
> **"When you say that people were 'afraid of him,' what do you mean? What does that look like?"**
> *"No one fucks with him. Not even the vampires, and they love roughing up werewolves."*

When you get more details about fat words—*tough* or *afraid*—they tend to solidify aspects of communities and individuals that you can draw on later. In the example, the MC has a bunch of information about Rico that's ready for use—he's tough, he's a killer, and even vampires don't fuck with him. Probably has some scars too.

»Exploring Generalities

When a player gives you a generality about a situation, place, or community, dig in deeper. Sometimes you might let one slide—as in the examples where words like "everyone" or "no one" went unchallenged to focus on unspecified nouns and fat words—but always circle back to them if possible.

If you say, "Tell me a little more about Rico's pack. You said they're *always* patrolling? Is it like a round-the-clock thing for all of them or do they set up shifts?"

"No one knows. They're just around a lot. Everyone says they're everywhere."

"Everyone? There's no one who says different?"
"Huh. Yeah, there's like one girl who says that she knows their schedule, that it's not random."

"Let's call her Leah. How do you know her?"
"I don't know her. People just say she says different."

"When you say people, do you mean like you heard about her from strangers or from a close friend?"
"No, Isaac. He's been my hookup before for this kind of info."

One trick for dealing with generalities is to give the player two options to think about. Most players won't pick either one, but triangulate some different answer that fits what they were trying to say. Your goal is to push them to be clear, not to drive them toward a specific place in the fiction.

DURING THE FIRST SESSION

After character creation (and all your questions), let the players know how things are going to go for the first session. Make it clear that you aren't going to run them through a plot or make them jump through hoops to finish an adventure. Say something like "*Urban Shadows* is all about playing to find out what happens, so we're going to figure out what's happening in the city together. I promise that, even though I don't have anything planned, the session is still going to be fun: you all are intriguing characters who lead interesting lives in a dramatic city. Just following you around is going to be fascinating, and we'll see where it takes us." Then MC the game with your principles and moves, pushing toward your agendas as much as you can.

Once things get moving, make heavy use of your MC worksheet: it's got all your principles and moves, places for you to write down NPCs, useful lists of names and drives, all that shit. Keep notes during the session so you can come back to them later to make Storms and Threats—we'll talk about these soon—out of the good stuff your players give you.

THINGS TO DO

MCing *Urban Shadows* is mostly about following your principles and making your moves—all in the service of your agendas—but here are a few things to focus on for the first session:

- Summon the shadows.
- Springboard off character creation.
- Ask questions constantly.
- Push on relationships and obligations.
- Call out moves when they happen.
- Offer moves when the players flinch.
- Frame scenes with multiple characters.
- Invoke every Faction.
- Let loose with some violence.

»Summon the shadows

Fill your city with monsters and demons, shadows and sacrifice. Show it to the players again and again; make sure they know that this is not a normal human metropolis, but a playground for the wizards and vampires and faeries that truly run the city. If you introduce a bar, make it a vampire bar where the ghoul bouncers require secret passcodes before admitting you; if you introduce a park, make it a hangout for trolls and fae-kin, all looking for a fix before they head back to Arcadia. Make the city something memorable by blanketing it in shadows that lie just outside of what normal mortals see everyday.

»Springboard off character creation

The players have given you a ton of hooks and mysteries to explore when making their characters: relationships that require attention, magical objects that attract thieves and scoundrels, conflicts with other PCs that are still unresolved. Grab something that interests you and bring it to bear immediately; show the players that you were listening when they said "I'm looking for my sister" or "My old mentor went crazy and disappeared." Make your early moves soft and obvious, softball pitches that tell your players exactly what's going on and telegraphs how they can "solve" the problem. Then follow the chaos they create!

»Ask questions constantly

Don't stop asking questions when you've finished character creation; make the question "What does that look like?" as common as "What do you do?" Ask for details about everything: their apartments, their clothes, their cars, their families. Take whatever they give you and write it down; reincorporate it right away if possible—"Yeah, this guy works for that werewolf pack you were talking about. Rico's the alpha of that pack, right?"—and then build on it later. Push them to define anything that's not defined; make them say what the city looks like as often as you tell them what they see in the shadows.

»Push on relationships and obligations

The PCs start the game with a bunch of history with each other and with the city. Most of this history manifests itself in the present as relationships and obligations that demand the PCs' attention. Players love to talk about how much control they have over all their little pieces, but you know that they're barely hanging on to their fragile little lives. Make your NPCs lean on the PCs in ways that make them scramble to hold on to everything, and offer opportunities for the PCs to gain the upper hand if they're willing to stretch their resources just a little bit further...

»Call out moves when they happen

Sometimes the players tell you what they want to do without making reference to the moves. Look for opportunities to say, "That sounds like you're trying to ***escape a situation***" or "If you want to ______, you'll have to make a move. I think ______ is a good fit." The players don't know all the moves yet, don't know when to pick up the dice, so call moves out as often as you can. Push them to roll the dice so that the mechanics of the game can kick in and drive the story forward. If players are avoiding moves, escalate your moves to the point that they have to act immediately to avoid disaster for themselves or someone they care about.

»Offer moves when the players flinch

Other times the players walk right up to a move and flinch at the last second, narrowly avoiding needing to roll something. Partly this is because they're nervous about committing to actions that might get them in trouble, but it's also because they don't know how far to push things. Look for places where they can get what they want by triggering a move—especially opportunities that fit the character really well—and push them to make the fucking move: "You're a big tough werewolf. Do you want to ***unleash an attack*** on this joker? It seem to me like he's just asking for you to rough him up for fucking with your territory."

»Frame scenes with multiple characters

Avoid any scene in the first session that starts with just one character. *Urban Shadows* characters are fairly self-sufficient for short periods of time, so a scene that's just supposed to set up a PC can sometimes end up going on for twenty minutes or more. That's fine later in the story, when everyone knows each other's characters and you're all fascinated by a tense scene featuring one character, but it's a real letdown to run a whole first session and not get a scene with another character. Push characters together early and often, even if it means using some **hard scene framing** (190) to get them into the same place.

»Invoke every Faction

Vary up the NPCs and plot threads you're bringing to the first session. Remember that the PCs need to deal with each Faction to advance, so leaving out Mortality or Power makes it hard for the characters to advance in the first session. Get characters from each Faction in scenes early—you can get players to trigger ***put a name to a face*** when an NPC mentions an important NPC or an important NPC is simply in a scene. If you're struggling to introduce a Night character to a mostly faerie plot, for example, frame a scene in which an important vampire or werewolf is on their way out of meeting with a faerie when the PCs show up. After all, the NPCs all know each other too, right?

»Let loose with some violence

Start a fight! The supernatural world isn't fucking around, and your PCs—especially The Hunter, The Veteran, The Wolf, and The Tainted—have plenty of their own firepower to hit back when attacked. You can even make the people attacking them a mystery: "This crew of demons rolls up on you, pistols out, knuckles cracked. What the fuck did you do to them?" If the player doesn't know, great! Now they've got a fight to survive *and* a mystery to solve. You don't have to build to violence; sometimes the violence comes looking for the PCs before they really understand what's happening.

TEACHING THE GAME

As you go through your first session, it's likely that you'll end up teaching the game to the players, either because they've never played a Powered by the Apocalypse game or because *Urban Shadows* is new to them. Here are some tips for teaching the game effectively in your first session:

»Pace Your Explanations

As the MC, you've got to walk the line between deluging the players with too much information and giving them so little guidance that they can't make informed decisions. It's tempting to sit down and explain every part of the Archetypes and basic moves before you start playing, but it would easily take you an hour just to go over everything. Instead, give the players the information they need to create their characters and leave the rest of it for when it comes up (or even for a later session).

For example, we find it best to explain the stats in broad terms when players are making characters—"Blood is about fighting and fleeing; bump it up if you think of your character as more physically capable in the face of danger"—instead of walking through each of the basic moves. It's much easier to explain exactly what Blood does the first time someone ***unleashes an attack*** or tries to ***escape a situation***. Give the players enough information to make choices, but structure that information so that it's not all coming at them at once.

»Be Generous and Patient

As the players are learning the game, they might find that a few of their choices at character creation are holding them back—The Wizard might decide that ***Teleport*** isn't that useful because it only goes a short distance or The Tainted might decide that *assassinating your patron's enemies* is a bit too serious a tone for the game. If a player finds that a choice they made on their Archetype doesn't work for them later, be generous and let them change it. New players often need some time to really internalize the mechanics in order to make choices.

In fact, patience and generosity are key to working with new players, period. Since you already know how the game works, the whole process of teaching the game can feel terribly slow and plodding. Be ready to explain a mechanic two or three times before folks get it; almost everyone needs to see a move work a few times before they fully grasp it. And let that patience extend to yourself as well; it sometimes takes a few sessions before even experienced MCs learn to run a new game really well. Give yourself the time to learn and teach!

»Model Great Behavior

Your players are probably awesome *people*—you picked them, right?—but that doesn't mean that they already know how to be awesome *players*.

During the first session, aggressively model for them what an awesome player looks like by acting as an engaged audience; talking as the NPCs and pushing the players for direct, in-character responses; and actively incorporating and reincorporating their contributions. Be excited when they trigger a move you weren't expecting or put forward an idea that has an interesting impact on the fiction.

Modeling good behavior is also about stepping in to address problems early. Use the X-Card (24) if you think a scene is going down a bad path, and directly address behavior at the table that's distracting or problematic—talking over other players, playing with a cell phone or computer—by talking openly and honestly about the group's norms. Other players at the table are counting on you to act as the authority, so look for opportunities to use that authority wisely or delegate it back to the group when necessary, e.g., "Are we all cool with using cell phones at the table?" or "Is it time for us to take a break?"

A NOTE ON ONE-SHOTS

It's possible that you end up playing *Urban Shadows* for just one session, maybe because your group is just trying out the system or you're at a gaming convention running for people who can't get together a second time. Either way, here are a few tips about making your only session count:

»Tie Everything Together

Look for opportunities to tie together NPCs, plot threads, and character relationships. Is someone looking for a powerful NPC who did them a favor? Maybe it's The Tainted's dark patron. Did someone recently move to the city for work? Perhaps another PC was the one offering a job. The tighter the web that binds the characters together, the faster things move in the fiction. Avoid giving any Debts to NPCs if possible, and keep things moving quickly through character creation.

On that same note, ask your players to focus their rumors and conflicts in the start of session move around a single issue in the city, perhaps even one you give to them. The characters all end up with different perspectives—usually people highlight a variety of Factions around the table—so you'll still end up with a solid mess of relationships and Debts, but you need to limit the spread of the plot so you can tell a coherent story in three to four hours.

»Go for the Throat

Make all your moves harder. Don't just threaten important NPCs, kill them; don't just hint at danger, crash into the PCs early and often. After all, none of this matters after the first session, right? It's not like you should be saving events for some Storm down the road or pacing the game like you're playing for five or six long sessions. Get there now or you run the risk of not getting there at all.

The same goes for your NPCs: introduce powerful characters who recklessly pursue their goals. Make this moment the culmination of years of planning, the moment at which things come together for the villains and scoundrels of your story. Catch the PCs up in the drama of political forces much larger than themselves, and put them into position to decide the fate of the city. Everything's in balance, all the forces posed against each other, and the PCs can tip things any way they want...assuming they're willing to live with the consequences.

»In Media Res

Above all else, start your players in the middle of things, narratively and mechanically. Frame scenes with multiple characters where they're already in the middle of shit and ask them to explain what happened—"Why *are* you two in the middle of stealing Watanabe's priceless sword? And what the hell went wrong?"—or put NPCs they care about in obvious harm's way and ask the PCs for help sorting it out. Don't be subtle here. Make it clear that you're jumping to the interesting stuff to make the session count.

Mechanically, start everyone with a free advance, three corruption, and a free corruption move. You want them to have a chance to earn an additional corruption advance during play, and sometimes an empty corruption track fills a bit slowly during the first session. You can skip going over advancement too, and just give everyone an additional advance halfway through the first session.

AFTER THE FIRST SESSION

Once you've played through the first session, start thinking about where things go from here. You've got a mess of relationships, a city in turmoil (it's always in turmoil, right? Fucking politics), and some hints at approaching danger—or maybe even some straight-up murderous fiends already heading for the PCs. Hopefully, all of this gets you and your players excited for the second session.

As all of this is bouncing around in your head, start to solidify the drama into Storms and Threats, complete with types, casts, and custom moves. See 260 in **The Storm** for the steps you need to create a Storm, but keep in mind that you're *not* writing a traditional plot, *not* setting up your players for a fall, *not* arranging all the fucking ducks in a row so things go the way you want. You're still going to **play to find out what happens**, even as you get a grasp on the politics and personalities that your city has to offer.

THE LONG EXAMPLE

What follows is an extended example of play that draws upon all the material in the book to this point. It calls out MC moves and principles throughout, as well as noting how the MC, Mark, is thinking about the emerging conflicts while the group plays to find out what happens. The session he's MCing is set in Boston and features three PCs:

- **The Hunter:** Susan—Black, female, casual clothing, friendly—a schoolteacher who hunts the fae for what they did to her brother. Played by Katherine.
- **The Oracle:** Daniel—White, male, warm clothing, paranoid—a distracted and nervous seer who is trying to master his increasingly violent visions. Played by John.
- **The Tainted:** Lana—Indigenous (Mohegan), female, dirty clothing, volatile—a transient demonic assassin and enforcer at the end of her rope. Played by Brendan.

This example is drawn from the first session of play. Earlier in the session, Susan put off Cora—a vampire who provides Susan with tools and supplies and who asked to meet with Daniel—because she became convinced that Cora was planning on hurting the seer. When Cora left her alone, Susan immediately rushed out to find Daniel and get him to a secure location.

Katherine says, "We need to get somewhere safe. I want to talk to some of my mortal allies about keeping Daniel away from Cora. We need to find a place to hole up until morning." She looks at John, and he nods. Katherine picks up the dice and gets ready to roll.

Mark says, "Sure, that sounds like **hitting the streets**. *Let's clarify what you're doing before you roll. Who are you going to?"*

"How about a local drug dealer? Manuel. He knows that I hunt things, so he trusts me. I think he could keep us safe." Mark nods. Katherine picks up the dice and rolls with Mortality. She's got Mortality +1, but ends up with a total of 5.

Mark reminds her to mark Mortality and looks over his moves. He considers **putting them in danger**, *but they're already on the run from Cora. That's sort of the same trouble a second time. He decides to* **surface a conflict, ancient or modern**; *Manuel and his lieutenants just died in a drug deal gone wrong, victims of a gang war they started last year. Mark's thinking offscreen—building fiction with characters that aren't standing in front of the PCs—but he knows it's all going to be revealed to Susan and Daniel when they show up at Manuel's looking for safety.*

"You roll up on Manuel's place, a squat two-story brick building in the heart of Dorchester. It's getting dark, and the streetlights on both sides of the street flicker at odd intervals. You've been here before?" Mark's setting up the punch, **asking loads of questions, and building on the answers**.

"Yeah, I met him here once when his guys found me out hunting. They brought me back here."

"Great. Does he usually post people around as lookouts?" Mark's letting Katherine build this place up, looking for ways to tell her things aren't normal when they get to the site.

Katherine nods. "Usually he has a few folks out on the street. They probably know me."

"None of them are out. The front door to his place is swinging open. As you step out of your car, you smell blood and gunpowder. You've got a bad feeling, like death visited too recently for your comfort. The street is deathly quiet. What do you do?"

"I pull out my magnum and approach slowly."

"How about you, Daniel? Do you stay in the car?" Mark's looking to get Daniel involved, sharing the spotlight to draw him further into the scene.

"No way," John says. "Daniel sticks with Susan."

Mark nods. Even when John talks in the third person about his character, Mark's still going to **address himself to the characters instead of the players**: *"You get the same bad feeling, Daniel. Your second sight is tingling hard, telling you that something happened here recently." Mark's* **being a fan of the characters**, *giving John's Oracle a lot of foreshadowing and encouraging him to make moves to get more information.*

But before John can do anything, Mark makes his move, revealing the conflict that killed Manuel. He's **cloaking the move in darkness**, *too: Katherine and John will see the deaths as the result of the fictional gang conflict rather than the result of an MC move selected off the list when Katherine missed: "As the two of you enter the building, Susan with her gun drawn ready for trouble, you see nearly a dozen bodies. No one is moving." John inhales a bit.*

John says, "Daniel scopes the place out, picking up and touching things that seem important. What happened here?"

"Are you **investigating a place of power**? *" Mark asks. John nods, and rolls with Mortality. He gets an 8, high enough to hit. Mark says, "Mark Mortality! On a 7-9, you see through to the 'reality underneath.' This was*

a deal gone bad between old enemies. A case of money is open on the table with a few kilos of cocaine next to it. It looks like everyone here died in a shootout. Ugly stuff. Manuel's body is in the corner, next to the bar."

"I point the drugs and money out to Susan," says John. "It looks like things went bad here."

Katherine frowns. "Crap. No safety here, then?" she asks Mark.

Mark smiles and **offers an opportunity with a cost**. *"Well…this whole place is basically a safehouse. Manuel could have locked it down, but he let these folks in trying to close a deal. If you got it cleaned up before all these bodies start to smell, you could probably stay here a long time. Do you know any demons who might be good at getting rid of corpses?" Mark's* **pushing the characters together**, *hoping to get Brendan's character involved in the scene.*

Katherine grins. "I call Lana." Everyone looks at Brendan.

"Yo, what's up?'

"I'm **cashing in a Debt** *for a moderate favor: 'Remember how you almost got me killed last week? I need to make a bunch of dead bodies disappear... tonight. That's something you can do, right?'"*

"Lana groans," Brendan says, "She says, 'I don't have time for something like that. I got stuff going on.'"

"Are you **refusing the Debt***?" Mark points at Brendan's dice. He nods vigorously and rolls. Snake eyes. Lana's got to honor the Debt or face some nasty consequences. Mark says, "Looks like she's not getting very far with you, Susan. What do you say back that closes the noose on her?"*

"Seriously, Lana. I need this. Now."

"Argh. Fine, where are you? I'll be there in a few minutes."

Since things seem to be getting a bit quiet (and all the PCs are getting along just a bit too well), Mark makes an MC move: **warn someone of approaching danger**.

"It takes you a few minutes, Lana, but you head over to the safehouse. As you park your motorcycle, you spot a vampire watching the place from across the street. He's talking on the phone, furtively glancing at the safehouse and Susan's car."

Brendan says, "I try to **figure him out**. *What's he doing here?" Brendan rolls and misses. Not his day.*

Mark decides to **mobilize resources to shift the odds**. *The vamp would love to get Daniel by himself, but the arrival of Lana makes that too hard. He'll get Cora and come back. "As you start to get a bead on the guy, he notices you. The car rumbles to life, and he drops it into gear and pulls out into the street. You're not sure why he was here."*

Brendan says, "Lana shrugs. No need to get worked up about some stupid vampire. I'll go in and start cleaning up bodies."

"Great. Let's jump forward a bit. Cool with everyone? You spend an hour or so cleaning things up and trying to make the place liveable. What do you do with the bodies, Lana?" **More questions**.

"I move them to a truck out front, wrapped in tarps. I'll probably **hit the streets** *with Wild to see if I can get a demon or faerie to take them off my hands."*

*"Sure, we'll get there in a minute." Mark's delaying that move, pushing it into the future to deal with the action right now. The city's moving, and Lana will have to keep up. "As you're loading the last of the bodies into the truck, though, you see a sedan pull up. A few vampires get out, two of them holding shotguns." Mark's making a Night move here (***display an aggressive show of force***), softly, to follow through on Brendan's miss earlier. "The woman who gets out of the passenger seat is Cora. Lana, go ahead and* **put a name to a face** *with her."*

Lana, rolling with Night, hits an 8 on **put a name to a face**. *Mark says, "You know her only by reputation. She's an up-and-coming vamp, trying to claim all of the industrial area by the river, the same neighborhood where Susan's warehouse is located. She's known for sudden, violent outbursts when she doesn't get what she wants. What do you do?"*

"I back up into the house and yell, 'Susan, someone here to see you.'"

Mark grins. "Cora waits patiently out front for Susan to come out. Susan, what do you do?" Mark's **giving them time to weigh in**, *letting Susan drive the action now that Cora is on the scene. He's made his moves, and he wants to see how they're going to play out.*

Katherine asks, "I'm still in the house, right?" Mark nods. "Okay, I tell Daniel to run."

John shakes his head. "No deal, Susan. I gotta stay with you."

"Daniel, you have to leave. They are going to do something horrible to you, I know it. Run. We'll cover you."

"I had a vision, Susan. If I leave, you and Lana both die."

Mark interjects: "That's a false prophecy, right? Mark corruption! What do you do, Susan?"

"I can't let him stay, even if he's got a prophecy. I **cash in a Debt** *and say, 'I've been protecting you, Daniel. That's not going to stop. You need to run.'" John frowns.*

"Do you want to **refuse to honor the Debt***, Daniel?" Mark asks. "Your Heart is -1, so you're not good at putting people off."*

"No, I'm good. I grab my stuff and run. Can I roll **escape***?"*

"Yeah, I think Susan heading out to meet with Cora is a good enough opportunity. You've got a pretty low Blood, though. Do you want to maybe **let it out** *first to look for the best path out and get a +1 forward?" Mark's suggesting moves, getting them used to the idea of the whole system without rushing them, and encouraging the players to make use of the advantages they can get.*

"Yes. Definitely."

"What does that look like?" **Questions, questions, questions.**

"I push myself to see into the future a bit in the hopes that it helps me get out of here. Let's see how it goes!" He rolls with Spirit +2 and gets a 10. John smiles: "I'll take the +1 forward and avoid marking corruption." Mark nods.

"You see a bunch of alternate futures rushing by you, some with you walking out the front door, others with you sneaking out a window. It's too much to process, but you know going out through the side window and up on the roof is the best bet. Cora probably doesn't have anyone there yet. Go ahead and roll **escape***." John rolls with his +1 forward and gets a 10. His +1 forward saves him from more messy complications with a 7-9.*

John picks you leave something important behind. *Mark says, "You're out the window, on the roof, and climbing onto the next building before you realize that you forgot your cell phone. Looks like you'll have to find some other way of getting in contact with Susan when you get somewhere safe. We'll come back to you soon!*

"Out front, Cora is direct about what she wants, Susan," Mark says, **offering an opportunity with a cost***. "She's on edge, maybe even a little high, and*

she's no longer asking: 'I want him, Susan. I've been keeping you equipped in your silly little war against the faeries, and it's time to pay up. Where is he?' She's **cashing in a Debt** *to get you to give her an honest answer."*

"Can I just lie to her?"

"You can try to **trick** *her, but first you've got to deal with the Debt. Remember that it has some weight with you in the fiction. You really do feel like you owe her."*

"Yeah, okay. I say, 'I can't tell you that, Cora. He's a friend.'" Katherine rolls to **refuse to honor the Debt** *and gets a 10+. She's in the clear for now.*

Mark says, "She looks like she's about to lose her shit. 'I've already talked to Wren. She says that Daniel is mine for as long as I want him. He's mine to take.'" Mark's pushing here, escalating by **revealing a deal done in her absence** *to put the characters at the center of conflicts. More soft moves that keep the tension up in the scene but still leave the action in the PCs' hands.*

"Now I lie. 'He's not here, Cora. I don't know where he is.'" Katherine rolls to **mislead, distract, or trick** *with Mind, but comes up short with a 4. Even Lana can't help. Ouch.*

"Cora laughs. She turns back to her vampire goons, and says 'Cute. She thinks she has friends.'"

"I pull out my gun."

"Hold on. Cora's not done." Mark's going to have the vampires make a Faction MC move **claim territory from the weak or foolish**, *but he's still* **cloaking moves in darkness**, *making it look like what Susan said actually changed Cora's opinion of her. He didn't plan for things to escalate here—he's* **playing to find out what happens**—*but Susan's blocked every attempt Cora's made to get to Daniel. Now Mark's got to say* **what the city demands**: *Cora's got power here and she's going to use it.*

"Before you can react, Cora's hand is around your throat, her nails piercing your skin. Take 1-harm. She pushes you back into the safehouse, out of sight of the street. 'He's mine,' she says. 'And if I can't have him, I'll take you and this house and whatever you're doing here.' Susan, you're disoriented by Cora's strength, but you'll pull yourself together in a moment. Lana, what do you do?"

"Fuck this, I follow them into the house and activate my demon form." Mark smiles. Brendan rolls a 10+ with Blood, and chooses Gain armor+1—*for a total of 2-armor with* **Tough as Nails**—*and* a 3-harm hand demonic weapon.

"What does your demon form look like?'

"Lana's got horns and spikes on her head, flames on her hands, feathered wings, rocklike charred flesh, and burning eyes. I'm pretty intimidating."

"Cora, still holding Susan up in the air by her throat, says, 'Erick, Felipe, Nadir, please kill her for me.'" Mark's **treating everyone according to their station***—playing to the idea that Lana is the biggest threat here—and* **naming everyone, giving them drives**. *Cora's drive (*to expand my territory*) is pushing these three vampires (*to serve the powerful*). "Lana, what do you do?"*

"My hands are on fire, right? I grab one of these assholes by the face." Brendan rolls with blood and gets a 9, just short of the 10+. "Okay, I'll inflict terrible harm, and… Hmm. I don't want to get put in a spot, *so I'll take* they inflict harm on me *and hope my armor holds up."*

Katherine says, "Wait! I can help, right?"

"Sure, what does that look like?" **More questions!**

"I grab my gun and shoot at them to distract them while Lana attacks them. Is that **distract** *or* **lend a hand***?"*

"It's **lend a hand**. *Since we're still resolving Lana's move, you're just* **lending a hand** *to her efforts. Roll with Wild!" Kathrine rolls with Wild +0 and comes up short. Snake eyes. "Ouch. As you try to get your gun out, Cora smiles and snatches it from you, dangling it just out of reach with her other hand. 'What are you planning on doing with this?'" Mark's* **activating her stuff's downside**, *reminding her that her guns and gear can be snatched away by a clever opponent.*

Mark turns to Brendan: "You grapple the first vampire that comes toward you, Lana, your flaming hands burning his skin to ash immediately. As the other two vampires lower their shotguns, you shift your grip directly to his face. He screams and his whole body starts to shake. You inflict 4-harm and drop him to the ground." Mark figures these guys can take 5-harm before they die, but 4-harm to the face is pretty crippling. He decides that the first vampire is out of the fight, unconscious and near death.

Mark continues: "The other two open fire, inflicting 2-harm total—3-harm from each shotgun minus your 2-armor. What do you do?"

"I don't want to fight all of them with Susan in such a bad spot. I yell at them to run away. Maybe **let it out***?"*

"Sounds to me like you're **persuading an NPC** *with threats."*

"Yeah, totally. I'm Heart +1, so that makes sense." Brendan rolls with Heart, but only gets a 5. He groans. "I guess they don't run away."

"It's a miss, not a failure," says Mark. "The two vampires totally book it. They just saw their friend get turned to ash while you shrugged off two shotgun blasts. They're out." Mark's **being a fan** *of Lana. She's supposed to be scary and awesome!*

"Okay…"

"But as they flee, you hear a sharp crack and feel a sudden pain in your side. There's Cora, Susan's gun outstretched toward you, her other hand holding Susan up in the air." Mark's **inflicting harm** *as established, escalating the tension of the scene by* **giving everything a price**. *How much longer will Lana keep fighting for Susan? "Susan, how much damage does your gun do?"*

"Uh. It's 3-harm...but it's also blessed."

Mark stops for a second. He hadn't thought about that. He thought he was just going to **inflict harm** *on a heavily armored character, but the blessed gun cuts right through that. Mark's* **playing to find out what happens**, *though, so he lets it ride.*

"Oh, man. Rough. That's enough to fill up your whole harm track, right?" Brendan nods. "You fall. Susan, you see Lana's demon form flicker, and blood spreads across the floor, red and thick. What do you do?"

"Can I slide away and **escape** *while Cora's distracted?"*

"She's got a hand on you, so I don't think you have an opportunity yet. You might be able to shake her off and get out of her immediate reach, though, by **keeping your cool**."

Katherine frowns. She doesn't have a good roll for that. "I really don't want to stay here and get killed. I'll squirm away."

"What are you trying to avoid?" Mark's following the move, even when Katherine's distracted, making sure she sets the stakes before the dice hit the table.

"I don't want to get eaten!" She rolls, and gets a 7.

Mark says, "Okay, here's what it's going to cost to **keep your cool** *and avoid Cora's fangs. You can squirm away, but Cora will take a shot at you with your own gun. 3-harm, right in the back." It's a hard bargain, but it's* **what the city demands**. *Cora's not going to let up now, not when she's got the upper hand.*

"Nah, I can't do it. Too much harm. Wait. If I let her feed on me, maybe I can get back my gun? She'd be distracted, right?"

Mark smiles. That's awesome. He's **a fan of the players' characters**, *both when they are terrifying and effective—Lana melting the vampire's face—and when the fiction puts them in terrible danger and they have to survive. "What does that look like?"*

"I struggle a bit in her grasp, but tilt my head toward the door so that my neck is exposed."

"Yeah, that's great. You see Cora look around the room, but her eyes are drawn to your neck. She says, 'Ah, this day is shit. You cost me a vamp, and I still don't have Daniel. At least I can get a meal in." Mark's making another Faction move: Cora's **making the best of a bad situation**. *It's a pillowy soft move, setting Katherine up for* **mislead, distract, or trick**. *"*

Katherine rolls and hits on a 9: she chooses create an opportunity *and* expose a weakness or flaw. *Mark says, "Her teeth sink into your neck. It's blissful, better than the best sex you've ever had...for both of you. The gun slips from Cora's fingers as she drinks deeply, and you hold yourself together long enough to grab it before it hits the floor. You have an opportunity to use the gun, but you also notice that her neck is exposed while she feeds. A shot there could be lethal, even for a vampire as strong as Cora. I'll give you +1-harm. That said, you take 2-harm as she sucks the life right out of you. "*

"I shoot her in the fucking throat!"

"Okay, before you roll **unleash an attack**, *I think this feeding counts as intimacy. What's your intimacy move?" Mark's* **dirtying the hands of all involved**, *reminding Susan that Cora is a person, not a thing, not a target. He wants Susan to kill her, but he also wants the death to stick with Susan and feel real.*

"It says 'ask them a question; they must answer it honestly. They will ask you a question in return; answer it honestly or mark corruption.' I ask, 'What do you want Daniel for?'"

"In between gulps of your blood, she whispers into your ear, 'I need his heart. It will show me how to kill my sire.' She pauses drinking for a moment, and says, 'Do you want me to kill you...or make you one of us?"

"I'm not going to answer that honestly. I'll mark the corruption, and say 'Fuck you' right before I kill her." Mark nods.

Susan rolls her **unleash** *and hits a 12. She chooses* Inflict terrible harm. *Mark says, "3-harm weapon, +1-harm for* Inflict terrible harm, *+1-harm for* *the weakness is 5-harm total. Cora dies, her body turning to ashes in your arms, like a lover vanishing in the wind. The last thing you feel is her lips on your neck. You drop to the floor, exhausted."*

Mark turns to Brendan: "Lana, you feel your last breaths shudder out from your body as the gunshot rings out through the safehouse. You die. Please read your death move." Mark's pushing the spotlight back to Lana; he knows that Lana's death move gives her a way out, so the fiction is going to snowball from here, not end.

Brendan smiles. "'When you die, cash in all the Debts your patron owes you to come back. If you have none, your patron will ask someone else to pay the Debt for you. If they refuse, time's up. It's been a good run.' I don't have any Debts on my patron yet."

Mark turns back to Katherine: "Susan, Cora may be dead, but you hear a low rumble in the quiet safehouse. You know that Lana is gone, her breathing stopped completely. In the darkness, you hear a chitinous chuckle, an otherworldly sound of some demon just out of reach. You know it's come to make a deal."

Mark makes the best move he's got: "Susan, what do you do?"

NINE
THE STORM

A CITY FULL OF STORMS

After the first session, you'll have all sorts of NPCs to play with and build up, people and organizations that fill your city with malice and hope, characters dripping with dark futures and impending catastrophes. In other words, you'll have the raw elements for a whole bunch of plots, each promising to take the PCs to interesting places.

Those plots are a great big fucking trap.

When you start thinking about how to get this PC into a room with that NPC or start figuring out how to frame a big scene that brings all the PCs together or start choosing which NPCs are expendable and which aren't...you aren't playing to find out what happens anymore. You're *deciding what happens* and turning the game into a rote exercise, a lie you tell your players to have them to jump through your hoops.

The city's too big for one person's head. Don't try to bottle it up. Don't try to control it. **Play to find out what happens**.

In between sessions—when you've got some time to think—you need to figure out what your city wants, and you need to decide which NPCs are plotting and scheming to get their way. You need to have interesting situations that bring the PCs together because they care about stakes—and not because you trick them into coming together—and you need to know what it means for the PCs to lose control. Prep isn't the same as control.

Instead of plots, you'll create Threats, forces that work to change the city according to their natures. As those Threats grow and build, you'll also create Storms, collections of linked Threats that unify and focus your story to bring the PCs together—on the same side or in conflict—to confront the city's future. This is your prep.

All of the prep work you do becomes part of the city, what the city demands. Remember that. What you commit to when you build your Threats is real. It's not to be tossed aside or undermined or ignored. These decisions matter as much as any decision the players make. The fiction you define here is part of the game, resolute and focused on its own future.

CREATING THREATS

Each Threat is an individual, organization, or magical phenomenon in the city that threatens the PCs, their interests, or things that matter to them. It might target the PCs directly, or it may work alongside their plans, altering the city in ways they might support or oppose. A rogue mage working to kill a rival is a Threat, so long as the PCs care about one of the two wizards, but so is a magical portal that seduces mortals into feeding it children in the hopes of acquiring great power. Most PCs, in our experience, tend to get upset when innocent people go missing.

When you create a new Threat:

- Choose a Threat type and subtype
- Create an NPC cast and description
- Assign stakes to a countdown clock (optional)
- Design any necessary custom moves (optional)

If you want to see a fully constructed Threat, skip ahead to 258 for "Ley Lines Loose," a sample Threat for a Kansas City-based *Urban Shadows* game.

CHOOSING THREAT TYPES

There are five types of Threats. When you create a Threat, choose one:

- Revolution
- Power Play
- Passion
- Ritual
- Territory

The Threat types describe the broad thrust of a Threat, the overall driving force behind the danger, and MC moves associated with the conflict. Remember that Threats may be individuals, organizations, or magical phenomena: a revolution might be a single powerful mage throwing off his chains of servitude or a collection of faeries who flee Arcadia in the hopes of setting up their own court. The Threat type describes how they threaten the status quo, not the structure or organization through which they work; all of that is up to you.

After you pick a Threat type, pick a subtype as well, a specific frame for the conflict you're building. Sometimes you come to this list looking for a subtype—"Hmmm. Which one best describes the way Rico's pack is behaving?"—and sometimes the subtypes will inspire new perspectives—"Huh. What if Rico is acting out of *love* for his territory rather than a lust for power?"

Each subtype comes with an **impulse**, a drive for the Threat similar to a drive for individual characters. Characters associated with the Threat still keep their personal drives, but your job is to make the Threat as a whole fulfill its impulse through basic MC moves and Threat moves—you might even note when characters have impulses associated with a Threat. A character caught between their own drive and their Threat's impulse may exhibit some strange, contradictory behavior, oscillating back and forth between two competing concerns, trying to meet both and failing to meet either.

In addition to impulses, Threat types also give you a list of Threat moves that can be made any time you would normally make a basic or Faction move, provided that the Threat itself can be brought to bear against the PCs. You can read more about how to use Threat moves on 254.

»Threat Type: Revolution

Revolutions attempt to upend the social order, making paupers into kings and plowshares into swords. They desire to thwart the status quo as a political project, and hope to find resources in those oft overlooked.

Threat Subtypes:

- Idealist (Impulse: craves sacrifice, its own or others)
- Revolt (Impulse: craves justice, bloody and swift)
- Strike (Impulse: craves respect and security)
- Mob (Impulse: craves violence and satiety)
- Infestation (Impulse: craves acceptance)

MC Moves for Revolution:

- Sacrifice to turn ripples into waves
- Display the nature of the world it inhabits
- Insult, affront, or offend someone powerful
- Offer, but with personal strings attached
- Offer, but with messy and uncertain outcomes
- Capture someone powerful and important
- Threaten something vulnerable and crucial
- Destroy a public figure/landmark/group
- Refuse aid: escalate with threats

A revolution, even in the best of conditions, is a wildfire, narrowly controlled by those who claim to speak for the masses. Many clever demagogues have found themselves on the receiving end of mob justice, caught between their egos and abilities.

»Threat Type: Power Play

Power Plays are forces set in motion by elders and elites, designed to leverage resources into bigger and better things. They are the clever and careful machinations of the powerful, sometimes pitted against other titans and sometimes turned on their own people.

Threat Subtypes:

- Coup (Impulse: to steal power in moments of weakness)
- Feint (Impulse: to draw an enemy into the open)
- Alliance (Impulse: to satisfy another to gain favor)
- Annexation (Impulse: to wrest control from others)
- Sabotage (Impulse: to create and exploit weaknesses)

MC Moves for Power Play:

- Reveal a plan too far gone to stop
- Offer an alliance, temporary or lasting
- Showcase a weakness for all to see
- Showcase a strength to a private audience
- Attack someone cautiously, holding reserves
- Attack someone suddenly, without warning
- Exploit hesitation or delays with decisive action
- Demand reparations or considerations
- Buy out someone's allies

Power plays are usually centered around a powerful NPC, but power is relative. An elder vampire lord might attempt to secure territory from other powerful wizards and warlocks, but a local community leader might also try to secure new resources for development in a low-income area from a city council or gang of vampires.

»Threat Type: Passion

Passion Threats are people, organizations, and phenomena motivated by a specific intense emotion. They burn bright and quick, caring nothing for the consequences others suffer for their actions and making the personal political wherever they go.

Threat Subtypes:

- Revenge (Impulse: to strike without warning)
- Love (Impulse: to protect)
- Beauty (Impulse: to sacrifice)
- Rage (Impulse: to victimize and cause pain)
- Envy (Impulse: to take more than its share)

MC Moves for Passion:

- Exhaust a resource, wastefully and completely
- Strike out with reckless abandon
- Display the contents of its heart
- Sacrifice a great deal for a crucial advantage
- Sacrifice a great deal to send a message
- Sacrifice a great deal for nothing
- Cling to reason, tradition, or injustice
- Beg someone for help with a dangerous problem
- Ruin something purposefully, callously, or stupidly

Passion Threats most often work through individuals in the throes of grief or rage or lust, people who care more for accomplishing their objective than they do for their own existence. They may find others like them to share in such pain or turn to magic and ritual for the power they need to accomplish their goals.

»Threat Type: Ritual

Ritual threats are a series of planned events or triggers that harness supernatural forces to accomplish a specific goal. Rituals are never accidental: someone must be behind the ritual, intentionally working towards its end.

Threat Subtypes:

- Theft (Impulse: to take something from another)
- Containment (Impulse: to capture and restrain)
- Destruction (Impulse: to wreak death and collapse)
- Link (Impulse: to create bridges and connections)
- Restore (Impulse: to heal and mend)

MC Moves for Ritual:

- Release something once sealed away
- Summon something new and original
- Unleash chaos, fear, or death
- Kill someone important, violently and publicly
- Kill someone meaningless, quietly and inconspicuously
- Bind someone or something to a place
- Snatch up resources, covertly or cleverly
- Alter or corrupt a facet of the city
- Exploit an unrelated conflict or conquest

Rituals must have a driving force behind them, so they tend to be pushed forward by powerful organizations or individuals who have the resources to unlock tremendous powers. They can be completed by any Faction, including Mortality, but they are often fragile and easily disrupted.

»Threat Type: Territory

Territory Threats represent a part of the city endangering the status quo, undermining the security of people living close by the locus of change. They are the city made living, pieces of a metropolis that work to disrupt the character's lives.

Threat Subtypes:

- Surge (Impulse: to burn or consume)
- Illusion (Impulse: to entice and enthrall)
- Stronghold (Impulse: to deny access)
- Expansion (Impulse: to create and multiply)
- Quagmire (impulse: to capture and imprison)

MC Moves for Territory:

- Shift, move, or rearrange a place
- Present a new path or structure
- Seal off something in an obviously magical way
- Seal off something in a mundane and pedestrian way
- Seize something, forcibly and quickly
- Infest and overtake everything in sight
- Display the reality underneath

The focus of a territory Threat can be as small as a single building or as large as the entire city, natural—like a park or ley line—or constructed—like a shopping mall or skyscraper. Characters may be responsible for the initial events that awake the Threat, but the territory itself must start to drive the fiction after the awakening. The affected area may itself be the Threat—a haunted house—or it may house the Threat—an illegal black market in fae organs.

MAKING THREAT MOVES

The Threat moves associated with each Threat type are yours to make, though they may make use of NPCs or physical features of the cityscape. If you choose to ***release something once sealed away*** as a part of a ritual Threat, it may be a demon intentionally released by vampire cultists as part of the ritual or an evil spirit that takes advantage of the situation to gain the upper hand on its bondage. You're the one making the move, not the cultists or the spirit or the demon, so you aren't bound by the intention or agency of the characters. You still **cloak your moves in darkness**, though, such that you'll often work through these agents to make your moves.

You can make a Threat move anytime you have an opportunity to make an MC move. See 189 in **The Master of Ceremonies** for a refresher on when to make an MC move.

Elora's been on the hunt for Rico for a while now, but he's moving fast, claiming territory left and right without regard for the consequences. Mark, the MC, has worked up Rico's pack as a **passion: envy (impulse: to take more than its share) Threat***, so the next time Elora's out hunting, Mark makes his move. He might have the Threat…*

*…***exhaust a resource, wastefully and completely***: "The park near Rico's territory is filled with dead animals, some gnawed down to the bone and others barely consumed. Wolf tracks. Feces. Blood. What do you do?"*

*…***strike out with reckless abandon***: "The first wolf lands on the front of your car like a freight train, crushing the engine. Your car shudders to a halt. You're in Watanabe's territory, but the pack doesn't seem to care. Three more wolves emerge from the darkness, growling and snarling. What do you do?"*

*…***display the content of its heart***: "You're not sure how Rico got your number, but it's definitely him on the voicemail. 'Stay out of my fucking territory, Elora. I'm the king here, not you. You're nothing. You're all nothing. Stay. The. Fuck. Out.' What do you do?"*

CAST AND DESCRIPTION

After you decide on a type and subtype for the Threat, add a **cast** and **description**. Threats aren't just ticking time bombs; they're conflicts that feature characters and aspects of the city pushing toward their own goals.

The cast is the list of NPCs who are associated with the Threat; some of them may already exist and some may be new creations that you're adding to the city. If someone in the cast has a group, like Rico's werewolf pack, give them tags based on the size and scope of the group (see 157 for more on groups); if they have gear or other magical tools, figure out what you need to know about those resources to present them effectively.

The description briefly fleshes out the nature of the conflict, explaining what the Threat is about and the stakes of the conflict. Make sure the central tension in the Threat is clear; who or what already opposes the primary actors in the Threat? What keeps them from simply getting what they want? Nothing new happens in the city without opposition, even if that opposition is unable to hold the line as the Threat advances.

COUNTDOWN CLOCKS

If a Threat has forward momentum—it has plans or designs to accomplish a goal rather than support the status quo—give it a **countdown clock**. A countdown clock is a way to remind yourself that the Threat wants to move, wants to push forward against opposition. Not every Threat gets one: if all Rico wants to do is hold his territory, he doesn't need a countdown clock.

Countdown clocks are prescriptive and descriptive—they tell you what will happen if the Threat is left unchecked and act as measuring stick for how much more time is left before the Threat is fully realized. If the Threat is ignored, you'll tick down each section of the clock, eventually reaching the Threat's 12:00 consequences, hard and irreversible (prescriptive); if something acts to reach a portion of the Threat's future plans early—like the PCs encouraging Rico to kill Anton early—move the clock directly to that section (descriptive).

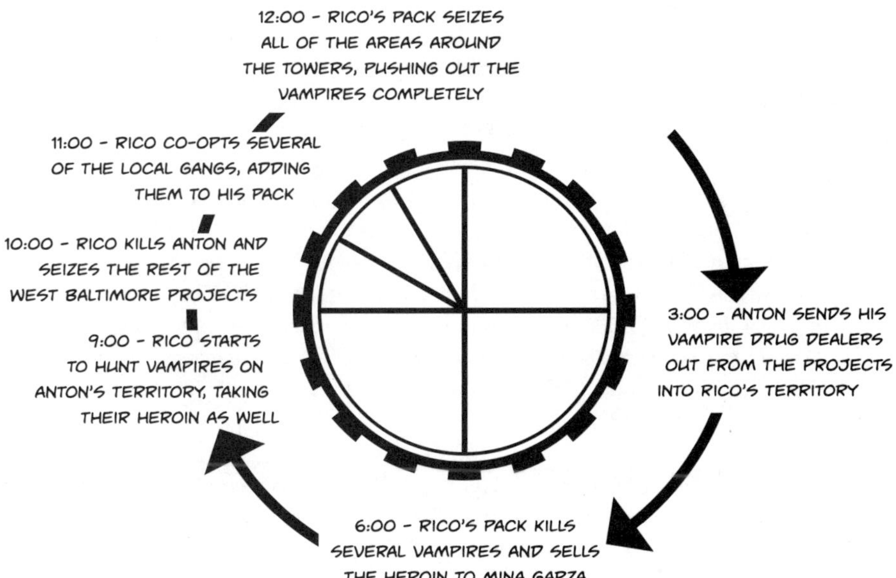

When you create a countdown clock, look at the Threat's future. What might happen? What stakes are in play? At what point does the Threat alter the city's future? At what point does it achieve its full expression? Note some points of obvious change around the clock, stuff the PCs would probably notice, in accordance with the following:

0:00–6:00–Rising action. The Threat is building, still reversible if the right moves are made.

9:00–The shift is coming. The signs are distinct and unmistakable. The Threat could still be interrupted, but the costs are mounting.

10:00–Irrevocable change. At this point, the Threat impacts the city in some nonreversible way.

11:00–Further down the road. Whatever changes occurred at 10:00 take real root.

12:00–Doom. Whatever the Threat wanted to bring to pass has come to pass.

These portents should be stuff that's outside the PCs' control. You're not trying to predict their actions or put them in specific scenes: each section of the clock notates the action that would occur if the PCs didn't exist or refused to interfere. The clock is an arrow, drawn back and ready to fire, waiting for the PCs to alter its course.

When you make a Threat move, consider making a move that advances one of your clocks. Advancing the clock isn't a move by itself—the clock is a measure of what *has* happened—but look at your clocks to see if there's a move that also might push the clock forward.

Mark has listed "Rico kills Anton and seizes the rest of the West Baltimore projects" as his 10:00 slot on Rico's countdown clock. When one of the PCs misses a roll to **investigate a place of power** *in the projects, Mark decides the Threat will* **sacrifice a great deal for a crucial advantage.** *He says, "As you're walking up to the lot surrounding the projects, Blue comes up to you. 'Hey, sister. You don't want to be here right now. Rico and Anton just got in a scrap. Rico lost some guys but Anton's fucking dead. Let's go.' What do you do?"*

Mark's made his move and adjusts his countdown clocks accordingly. Rico's Threat has advanced to the point that there's no turning back. No matter what the PCs do, Rico's altered the city's future forever, and upended the status quo. How much further will they let him push?

Feel free to alter or rewrite a section of the clock if it's no longer relevant—like if Anton gets killed by a PC at the start of the second session—but allow the PCs to disrupt or derail a Threat with concentrated action. It's possible that one of Rico's lieutenants would pursue some of his goals in his absence, but it's likely that no one could rally the troops and follow through on a plan if Rico dies.

CUSTOM MOVES

If you want to further develop a Threat, add custom moves. Note that these moves aren't for you; you already got a new set of MC moves when you picked the Threat's type. Instead, these are for the PCs, additional options or restrictions on their engagement with the Threat. Generally, moves have the following parts:

- **a trigger:** "When X happens..."
- **an outcome:** "...then Y." Sometimes it's a roll, other times it's just an outcome.
- **stakes:** if it has a roll, define 10+, 7-9, and 6-.

If a move involves a roll, 10+ means things work out fine for the PC, 7-9 means they pay some costs or endure some complications, and 6- means that things go to shit. But it's all relative. You might want things to be pretty soft all over—6- is just rough, not tragic—or for even the 10+ to be pretty fucking bad.

> *When you* **sample Anton's heroin**, *roll with Spirit. On a 10+, you feel his blood through the drugs: ask him a question and he'll answer it honestly. On a 7-9, you only get an impression: the MC will tell you what you see. On a miss, Anton knows you're using: he gets to ask you a question that you must answer honestly.*

> *When you* **enter Rico's territory**, *roll with Mind. On a 10+, the werewolves come at you hard, but you see them coming. On a 7-9, you catch wind of them, but only moments before they strike. On a miss, you're vulnerable and separated from the others when the pack strikes.*

You can even ape the structure from Archetype moves:

> **Claw and Tooth:** *When you* **unleash an attack** *on Rico with a close or hand weapon, pick an additional option off the 7-9 list, even on a miss.*

> **Reaper:** *When you try to* **figure Anton out**, *roll with Blood instead of Mind. He's a predator, and he hides his intentions from all those who are prey.*

See **The Shadows** on 271 for more on writing custom moves. If you write up custom moves for your sessions, please share them in our G+ Community (bit.ly/usgplus)!

SAMPLE THREAT: LEY LINES LOOSE

We designed the following Threat for Jahmal to use in his Kansas City-based *Urban Shadows* game. He's generously allowed us to reprint it here:

Name: Ley Lines Loose

Type: territory (surge)

Impulse: to burn or consume

Cast: Melissa Bachnall, the oldest and most respected wizard in Kansas City (Power); Edwin Gonzales, city councilman in the pocket of the wizards (Mortality); Kip Erhart, *Kansas City Star* freelance reporter (Mortality); Lucy Davies, city planner and geomancer, architect of the reconstructions (Power).

Description: Melissa Bachnall and Lucy Davies are spearheading a campaign—using their sway within the city council through Edwin Gonzales—to reconstruct the city's ley lines to create a powerful focal point in downtown. They think this focus will give them tremendous power over the city and seal their hold on the core, but the power of the ley lines is beyond even their control.

Countdown Clock:

- 3:00–The wizards arrange for Gonzales to push through a redevelopment plan that reconfigures the city's ley lines. Work begins immediately.
- 6:00–The ley lines produce occasional "time spikes"; people are reporting lost time and visions of 1930's Kansas City.
- 9:00–A local reporter, Kip Erhart, posts video to the *Kansas City Star* website documenting one of the ley lines surging.
- 10:00–Buildings and people start to disappear around the ley lines.
- 11:00–The ley lines begin to burn out; strange time loops and paradoxes occur in their wake.
- 12:00–The old and new ley lines are burnt out, a magical dead zone exists throughout downtown Kansas City.

Custom Moves

Overwhelming: When you ***let it out*** near an exposed ley line, treat any 12+ as if you had already advanced ***let it out*** before rolling.

Timetrip: When you ***trigger a ley line surge***, roll with Spirit. On a 10+, you see what the past has to offer from a comfortable metaphysical distance. On a 7-9, you're right there in the past, exposed and vulnerable, but only for a few minutes. On a miss, enjoy 1939.

Archmage: When you ***unleash an attack*** on Melissa Bachnall, roll with Spirit instead of Blood. Her magicks grant her powerful protection from the weak-willed and mundane.

Note that this Threat has real stakes—failure to stop the wizards will create a magical deadzone in downtown Kansas City—but it doesn't demand that the PCs necessarily take a particular side. Some PCs in the Mortality faction might love to have a magical deadzone occupy the center of the city, creating a delicious PC-Threat-PC triangle for you to exploit. Threats that target PCs or their immediate interests are fine, but sometimes work orthogonally to the PCs, demanding attention but offering multiple avenues of engagement.

CREATING STORMS

Once you've got a number of Threats written up and working, each pursuing their impulses and drives, you've got a **Storm** brewing. Threats focus on individual actors and specific dangers, but Storms unite those different Threats into a cohesive whole across the city, placing each Threat in context with the other Threats and looking for opportunities to flesh out the city's political ecosystem.

Each Storm is anchored to a fundamental **obligation**, a theme around which the Storm revolves both literally and metaphorically: a Storm focused on *justice* could feature a hunter seeking revenge against a vampire, a community organization unseating a corrupt city councilor, and a house haunted by a woman murdered by her husband 50 years ago. Each Threat is a meditation on the obligation, a conflict that urges the PCs to reflect on their own understanding.

At the center of the Storm is the **Eye**, a Threat that's driving the hardest toward the obligation; each Threat in the story is tied to the Eye. Eyes aren't necessarily more important than other Threats, but they make the city feel real and interconnected. The goal of these connections isn't to build up an unrealistic world where everyone knows everyone, but instead to ensure that no matter which Threat the PCs engage they'll all be carrying similar references and playing to the chosen theme.

Storms and Threats may look mechanical, but they're really conceptual, fueling interesting conversation when you're stuck and giving you tools that push characters back together instead of letting them drift apart. Rather than attempt to force characters to care about the same Threats—even when those Threats don't affect the things the PCs care about—your Storms reveal the literal and metaphorical connectedness of the city, drawing lines between Threats that focus the characters on the conflicts that matter.

When you create a new Storm:

- Choose a fundamental obligation
- Assign Threats to the Storm
- Create additional Threats (optional)
- Select an Eye and draw connections

CHOOSING AN OBLIGATION

Each Storm is concerned with a fundamental obligation, a unifying theme that ties multiple Threats to the PCs. When you create a Storm, choose 1:

- Community
- Duty
- Family
- Fealty
- Fellowship
- Honor
- Justice

Choosing a fundamental obligation is a bit like selecting a type for your Threats: you may come to the list with some ideas in mind for Threats you want to explore more deeply or you may be prompted by the list to think differently about your Threats. Look for common threads in the Threats you already have, thematic linkages that tell you what the Storm could be about if you focused and connected the Threats together.

> *Mark's got a bunch of Threats on the table after MCing his first session with a new group: Rico's pack moving on Anton's territory (passion: envy), an order of wizards seeking to reclaim a lost citadel (ritual: restore), a reporter trying to expose an elder vampire's criminal empire (revolution: idealist), and a faerie monarch plotting to dethrone her counterpart in a rival court (power play: coup). He works up each Threat, complete with countdown clocks and custom moves as appropriate.*
>
> *He looks them over and decides that one of the major themes of the collection is* family. *Rico's loyalty to his pack, the reporter's motivation—the vampire killed her brother—and the weird organizational structure of the wizard coven all point toward issues of family. He selects* family *for his Storm's fundamental obligation.*

ASSIGNING THREATS

Once you've chosen the Storm's fundamental obligation, pick Threats that tie into, represent, or embody that obligation. Sometimes this engagement is literal—a demon is trying to free his master (fealty) or a hunter seeks to kill an evil vampire lord (justice)—but it can also be metaphorical—a werewolf pack builds power by acquiring territory (family) or an abandoned apartment building attempts to consume the nearby populace (community).

Not every Threat needs to go into your first Storm. In fact, you'll probably have multiple Storms active and engaged at one time, although you probably want to focus on presenting one Storm at a time until you've played a few sessions. Threats that aren't added to this Storm can be added to another Storm at a later date, so they won't be wasted.

Mark decides that Rico's pack and the reporter are a perfect fit for the Storm. He thinks that maybe the faerie Threat isn't a good fit, but then it occurs to him that the two monarchs at war could be sisters! He likes that a lot because it gives the political drama a personal dimension, and puts The Fae in his game **in the middle of conflicts, political and personal**. *Turns out that conflict is about family after all.*

Mark thought that the wizard Threat would be a good fit, but the family link doesn't seem as strong as he thought it might be. The wizards are a motley crew (like a family), but their motivations and drives have much more to do with restoring their order's honor than it does with their own family connections. He decides to set aside that Threat for a different Storm.

CREATING ADDITIONAL THREATS

If a Storm needs additional Threats—either because some important aspect of it is unaddressed or it doesn't reach enough of the PCs—design additional Threats and add them to the Storm. Usually these kinds of Threats fill in holes or address unaddressed issues, so they are fairly simple to envision and add.

Mark's got four PCs involved in his current game, but the Threats only really engage The Hunter, The Fae, and The Aware. The Oracle is largely left out of the current set of Threats, so Mark decides to design a Threat attached to the Storm that will focus on her interests (even though she'll probably be dragged into the action through one of the other PCs).

The Storm already has passion, power play, and revolution Threats. Mark decides to add a secret library that will wall itself off after remaining open for a 100 years and a day because the family line that maintains the space refuses to train new caretakers (territory: stronghold). Mark creates a cast, description, countdown clock, and custom moves for the Threat, and places it in the Storm with his other Threats.

Mark also ponders expressing family in a different way. Right now he's got family as a resource (werewolves), family as a potential bond (faeries), family as motivator (reporter), and family as limit (library), but he doesn't see family as conflict represented. Mark decides to add a fifth Threat, a ghost named Omar who is tormenting Raquel, a PC's lover, and driving away her friends and loved ones to "protect" her (passion: love). Again, Mark creates a cast, description, countdown clock, and custom moves for the Threat, and places it in the Storm with his other Threats.

Don't feel obligated to add extra Threats if you've already got enough; you can return to this step whenever the Storm feels incomplete or insufficient. Since you control the pace at which the Threats advance, include as many or as few Threats as you need. Generally, we find that six Threats is the upper limit and that fewer than three Threats isn't sufficiently complex.

SELECTING AN EYE AND DRAWING CONNECTIONS

Finally, structure the Storm by selecting a Threat to act as the Eye, the Threat that takes a central position in the Storm. The Eye is the Threat that's most likely to make itself known, to interfere with the players' plans, and to be interesting to you as you explore the city. Throughout the life of the Storm, the Eye is the Threat around which the other Threats revolve; each Threat has a connection to the Eye, even if they don't have a connection to each other.

Choose a Threat that strongly expresses the fundamental obligation, and move it to the middle of the Storm. You can use the Storm worksheet to track the Storm, including the individual Threats and connections.

Mark looks over the Threats he's got and decides that Rico's pack is a great Eye for the Storm. Some of the other Threats do a good job of expressing the core obligation, but Rico's move on Anton's territory can have some rich connections to other Threats since Rico is shaking up the status quo quite a bit. Mark also thinks that Rico's pack is fun to portray, and he's excited about the idea of focusing on that conflict for a few sessions.

After you've decided on an Eye, draw connections between the Eye and the other Threats. Look for opportunities to express the political ecosystem of the city or to show how one power center is supported by resources obtained in a different environment. Start by working out a connection between the Eye and each other Threat, imagining how changes in one might affect the other:

Mark creates the following connections to Rico's pack:

Rico is feeding information to the reporter to keep the vampire lord—Anton's sire—off balance. The reporter's success or failure will dramatically affect Anton's resources to oppose Rico.

Both faerie monarchs are talking to Rico (and his pack) about fighting for them in the coming faerie war that will erupt if control between the courts doesn't shift. Rico may split his pack (temporarily weakening his position) if he thinks that the faeries have resources he wants...

One of Rico's pack members is friends with the family who's maintaining the library. He's tried to push them to expand their lineage, with little success. He's trying to persuade Rico to offer help, and he's on the lookout for PCs that might be willing to solve the problem.

Raquel lives in Rico's territory; she owns a house just a block away from some of the projects. Anyone who comes to deal with the ghost will surely run into Rico's pack, for better or worse.

You can also look for connections between Threats, aside from the Eye:

Mark notices that the library is still disconnected from the other Threats. He decides that Raquel is part of the family that runs the library, although she hasn't seen them in some time. They think she's dead, and they're too fucking self-absorbed to go look for her a few blocks away.

Mark also thinks that the faerie court connection is a bit weak; if negotiations go poorly, Rico's just going to ignore that conflict and focus on Anton. Mark decides to add a connection between the faeries and the reporter to keep them interesting and involved in the Storm: the new monarch is in love with the reporter, and wants to take her away to Arcadia if she would willingly go.

Note that these connections aren't new plots or plans on their own; they don't require their own countdown clocks to track. Instead they're more like triggers—relationships and interests that might be used to alter the path of things and push the PCs toward the other parts of the Storm and each other.

SAMPLE STORM: ALL THE KING'S VAMPS

In order to demonstrate how Storms and Threats come together, we've provided a sample Storm drawn from the examples in this chapter. The Storm—titled "All the King's Vamps"—is set in Baltimore, Maryland, an urban area that plays host to the best and worst that cities have to offer; the city is legendary for its culture and crime in equal measures.

The Eye of this Storm is centered around Rico, a charismatic werewolf alpha who decides to claim new territory from a weakened vampire cartel led by Anton Rivera. As the politics around Anton's territory turn violent, other conflicts swirl in the Storm: a ghost that haunts a young woman in her new apartment, a library that threatens to lock away its secrets for all time, a nosy reporter threatening to expose an undead vampire lord, and a pair of faerie sisters vying for a ritual throne.

Many of the details in this Storm could be adapted for your game; feel free to make use of what works for you here in your own games. If you're looking to build your own Storms, this sample can be a useful tool for understanding how it all comes together.

Threat: Lobos del Rico, Eye of the Storm

Type: passion (envy)

Impulse: to take more than its share

Cast: Anton Rivera, a vampire who controls the West Baltimore projects (Night); Rico, the alpha of a werewolf pack located in West Baltimore (Night); and Mina Garza, an oracle who often acts as a black market entrepreneur for illegal goods (Power); Rico's pack: 2-harm medium group 1-armor savage clever

Description: Rico's been eyeing Anton's territory for months, his jealousy mounting. When Anton sends out runners into Rico's territory, it's all the excuse Rico needs to start making his own moves to take what he wants. Can Anton hold his own against a wolf pack on the hunt?

Countdown Clock:

- 3:00–Anton sends his vampire drug dealers out from the projects into Rico's territory.
- 6:00–Rico's pack kills several vampires and sells the heroin to Mina Garza.
- 9:00–Rico starts to hunt vampires on Anton's territory, taking their heroin as well.
- 10:00–Rico kills Anton and seizes the rest of the West Baltimore projects.
- 11:00–Rico co-opts several of the local gangs, adding them to his pack.
- 12:00–Rico's pack seizes all of the areas around the towers, pushing out the vampires completely.

Custom Moves

Killer Instincts: When you try to ***mislead, distract, or trick*** Rico on his territory, roll with Blood instead of Mind. He's a soldier, through and through.

Trespass: When you ***enter Rico's territory***, roll with Mind. On a 10+, the werewolves come at you hard, but you see them coming. On a 7-9, you catch wind of them, but only moments before they strike. On a miss, you're vulnerable and separated from the others when the pack strikes.

First One's Free: When you ***sample Anton's heroin***, roll with Spirit. On a 10+, you feel his blood through the drugs: ask him a question and he'll answer it honestly. On a 7-9, you only get an impression: the MC will tell you what you see. On a miss, Anton knows you're using: he gets to ask you a question that you must answer honestly.

Threat: Overdrawn

Type: territory (stronghold)

Impulse: to deny access

Cast: Alex O'Sullivan, a young man from the O'Sullivan family of caretakers (Power); Alder O'Sullivan, the oldest member of the caretakers (Power); Diego Ruiz, a shaman from Rico's pack (Night).

Description: The O'Sullivans were charged with serving the Elrach Library by Reyna Douglas, a powerful wizard who bound the family to the site in the late 1800s. Today, the O'Sullivan clan is dying out, and the Elrach Library is starting to close itself off to the outside world. Can a new caretaker be found that the Library will accept before it's too late?

Countdown Clock:

- 3:00–Alex O'Sullivan goes outside the family to seek help with the upcoming closure, perhaps to one of the PCs.
- 6:00–Alex is captured upon his return to the library. He's punished by Alder O'Sullivan, banished to the far west wing for his troubles.
- 9:00–All books that have been removed from the library are instantaneously returned, as if by magic, ripped from their current locations and placed on the shelves of the library.
- 10:00–The west wing of the library closes; anyone inside vanishes completely, lost to some horror dimension.
- 11:00–The east wing of the library closes; major exhibits come to life to guard the doors, sealing off that wing by force.
- 12:00–The library closes entirely, denying access to anyone not of the O'Sullivan bloodline.

Custom Moves

Checkout: When you ***go to the library for valuable information***, roll with Mind. On a hit, you find a relevant book or tome. On a 10+, the library delivers a book to you that reveals several important secrets; ask the MC three questions about the situation at hand. On a 7-9, the tome is difficult to understand; you'll need assistance with the book to get your answers. On a miss, the information you find reveals a dark prophecy that will soon come to pass.

The Help: When you ***lay hands on a caretaker***, roll with Spirit. On a 10+, the library issues warnings and threats, but does not interfere. On a 7-9, the library makes a show of force: release the caretaker or suffer 2-harm (ap). On a miss, the library swallows you up: you're bound and trapped by its magical powers until a caretaker releases you.

Threat: Two Queens, One Throne

Type: power play (coup)

Impulse: to steal power in moments of weakness

Cast: The Queen of Summer, the coming monarch of Baltimore (Wild); The Queen of Winter, the retreating monarch of Baltimore (Wild); Ansu Han, the chosen Knight of Summer (Wild).

Description: The Queen of Summer and the Queen of Winter are faerie sisters who pass their throne back and forth, but their sibling rivalries have been kept in check by their elderly father, Brion. Since Brion retired to Arcadia for ten years and a day, Winter has plotted to steal the throne from Summer. Will she succeed now that their father is no longer keeping the peace?

Countdown Clock:

- 3:00–Summer snubs Winter at a courtly gathering, refusing to publicly thank her for handing over the crown on schedule.
- 6:00–Summer's knight, Han, is found dead in a parked car under a bridge.
- 9:00–Han's death prompts the Queen of Summer to lash out at Winter, destroying several key loci belonging to her sister.
- 10:00–Winter usurps Summer completely, imprisoning her and bringing an early coldfront to Baltimore.
- 11:00–The continuing imbalance weakens many of the portals to Arcadia around the city, breaking some irrevocably and leaving others barely functioning.
- 12:00–Winter executes Summer, publicly, and establishes herself as the sole faerie queen of Baltimore.

Custom Moves

Hospitality: When you ***present a worthy gift to a faerie queen***, you may act as if you ***cashed in a Debt*** with her when you ***persuade*** her to do you a favor or select any other item off the ***cash in a Debt*** list for NPCs.

Faeseeker: When you ***seek a courtly gathering of fae***, roll with Mind. On a 10+, you find your way there without trouble; the MC will tell you what you find. On a 7-9, the way forward is blocked to you, but you know which way to travel. On a miss, you're caught nearby, exposed and vulnerable, by the fae or something worse.

Threat: Chaperone

Type: passion (love)

Impulse: to protect

Cast: Raquel O'Sullivan, estranged daughter of the O'Sullivan clan and powerful seer (Power); Omar, a ghost determined to protect those living in his house at all costs (Night).

Description: Raquel's newly purchased home hides a dangerous secret; the last resident was murdered in cold blood by his jealous lover. Now the ghostly remnant of the murdered man, calling himself Omar, has begun to haunt Raquel's dreams, working to push away those who love and care for Raquel.

Countdown Clock: None. Omar is content to push Raquel's friends away indefinitely, and Raquel is unwilling to move.

Custom Moves

Exorcism: When you try to ***exorcise Omar from the apartment***, roll with Spirit. On a 10+, pick 2. On a 7-9, pick 1.

- He doesn't assault your mind
- He doesn't assault your body
- He doesn't escape the ritual

On a miss, Omar transfers his "protection" to another character present, manifesting later when they are at their most vulnerable.

Ghostface: When you try to ***figure Omar out***, roll with Spirit instead of Mind. His ghostly nature makes him difficult to read.

Threat: Fit to Print

Type: revolution (idealist)

Impulse: craves sacrifice, its own or others

Cast: Kazue Kimura, investigative reporter for a local newspaper (Mortality); Bosede Carter, an elder vampire responsible for Kazue's brother's death (Night).

Description: Kazue Kimura is looking for vengeance against Bosede Carter for murdering her brother last year. Careful and patient, Kazue has decided to use the resources she knows—the news media—to sabotage Carter's profitable financial empire. Meanwhile, Carter's forces are beseiged on all sides by those who wish to steal her territory.

Countdown Clock:

- 3:00–Kazue receives a visit from Rico, who explains that Bosede had her brother killed to keep her vampiric secrets.
- 6:00–Kazue digs deeper into Bosede's business dealings and finds evidence of widespread corruption and bribery. She steals a number of financial records from one of Bosede's office parks.
- 9:00–Kazue helps a criminal witness escape from Bosede's reach, matching the witness up with local cops that get the witness processed through before Bosede can react.
- 10:00–Kazue exposes Bosede's criminal financial enterprise in the paper, but finds that no one will print anything about Bosede's vampirism.
- 11:00–Bosede kills Kazue and flees into the nearby woods, disgraced and animalistic, quickly losing touch with her human nature.
- 12:00–Bosede takes up permanent residence in the woods—a fallen soul preying upon mortals foolish enough to travel alone at night.

Custom Moves

None.

MORE STORMS, MORE THREATS

As your story goes on, you'll resolve some Storms and Threats, creating new ones to fill the void left by the resolution of old conflicts. We prefer running the game with just one or two full Storms in play, but you might find you're able to juggle more. If you come up with some interesting ideas, please share them online in our G+ Community (bit.ly/usgplus)! A good Storm is always educational, even if it's tied strongly to your PCs and their stories.

TEN
THE SHADOWS

CALLING THE SHADOWS

Custom moves have the power to define your city, offer your players new arenas of conflicts, and even add new depth and complexity to the existing Archetypes. Here's an example:

When you ***enter the abandoned subway tunnels***, roll with Spirit. On a 10+, you're fine but you're sure someone's watching. On a 7-9, you hear whispers all around; mark corruption to move in deeper or flee the scene. On a miss, you are overcome by the monsters that haunt the undercity; the MC will tell you where in the sewers you end up.

This kind of move could be tied to a Threat or Storm, something menacing lurking underneath the city that the characters have to confront to keep the city whole. But the move also works *entirely independently of a Threat*; it's a bit of your city made real, a custom move that promises your players that something interesting will happen if they venture down to the abandoned tunnels.

That's what a move is, after all: a promise between you and the players. Custom moves let you make new promises all your own. Just for your city. Just for your players. Just for you.

BUILDING CUSTOM MOVES

As we said in **The Storm** on 257, custom moves have the following structure:

- **a trigger:** "When X happens..."
- **an outcome:** "...then Y." Sometimes it's a roll, other times it's just an outcome.
- **stakes:** if it has a roll, define 10+, 7-9, and 6-.

If a move involves a roll, 10+ means things work out fine for the PC, 7-9 means they pay some costs or endure some complications, and 6- means that things go to shit. But it's all relative. You might want things to be pretty soft all over—6- is just rough, not tragic—or for even the 10+ to be pretty fucking bad.

Moves state concrete relationships between a trigger and an outcome, a flow of fiction that pushes the characters forward into new and interesting situations. It's vital that these two elements serve each other—raising the action to a level of uncertainty to trigger the move and pushing the fiction forward with the effects—and your setting overall.

CUSTOM TRIGGERS

The first half of a move is the trigger, the "when X happens" part of the formula that sets up when the move is set to go off. It's important to make the trigger itself evocative and specific; it should draw the player into the world you're creating together, raise the action to an uncertain level, and be specific enough for the player to say, "I know how to trigger this move in the fiction..."

Here's an example of a move with a boring and nonspecific trigger:

> **Honest Eyes**: When you ***tell the truth to someone***, roll with Heart. On a 10+, they believe you. On a 7-9, they are willing to accept it, but they don't fully trust you. On a miss, they doubt your sincerity and demand proof.

There's some good stuff that might come out of this move, but it's going to trigger at times when nothing is at stake (and the results don't push the fiction forward in interesting ways either). It could be greatly improved by getting specific: ***when you confess your sins*** or ***when you reveal the truth to a spouse or lover***.

Here's an example of a move with an evocative and specific trigger:

> **Fast and Furious**: When you ***race for pinks***, roll with Mind. On a 10+, you win the race cleanly, no harm to either car. On a 7-9, you win, but either their car or your car gets messed up during the race, your choice. On a miss, you total your car in an embarrassing loss. Tough break.

You could say ***when you enter a car race*** or ***when you try to win a car race***, but neither is as pointed and riveting as ***when you race for pinks***. It's clear when the move does or does not trigger, and the trigger itself is evocative and uncertain. Remember that uncertainty is at the core of moves: a move with a boring trigger is likely to fall apart in actual play.

Sample Triggers

When a character acts (usually in specific circumstances):

Moves can trigger when a character takes a particular action in the fiction, usually tied to a location, item, or person.

Lights Out: When you ***hack into Anton's security system***, roll with Mind. On a 10+, you shut it all down, no problem. On a 7-9, you shut down two systems, your choice: infrared sensors, motion detector, window alarms, or video cameras. On a miss, you trip the alarm directly; Anton's goons will be here momentarily.

When circumstances dictate:

Sometimes the actor is an NPC or the environment, although a PC usually has to do something in the fiction to get the environment working.

Tarot Tea: When ***Madam Laroux reads your tarot***, roll with Spirit. On a hit, she reads you clean and clear: ask one question about your future and she will answer it. On a 10+, she demands no payment or Debt, provided you know how to thank her properly. On a miss, she sees something dark and foreboding in your cards that she must share with you, regardless of what you sought her out to learn.

When an item is used:

Using an item is like taking a particular action, but the focus is on what the item can do in the fiction instead of what the character is able to do.

Bloodblade: When ***Watanabe's knife spills your blood***, roll with harm you inflict on yourself (max +3). On a hit, you create a weapon from your blood that lasts for a scene (3-harm close messy demonic). On a 10+, you can recall the weapon into your body at any time; when you do, heal the harm you inflicted on yourself to create the weapon. On a miss, the knife makes a demand; promise to fulfill it, and the knife will create the weapon and serve you.

From now on:

This move doesn't need an explicit trigger. When a character takes it, the move takes effect. Those effects go on for as long as the move indicates.

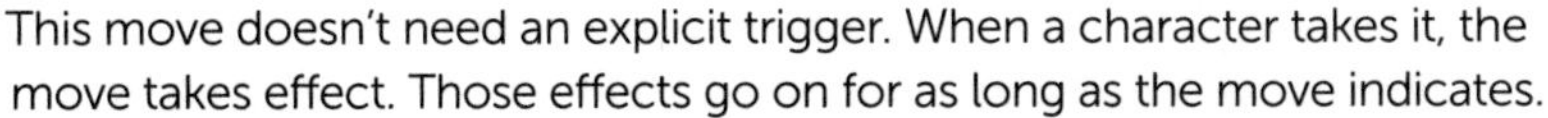

Frostkin: [When you take this move...] Swear a lifetime oath to the Queen of Winter; take +1 ongoing to all rolls defending her interests for the duration of your oath. If you break this oath, suffer 4-harm (ap).

Right now and done:

Again, the trigger here is implicit. No need to state it because it's clear that the effect takes place when you take the move.

Unholy Restoration: [When you take this move...] Erase a Scar and scratch out an unmarked corruption advance. You can't scratch out "Retire your character." Anyone with magical sight can look upon you and know that you have healed yourself through the dark arts. You can take this move more than once.

»Wasted Triggers

The key to good triggers is to connect them to the overall flow of fiction within the move. Good triggers need to be specific. Specific triggers let you build specific outcomes; specific outcomes mean interesting fiction. Broad triggers can't do the work of lifting the action into uncertainty, so the move ends up pushing the characters away from the tense action that makes *Urban Shadows* fun.

Here's a problematic move a player might get after picking up a dead PC's custom bow:

When you ***shoot an arrow with Elora's bow***, roll with Blood. On a hit, inflict harm as established. On a 7-9, pick one.

- You're out of ammo
- You inflict less harm
- You get put in a spot

"Shoot an arrow" is far too broad a trigger for *Urban Shadows*; there's no guarantee that something interesting is happening when you use the bow, so the move is likely to trigger at inappropriate times. You can see that the non-specific trigger leads to outcomes that can't push the fiction forward in ways that are specific and evocative. The players will usually pick *you're out of ammo*—they can grab more at a store in the city—or *inflict less harm*, leading to mechanical outcomes (ammo or harm) without meaningful engagement with the fiction (the bow).

Here are three versions of a move built around Elora's bow that push the fiction forward in more interesting ways:

When you ***kill someone with Elora's bow***, ask the player of the character you killed if Elora would have approved. If they say "yes," mark Mortality; if they say "No," mark corruption.

When you ***unleash an attack*** on someone with Elora's bow, roll with Mind instead of Blood. On a miss, the bow betrays you to mortal hunters at the next opportunity.

When you ***go into battle with Elora's bow***, roll with Blood. On a hit, you have a vision. The MC will make your vision come true, if it's remotely possible. On a 10+, you know one NPC who will die and one who will live. On a 7-9, your vision is incomplete: choose one who will live or one who will die, but not both. On a miss, you foresee your own death; take a -1 ongoing throughout the battle.

Each trigger in these moves is specific, evocative, and tuned to uncertainty, sometimes riding on the back of an existing move and sometimes engaging the broader mechanical systems like corruption and advancement. Each trigger leads to an outcome that pushes the fiction forward toward additional conflicts and moves down the road.

CUSTOM EFFECTS

As the second half of the move, effects have an equal burden to bear: the trigger has to be evocative and specific and the effect has to push the fiction forward in a meaningful way. That's partially about being evocative and specific as well, but it's also a function of what paths the move might lead to in the fiction.

Here's an example of a move that fails to push the fiction forward with its effects:

> When you ***confess your sins to your parish priest***, roll with Heart. On a 10+, he forgives you; go in peace. On a 7-9, he offers you forgiveness, but demands a penance. On a miss, he doesn't forgive you.

At first glance, these all sound interesting, but do they really matter? Is the priest such a central character that the lack of forgiveness drives new scenes (and new moves in those future scenes)? There's some promise around the 7-9 result, but it's meager at best. There's also a missed opportunity around the miss: 6- shouldn't just mean failure when you have the opportunity to do something that fits the theme of the move.

Here's an example of a move that pushes the fiction forward with its effects (even on a miss):

> When you ***conspire with one of Watanabe's underlings***, roll with Mind. On a hit, they offer you an opportunity to get close to him or reveal a weakness or flaw in his organization, your choice. On a 7-9, the advantage they confer is short-lived; seize it soon or it will fade. On a miss, all of this was a trap; the underling has lured you into a vulnerable position in order to strike.

The outcomes here rely on fictional positioning; very little mechanical action is taking place within the move (+1 forward, armor, harm). But the outcomes it proposes will almost certainly lead to interesting scenes and fiction down the road, and the mechanical effects of a move are only important insofar as they push toward new scenes and new moves. Either the PCs get a chance to strike at Watanabe or they are put into a dangerous trap; either way, the next set of moves is just over the horizon. A +1 ongoing against Watanabe sounds attractive, but it doesn't necessarily lead to any of that.

Sample Effects

Direct Effects:

Moves can stipulate direct effects in the fiction (and sometimes choices that will lead to direct effects as a result of a roll). Note that the 10+ effect here is really meaty; the player is offered a full advance to cooperate, but the Lake will certainly ask for something bloody and tragic.

The Gray Lake: When you ***seek the counsel of the Gray Lake***, roll with Heart. On a 10+, the Lake offers you hard advice; mark an advance if you follow it. On a 7-9, the Lake has cold tidings and a few answers; mark Power if you follow the trail it lays out and corruption if you don't. On a miss, the Lake reveals the only path forward, dark and bloody; mark a corruption advance if you turn away from this fate.

Stat swap:

Like some Archetype moves, stat swap moves allow a character to roll with a different stat than is presented in the basic moves. Make sure there's some focus here on the trigger, or these can quickly become a way for characters to ignore a stat completely.

Demon Tricks: After you ***sign a contract with Balthazar for power***, roll with Wild instead of Mind when you try to ***mislead, distract, or trick*** someone, provided you still honor the contract.

Add options to an existing move:

Like the stat swap, a move that adds options allows characters to make broader use of an existing mechanic.

Witchhunter: Add the following option to ***let it out***:

- Reveal a supernatural effect or presence to nearby mortals

Inflict harm/corruption:

It's worth calling out that a move can inflict purely mechanical effects on PCs or NPCs. Be careful here: it's only interesting to inflict harm or corruption if they limit a character's options or escalate tension.

The Word of the Lord: When you ***offer true forgiveness to the corrupted or monstrous***, ask them to accept the grace of your faith. If they reject it, they take 2-harm (ap); if they accept it, mark their Faction and take +1 ongoing against them for the scene.

Choose options:

Some moves allow players to choose options from a list. These choices structure the fiction moving forward, and usually give players more options on a 10+.

Mercado: When you ***open a booth in the goblin market***, roll with Wild. On a 10+, pick 2. On a 7-9, pick 1.

- Someone offers you a Debt for your wares
- Someone offers you trade for your wares
- Someone offers you information for your wares

On a miss, you see someone walk away with something precious and rare from your booth.

Hold and spend:

Moves that rely on hold give players an opportunity to structure the fiction moving forward, but in a time delayed way. Rather than picking all the options at once, hold allows the PC to use the options whenever it's appropriate.

Trapper: When you ***set up security measures to protect a stronghold***, roll with Mind. On a 10+, hold 3. On a 7-9, hold 1. When the stronghold is under attack, you can spend that hold 1 for 1 to:

- Inflict 2-harm (ap) on a single NPC
- Delay, disarm, or disable an NPC
- Create an opportunity for another PC

On a miss, whatever you were hoping to defend against finds you alone while you're arranging the defenses.

Ask and answer:

Moves that allow characters to ask questions are sometimes immediate—as below—and sometimes delayed using hold. Either way, the questions drive fiction only so much as they prompt interesting answers.

Sciencesight: When you ***bring a supernatural item back to the university lab for study***, roll with Mind. On a 10+, ask 2. On a 7-9, ask 1.

- How could I neutralize this item?
- What fuels or powers this item?
- Who does this item belong to?
- When was this item created?

On a miss, the item attracts the devoted attention of the innocent or uninvolved before you can intervene.

»Wasted Effects

One of the biggest risks with designing the effect of a custom move is falling into the trap of mechanics. Sometimes the effects of custom moves become entirely mechanical, lacking any real push forward in the fiction. Here's an example:

When you're facing an uphill battle to get something done, take -1 to the roll. If whatever you're trying to do is incredibly easy, add +2 to your roll. The MC gets to decide when something is an uphill battle or incredibly easy.

This move doesn't change anything in the fiction; nothing about the outcome snowballs into more moves. A few more failures, a few more successes, sure. But it's pretty fucking boring. Moves have to bring the fiction and the mechanics together to advance the story. Tracking holds, and forwards, and bonuses without also tracking something interesting in the fiction turns the game into urban bookkeeping instead of urban fantasy.

Here are the three examples tied to Elora's bow again. Note how each works to push the fiction forward, offering opportunities for more moves and scenes down the road:

When you ***kill someone with Elora's bow***, ask the player of the character you killed if Elora would have approved. If they say "yes," mark Mortality; if they say "No," mark corruption.

When you ***unleash an attack*** on someone with Elora's bow, roll with Mind instead of Blood. On a miss, the bow betrays you to mortal hunters at the next opportunity.

When you ***go into battle with Elora's bow***, roll with Blood. On a hit, you have a vision. The MC will make your vision come true, if it's remotely possible. On a 10+, you know one NPC who will die and one who will live. On a 7-9, your vision is incomplete: choose one who will live or one who will die, but not both. On a miss, you foresee your own death; take a -1 ongoing throughout the battle.

Each of those moves has an effect that drives the fiction forward in an interesting way. Even when a mechanical system is engaged—corruption, -1 ongoing, etc.—it's pushing the characters toward hard and interesting choices in future scenes instead of applying a fictionally meaningless cost or bonus.

BUILDING LISTS

As you're building effects for your custom moves, you'll find that that lists often work well for generating fiction and offering players control over the outcomes. In other words, offering the players multiple paths forward ensures that the players are driving the action and that the fiction is going somewhere productive. Here are a few models for lists that you might find useful:

»Multiple Juicy Options

One way to a make a list interesting is to present multiple juicy options to the players, similar to moves like ***mislead, distract, or trick*** or ***let it out***:

The Seer Jong: When you ***go to Jong for prophecy and portent***, bearing gifts, roll with Power. On a hit, she offers you a vision. On a 10+, choose 2. On a 7-9, choose 1.

- She offers you a clear enemy; take +1 forward against your foe
- She offers you additional information; ask a followup question
- She offers you a potential ally; take +1 forward to ***hit the streets***

On a miss, she reveals the terrifying scope and scale of the foes you face; -1 ongoing to ***keep your cool*** until you have a chance to rest and relax in safety.

When you create this type of list as an effect, make the 10+ result one short of the full list and the 7-9 result a bit shorter than that. Give them almost everything they want, but never all of it. Or offer them all of it for a bit of corruption or harm, like ***The Devil Inside*** (142).

»Arenas of Conflict

Some moves define arenas of conflict with the choices, like ***Pack Alpha*** (116) or ***Manifest*** (104); each option sets up future conflicts (or excludes future conflicts) based on your choices, even if you weren't thinking about that arena of conflict before making the move. In this move, we're defining the areas of conflict: the PC's lover might ask questions, demand payments, or expose the PC to danger instead of just offering comfort:

Home Sweet Home: When you ***seek refuge from the world*** in the arms of your lover, roll with Heart. On a 10+, all 3. On a 7-9, only 1.

- He doesn't ask any questions
- He doesn't demand a Debt or payment
- He doesn't accidentally expose you to danger

On a miss, your enemies knew you would come here. He's missing and they're already one step ahead.

The setup for these types of moves is almost always all three on a 10+ result and only one on a 7-9. Keep that in mind when you design the move; if two of the three options don't make sense together, then the move will result in incoherent fiction a good portion of the time. Set things up so that a 10+ means that the player avoids the conflicts inherent in the move and a 7-9 means that two of the three arenas of conflict entangle the PC without canceling each other out.

»An Oddball Choice

Some lists contain an odd or jarring choice, like ***Eternal Hunger*** (109). It's usually the last choice in the list, and it stands out like a sore thumb:

Ghoul: When you ***feed at least a pint of your vampiric blood to a mortal***, roll with Blood. On a hit, they transform into your servant, eager to please you and loyal to your cause. On a 10+, pick 3. On a 7-9, pick 2.

- They can serve your will at a distance
- They do not hunger constantly for your blood
- They are not jealous of the others who serve you
- You don't have to mark corruption

The key here is that the oddball choice makes the player make a concrete decision about their character every time they use the move. They can have everything they want, provided they are willing to give up a little piece of their soul to get it. Only use oddball choices like this when they lead to such concrete choices and statements about the nature of the move.

SHADOWS EVERYWHERE

Custom moves work everywhere in *Urban Shadows*: special situations or locations, magic items, new character moves, scene framing moves, and more. The basic moves, Faction moves, and Debt moves from the core game will always be enough to get you through a session, but custom moves can make your city sing.

In general, these moves are best prepared between sessions—your players would certainly appreciate a handout with new moves on it at the table—but you might occasionally draw one up on the fly. Either way, remember to let the players know they're available so they know to trigger them!

SITUATION MOVES

One of the primary uses for custom moves is to fill in holes in the game, spots where you feel like ***keep your cool*** or ***let it out***—the default moves for resolving broad uncertainty—aren't sufficient:

When you ***stand trial in front of the Wizard's Council***, roll with Heart. On a 10+, they find you innocent of the charges brought against you. On a 7-9, they find you guilty of only a minor offense and impose a minor punishment. On a miss, your defense falls short; the Council finds you guilty and levies a stiff penalty for your criminality.

When you ***try to reach a hellplane through the cursed electric chair***, roll with Spirit. On a hit, you cross over. On a 10+, pick 2. On a 7-9, pick 1.

- You don't attract any immediate attention
- You don't get stuck on the other side
- You don't bring anything back with you

On a miss, you end up on a different plane altogether, one you were hoping to avoid.

When you ***try to get into the werewolf bar***, roll with Blood. On a 10+, the bouncer knows your pack; flex and you're legit. On a 7-9, the bouncer just laughs; shut his mouth with your fists or take a walk. On a miss, you're in over your head; your attempt has left you exposed, vulnerable, or alone at the worst moment.

Each one of these moves is designed to flesh out the world, giving the players a specific, concrete theme for the location, conflict, or opportunity. It's easy to say, "Oh, it's tough to get into this bar," and follow up on that with moves and fiction that reflects that truth, but the custom move drives home what that actually looks like to players really quickly.

»Custom Moves for Threats

Don't forget custom moves for Threats (254)! These are custom moves just like any other, but tied to a specific situation revolving around a Threat. As you get more comfortable with Threat moves, you can try alternate triggers and effects, stuff that pushes your players a bit harder than just offering them opportunities. Here's an example:

> When Cassie—the psychic girl—enters a scene, she can ask every character in the room a question from ***figure someone out***. She doesn't need to interact with them; she just needs to see them clearly.

That's a legit move, but it might make your players feel a bit pushed around, especially if they tend to travel in big groups where everyone's getting questions asked at the same time. You might try to bend it back toward a **player-facing stance**, meaning that the players are the ones who trigger it instead of Cassie:

> When you try to ***mislead, distract, or trick*** Cassie—the psychic girl—roll with Spirit instead of Mind. On a 10+, you keep yourself to yourself, but just barely. On a 7-9, she's fooled, but move quick 'cause it ain't gonna last long. On a miss, she asks you a question from ***figure someone out*** and everyone in the room knows your answer.

It's effectively the same kind of move, but the focus is on the PCs and their actions. It's not hard, however, to push them toward lying to her; you've still got your MC moves, driving them toward interesting places and conflicts.

EQUIPMENT MOVES

In addition to building the world at large, you can also use custom moves to give magic items, equipment, or spells more concrete mechanics:

> When you ***look deeply into the Eye of Eranth'adi***, roll with Mind. On a hit, the Eye shows you whatever you were seeking, regardless of time or distance. On a 10+, pick 1. On a 7-9, pick 2:
>
> - The Eye attacks your body; mark 2-harm (ap)
> - The Eye attacks your soul: mark corruption
> - The Eye attacks your mind; take -1 ongoing until you sleep
>
> On a miss, the Eye attacks your heart: it reveals something true and awful you've been trying to avoid.

Note that the Eye moves the fiction forward in every instance; all the rolls that engage the eye lead the character toward interesting fiction instead of imposing shallow mechanical costs. Here are the options:

- **10+:** You get to see the thing you seek at some cost. The MC will show you something interesting.
- **7-9:** You get to see the thing you seek with great costs. The MC will show you something interesting.
- **6-:** You don't get to see the thing you seek, but you get some other vision that will probably move you to action in an unexpected way. In other words, the MC will *still* show you something interesting.

Creating custom moves around magic items is especially useful because it puts the decisions around those items directly into the hands of your players: they get to trigger the move and make the tough choices instead of getting hammered for owning a special snowflake bit of fiction. Attaching moves to your players' items also means that sometimes your players miss their rolls—perfect opportunities for you to ***activate their stuff's downside*** in interesting ways.

CHARACTER MOVES

In addition to adding moves to the world at large or to items the PCs possess, you can also add new moves directly to the PCs themselves, either as the result of changes in the fiction or as advancements. Roxy, for example, might need a new move if she formally befriends her territory's spirit guardians or puts them in her Debt:

When you ***howl to the spirits of your territory for aid***, roll with Spirit. On a 10+, they come directly in exchange for chiminage at a later date; the MC will detail their form and function. On a 7-9, they offer their services, but they need tribute and offerings first. On a miss, your request offends; you must perform the rite of regret before you can ask again.

If Roxy's player earns this move in play, give it to her. If she wants a move like this as an advancement, that's cool too. Work with your players to make their new moves at least as awesome as what's already on their Archetype.

FRAMING SCENES

Custom moves can be used to frame scenes and set up conflicts as well, allowing you to jump to the middle of something interesting rather than wading in with every detail. ***Hit the streets*** serves a similar function in the Faction moves, giving players the option to skip ahead to the interesting part of looking for allies or resources. Here's an example—loosely based on John Harper's engagement move from *The Regiment*—that skips all the boring stuff that comes with executing a complex plan:

Saboteur: When you ***harry a gang from the shadows*** to disrupt their operations, tell the MC your plan and roll with Mind. On a 10+, pick 2. On a 7-9, pick 1. You start the next scene in the middle of your plan:

- Your forces are perfectly positioned
- You've suffered no major losses
- You have the element of surprise

On a miss, your plan gets you into serious trouble; your attempts to disrupt their operations lead you right into a trap.

Or you might use a scene framing move to put constant pressure on a PC:

Hunted: So long as the Brotherhood of the Blood hunts you, at the beginning of the session, roll with Mind. On a 10+, you evade their clutches, but you know that they draw nearer every day. On a 7-9, they've found you; you've got time to get away, but the noose tightens. On a miss, they catch you when you least expect it; the MC will tell you how and when.

Sometimes this move results in signs and portents, evidence that the Brotherhood is getting closer, but no scene. When the PC misses, though, the MC has permission to frame a scene fast and hard, a pivotal moment in a long game of cat and mouse.

LOVE LETTERS

Another use for custom moves is to get caught up with players who missed a session or ended on a serious cliffhanger. Since these require a bit more explanation than a typical lean move, we call them **love letters**. If you're looking to push your players right into the thick of things from their first roll, give them a love letter at the start of game—direct from you to them—bloody fingerprints and all.

Dear Desmond,

When we last left you, you were in seriously bad shape, bleeding all over the sidewalk and drifting into darkness. The good news is the paramedics got to you before your heart stopped, but someone in your condition is always in danger of the big sleep.

You're a bloody mess, so roll with Blood. On a hit, you're stabilized and wake up in a hospital bed. On a 10+, you heal 2-harm as well. On a miss, you died on the operating table...unless you mark a scar.

Hugs and Kisses,

Your MC

Here's a letter Andrew used to catch up Sam, who missed a session in a long-running game:

Dear Sam,

Last time anyone saw you, you were headed to see Jean Paul about that old book you found in Dawon's library. Let's see how that went and what you found out. Roll with Power.

On a 10+, you learned the secret origin of the book and why the Ordo Draconis is looking for it. On a 7-9, Jean Paul could tell you a few things about the book, but you've got more questions than answers. On a miss, you found Jean Paul dead in his office, the sign of the Ordo cut into his forehead...

Hugs and Kisses,

Your MC

You can also use love letters to set up conflicts, perhaps for a one-shot or because you think things are getting slow:

Dear Wizard,

Go ahead and create your character, following the Archetype instructions, with two quick exceptions: your sanctum is an apothecary and your focus gives armor+1 when you have hold from Channeling.

As the only wizard living in Hyde Park at the moment, you're constantly on the hook. People come to you with problems, concerns, and issues, even if it feels like maybe they should go see someone else who gives a shit. Lately, Mona has been coming to you looking for a potion that will make her forget her terrible marriage, and you've been telling her she needs therapy, not a memory wipe. The other day, you came home to find that someone broke into your apartment and stole a bunch of the ingredients you would need to make such a potion. Fucking Mona.

After you've made your character, before the session starts, I'll ask you what you know about the theft. Roll with Mind. On a 10+, tell me who broke in here and how you know they did it. Might be Mona. Might be someone completely new. On a 7-9, tell me who you suspect, and I'll tell you what evidence is pushing you in that direction. On a miss, tell me that you have no fucking clue, and I'll tell you what evidence you found that's throwing you for a loop.

I'll also ask you about the stuff that was taken. Roll with Spirit. On a 10+, pick 2. On a 7-9, pick 1.

- *Nothing that was taken was particularly valuable*
- *Nothing that was taken was needed for a pressing ritual*
- *Nothing that was taken wasn't yours.*
- *Nothing else was broken in the taking*

On a miss, all four are false! Tough break.

Hugs and Kisses,

Your MC

If you're looking to spin things up fast in a one-shot, skip the start of session moves and write up love letters to each character, all tied into the same Threat. It's a bit of work, but nothing makes a game hum like the momentum that comes from a few starting love letters.

BREAKING THE MOLD

All well and good, you might say, but what about really messing with the system? Is it possible to do more with custom moves? What's the limit here?

Oh, yes. You can do more. Much more. Anything you want, in fact.

GOING SOLO

Let's say you're running a game of *Urban Shadows* with only one PC. Brendan and Jenn play this way, and they've found a few holes that arise when there aren't any other PCs in the game. Let's spot some problems and invent a few custom moves to overcome them.

»Solo Fights

First, fights and physical violence can be tough for characters who don't have any physical force of their own; they can call in allies to help out, but since Jenn still has to ***unleash an attack*** with Blood to fight, those extra allies aren't much mechanical help. The MC can always say, "The NPCs inflict their damage!" but that starts to feel a bit like watching NPCs punch each other. Here's a move that makes Jenn's allies relevant while still keeping the power in her hands:

When you ***bring friends to a fight***, roll with Allies. On a 10+, pick 3. On a 7-9, pick 2.

- You suffer little harm
- Your allies suffer little harm
- Your enemies suffer terrible harm
- You take something from your enemies

Since Allies is a new stat we just made up, its value can depend on the fiction instead of the PC's stats. Maybe a big, bad werewolf matriarch is a +2 and a teenage apprentice is a +0 or -1: both the number and the quality of allies Jenn gets makes a difference when she goes into a fight. Or maybe it's just the sheer number of allies that show up to fight on her behalf. Your call.

The options for this move put narrative control of the fight back into Jenn's hands as well. The last option—*you take something from your enemies*—gives her the flexibility to take positions, items, or even the momentum from the opposition, while still making her face tough tradeoffs around suffering or inflicting harm.

MANAGING DEBTS

Of course, playing with only one PC means that ***cashing in Debts*** loses a lot of punch. If you're a low Heart character, it's a double whammy—you're not good at ***persuading*** NPCs (even with Debts) and you're bad at refusing NPCs who ***cash in Debts*** on you. Here's a move that replaces ***cash in a Debt*** for a solo game:

> When you ***cash in a Debt*** with an NPC for anything off the list, roll with Debts (max +3). On a 10+, they'll do what you ask to pay their interest; mark their Faction, but keep the Debt. On a 7-9, they'll do it, but it's costly; mark their Faction and lose the Debt. On a miss, they push you off until another day: keep the Debt, but take -1 ongoing against them for the rest of the scene.

This shifts Debts to ongoing relationships instead of transactional holdings. A character who owes Jenn a few Debts is going to have a hard time getting out from under her thumb; someone she's only got a minor hold on might be able to put her off for a while or pay it off without risking too much.

»Changes, Changes, Changes

Don't be confused here: these are major, major changes to the game. But they're what you need to set things up to run for just one PC. If you want to make similar changes—a new setting, a world of only vampires, etc.—you gotta be brave enough to rip stuff out and design custom moves to make it work.

THE END OF SHADOWS

There's seriously no end to what you can do with custom moves. Check out **Advanced Fuckery** (pages 267-284) in *Apocalypse World* for the full rundown on Vincent's framework. Remember that *Urban Shadows* itself is basically a collection of custom moves that bring *Apocalypse World* out of the post-apocalyptic future and into the urban fantasy present!

Good luck!

APPENDIX
STAFF AND THANKS

CREDITS

Liz Bauman is a copywriter and indexer living in suburban Maryland with her husband, two awesome kids, and lazy dog. Her fondness for online communities and social media inspired her to found #RPGchat, a weekly Twitter chat all about games, more than three years ago. She's a lover of story games, high fantasy ass-kicking, and supers roleplaying. She adores convention-going, running *Dread* and *Fiasco*, and playing paladins. Check out her daily life Twitter and Instagram @d20blonde, read some of her stuff about games on TheIlluminerdy.com, or get to know her at LizBauman.com.

Brendan Conway is a professional writer and co-owner of Magpie Games. He has worked on the *Firefly RPG, The Fate Codex, Bulldogs Fate Core, Wicked Fate*, and his own series of weird fantasy settings for *Dungeon World*, starting with *The Last Days of Anglekite*. He believes in the virtue of verbosity, the power of prolixity, and he doesn't understand what the big deal is about sprinkles.

Thomas Deeny is a graphic designer who specializes in book layout and game design. His layout and design work can be found in Growling Door Games' *Chill RPG*, Dead Gentlemen's *Demon Hunters RPG*, Margaret Weis Productions' *Firefly RPG* line, AEG's *Nightfall* and *Tempest* game lines, and upcoming titles from Tasty Minstrel Games. Thomas is an evangelist for hobby gaming, and helped to organize the gaming community in southern Arizona, working with manufacturers, retailers, and gamers to develop community awareness of the hobby. You can review his published works at denaghdesign.com and follow him on Twitter at @denaghdesign.

Shelley Harlan has been a professional editor for over 15 years. In the roleplaying genre, she is the editor for the indie gaming company Faster Monkey Games, and has done freelance work for Magpie Games and *Call of Catthulhu*. She will defend the Oxford comma and the four-dot ellipsis passionately, can tell you the difference between the verbs *accept* and *except*, and is a lot of fun at parties.

Marissa Kelly is the co-founder of Magpie Games and the author of *Epyllion*, a dragon epic RPG. She is currently involved in several collaborations: *Bluebeard's Bride* with Whitney "Strix" Beltrán and Sarah Richardson and *Galaxy XXX* with John Wick. In addition to her design work, Marissa also handles art direction for Magpie Games, Evil Hat Productions (Fate, *The Dresden Files*) and Storium. Marissa works as a paleontology intern throughout the year, spending summers in Montana and Wyoming doing field work.

Andrew Medeiros is a fan of all things game: video, tabletop, board game, larp, they're all fair game! His true gaming love is tabletop roleplaying games and he enjoys sharing that love with others. Andrew lives in Ontario, Canada, and likes being "that weird Canadian" at international conventions. His favorite animals are, in order: the Wolf, the Falcon, and the Dolphin. *Urban Shadows* is his first published product but he has created several free games also Powered by the Apocalypse, including *Star Wars World* and *A World of Ice and Fire*. He has plans for many other projects that he has been working on in his spare time and can't wait to share them with the world!

Juan Ochoa is a recovering post-production artist in Colombia, South America, who now makes a living drawing dragons and robots. He's been gaming since 1982 and would have probably chosen a career in the sciences if he had not come across RPG art and issues of *Metal Hurlant*. You can find his work at www.juanochoa.co.

Mark Diaz Truman is an Ennie award-winning game developer, a co-owner of Magpie Games (magpiegames.com), and the Editor in Chief for *The Fate Codex*. Mark authored two indie RPGs before *Urban Shadows*—*The Play's the Thing* and *Our Last Best Hope*—and has written a number of pieces for Evil Hat Productions, including parts of *The Fate Toolkit*, *Timeworks*, and the upcoming *Do: Fate of the Flying Temple*. In addition to his work as a designer and writer, Mark has worked as a developmental editor on the *Firefly RPG*, *A World of Dew*, and *No Country for Old Kobolds*, and as an organizer and activist with Gaming as Other. You can find him on Twitter (@trumonz).

Amanda Valentine is a freelance RPG editor and developer. Her work includes *The Dresden Files RPG*, *Marvel Heroic Roleplaying*, *Fate Accelerated Edition*, *Little Wizards*, *The Fate Codex*, Storium, and many others. She also edits fiction. She blogs sporadically at ayvalentine.com about editing, parenting, and gaming. At reads4tweens.com she writes spoilerific book reviews for adults who care about what the kids in their lives are reading. You can find her on Twitter as @ayvalentine and @reads4tweens.

CITY CHAMPIONS

At the close of our Kickstarter campaign, several of our backers volunteered to run extended playtests to explore long-term *Urban Shadows* play. Their feedback was a vital part of our design and writing process. Thank you, City Champions!

- **Canberra Creatures:** Jarrod Farquhar-Nicol, Suzanne Richardson, Ian Urquhart, Melissa Holz, Nathan Holz.
- **Cedar Street Gamers:** Ian Howard, Josh Blake, Justin Howard, Maggie Samuels, Martin Long, Maxim Delaney, Maximilian Howard, Mike Lawson, Patrick Martell, Tom Burpee.
- **The Intercontinental Crew:** Julia (Jules) Nienaber, Jonna Hind, Bodil Prinz, Alex Prinz, Rich Rogers, Jan Van Zon.
- **London Falling:** Daniel Scribner, Cara Arcuni, Anthony Ponzio, Bill Mullen, Kelly McWilliams, Melissa Spangenberg.
- **Ottawa Pen & Paper Gamers:** Kevin "Chroma" Petker, Catherine Hariton, Savannah Soule, Shawn Roske, Paul Towler, Kurt Sharma, Eric Wilkinson.
- **The Overeager:** Brian Poe, Alexsondra Schrock, Marty Oas, Laren Stock, James Davenport.
- **Saga Inc.:** Robert Vincent, Starky, John, Sam, Karel.
- **Spicejar Branch:** Steven Schwartz, Debbie Notkin, Alan Bostick.
- **Steel City Shadows:** Stras Acimovic, Jeff Kosko, Heather Yilmaz, Brianna Sheldon, John Sheldon, John LeBoeuf-Little, Kit LaTouche, Allie McCarthy.
- **Toronto Area Gamers:** Rob Deobald, Rachelle Shelkey, Kate Bullock, Erica Stevenson, Angela Duvall-Morgan, ronBunxious, Tomas Andrijauskas, George Kaldis.

INDEX

INDEX OF NAMED MOVES

BASIC MOVES

FACTION MOVES

ARCHETYPE MOVES

DRAMA MOVES

Corruption Moves

Debt Moves

Intimacy Moves

See Archetypes in Index